MODERNISM, CULTURAL PRODUCTION, AND THE BRITISH AVANT-GARDE

Edward Comentale exposes the links between art, literature and early twentieth-century capitalism. Comentale shows how apparently progressive avant-garde movements in their celebration of individualism, competition, and labor worked hand in hand with a market defined by a monstrous increase in production and consumption. Most importantly, he unearths an alternative modernist practice based on a special kind of production that both critiques and challenges economic production at large. He goes on to argue that the British avant-garde, which has often been criticized for its emphasis on classical stasis and restraint, sought to halt this market activity and to think of less destructive ways of communal belonging. Comentale provides an interdisciplinary study examining art and sculpture as well as writing by Virginia Woolf, T. S. Eliot, and H. D., among others, in the light of psychoanalytic, economic, and political theory. This book will be of interest to scholars of literary and cultural modernism.

EDWARD P. COMENTALE is Assistant Professor of Literature in the Department of English at Indiana University. He is the author of articles on international modernism, the avant-garde, and twentieth-century film.

MODERNISM, CULTURAL PRODUCTION, AND THE BRITISH AVANT-GARDE

EDWARD P. COMENTALE

Indiana University

CAMBRIDGE
UNIVERSITY PRESS

PUBLISHED BY THE PRESS SYNDICATE OF THE UNIVERSITY OF CAMBRIDGE
The Pitt Building, Trumpington Street, Cambridge, United Kingdom

CAMBRIDGE UNIVERSITY PRESS
The Edinburgh Building, Cambridge, CB2 2RU, UK
40 West 20th Street, New York, NY 10011–4211, USA
477 Williamstown Road, Port Melbourne, VIC 3207, Australia
Ruiz de Alarcón 13, 28014 Madrid, Spain
Dock House, The Waterfront, Cape Town 8001, South Africa

http://www.cambridge.org

First published 2004

Printed in the United Kingdom at the University Press, Cambridge

Typeface Adobe Garamond 11/12.5 pt.   *System* LATEX 2$_\varepsilon$ [TB]

A catalogue record for this book is available from the British Library

Library of Congress cataloging in publication data
Comentale, Edward P.
Modernism, cultural production, and the British avant-garde / Edward P. Comentale.
p.   cm.
Includes bibliographical references and index.
ISBN 0 521 83589 5 (hardback)
1. Arts, British – 20th century.   2. Modernism (Aesthetics) – Great Britain –
History – 20th century.   I. Title.
NX543.C65   2004
700′.941′09041 – dc22   2003063050

ISBN 0 521 83589 5 hardback

For Kimberly Munroe

Contents

Illustrations

viii

Acknowledgments

Much of this book bemoans the loss of collaborative work and community, and yet the final product stands as a testament to the opposite. My project allowed me to work with kind scholars from all ranks and many different fields and has proven the generosity of institutions on both sides of the Atlantic.

For assistance with research, I thank the Mark Diamond Research Grant Program at SUNY-Buffalo, for their early support, and Indiana University, for treating new faculty members so well. I also thank Matthew Gale at the Tate Modern and Michael Moody at the Imperial War Museum, who kindly made accessible materials that are not readily available; also, for permissions, Norma Watt and the Norwich Castle Museum, Maree Allitt and Kettle's Yard, Lucy Pringle and the Museum of London, Gillian Raffles and the Mercury Gallery, the staff at the Rare Book Collection, University of North Carolina at Chapel Hill, and David Finn for his beautiful photos. Many thanks also to my readers at Cambridge University Press, to my editor Ray Ryan, and to Rachel de Wachter and Maureen Leach.

Gratitude is also extended to my more or less formal advisors at SUNY-Buffalo, Joseph Conte, Henry Sussman, and David Schmid; at Indiana University, Helen Sword, Jonathan Elmer, Deidre Lynch, Janet Sorensen, and Susan Gubar; and elsewhere, Eileen Gregory, Cassandra Laity, and Judith Roof. A special word of gratitude must go out to Andrew Hewitt, for his inspiring rigor, and to Steve Watt, for his insight, support, and kindness. I am also grateful for the intelligence and enthusiasm of my colleagues and friends Heidi Hartwig and Lawrence Shine. And for the contentious brilliance of my modernist co-conspirators Justus Nieland, Stephan Wender, and Aaron Jaffe. My deepest thanks go out to Andrzej Gasiorek, the finest colleague in the business, and Bob Devens, the finest colleague out of it.

I must thank Gerry, for lugging a three-volume set home from Ireland; Phil, for driving me back and forth to Boston and Buffalo; Jeanette, for going back to school herself. For Kimberly, who was the best reader of all and who never stinted with her time. For Margaret, who taught me some hard facts about the ego-ideal. And for Delia, who took me to the park.

Introduction
On the nature of being otherwise

> One of the pre-eminently "classical" attributes is *an indifference to originality*. Indeed, in the classical artist, originality would be a fault. He is given, he is served out, with all he is supposed to require for his task: not his to reason why, but to "get on with the job" . . . He is tied hand and foot therefore to the values of his patrons. Their morals are his morals; it is the *Weltanschauung* that perforce he holds in common with them that is his subject-matter.
>
> Wyndham Lewis, *Men Without Art*[1]

In the fall of 1999, the Modernist Studies Association held its Inaugural Conference, aptly titled *The New Modernisms*. With this seminal event, late-twentieth-century scholarship turned back to its origins and proclaimed renewal. Echoing the progressive literature they aimed to explore, organizers and participants declared their commitment to an "international and interdisciplinary forum" and a "revitalized and rapidly changing field." Certainly, the conference lived up to its aims. As panel after panel announced, modernism was being "redefined," "reassessed," "recontextualized," "historicized," "hystericized," and, of course, "modernized." The work showcased not only new evaluations of old favorites – Woolf, Pound, and Joyce – but also first-time discussions of relatively unknown figures – Frantissek Kupka, Philippe Lamour, and Mulk Raj Anand. The field of inquiry spread from traditional centers of modernist activity – London, Paris, and New York – to the less traveled worlds of Harlem, India, and Mexico. Temporal boundaries were similarly reconstituted, widened from Wilde to Ginsberg and stretched to incorporate a few historical oddities such as Cervantes, Hopkins, and Handel. Most importantly, the period was opened to a dizzying array of postmodern paradigms and critical models, not only posthumanism, postcolonialism, and postfeminism, but also new economic criticism and geopolitical theory. Modernism, a category once bound by traditional configurations of space and time, would no longer be the same. It was poked and pulled, preened and polished for the new century. The discussion was exciting, revolutionary, and, well, inspiring. As a review in *The Chronicle of Higher Education* explained, "scholars of modernism, who, after years of being associated with the fusty and retrograde, suddenly found themselves energized and optimistic."[2]

And yet, attending the conference, one could not escape the feeling that all this good cheer was perhaps a bit forced. Surely, any inaugural ceremony serves to define and unite its various participants. But, here, the act of renewal was accompanied by a rather anxious need for differentiation and disavowal. Now, at last, a "new," brighter modernism would lay to rest the specter of fascism. For once and for all, modernist scholars would slough off the reactionary politics of their field. Thus, the revived authors and spaces mentioned above performed the double work of renewal and denial. These figures of "otherness," "alterity," and "difference" at once redeemed and obscured. This was clearly established in the seminar I attended, "Recontextualizations of Modernism, II." Here, the debate quickly turned to the issue of whether or not the term "modernism" should be expanded to include literary phenomena that occurred before the death of Edward VII and after World War II. For most participants, "modernism" was understood as a "floating signifier" or an "umbrella term," a loose set of attributes that can be applied to authors working within a variety of historical periods and geographical spaces. It was argued that we needed an open-ended, postmodern modernism, much like that which was being constructed at the conference. Its circularity aside, what was most telling about this argument was the manner in which it quickly and rigorously polarized points of view. Difference was privileged for its correctness, while any attempt to establish the historical or ideological integrity of the period, even as it might have been experienced by the moderns themselves, was met with disapproval. This latter position was criticized as elitist and reactionary, blind to the multiplicity and diversity of the ("new") modernist experience.

Needless to say, I also arrived at the inaugural conference with my own group of dissident others – T. E. Hulme, Henri Gaudier-Brzeska, and Jacob Epstein. I produced a new modernism of my own that focused on what seemed to be a very obscure area of aesthetic activity and debate: Wilhelm Worringer's influence on British sculptors who fought in World War I. The unspoken impulses of my own work, though, as I then began to realize them, raised new perplexing questions for me, which quickly took shape as the chapters in this book. I am certainly not the first scholar to recognize that the tragic history of the early twentieth century and its very proximity to the present continue to vex our responses to modernism. It is difficult to navigate not only the difficult political terrain of the modernist period, but also the possible critical models that seem to derive from that period, such as deconstruction, feminism, and postcolonialism. However, I am specifically concerned with whether the oppositional impulse of recent responses can maintain any critical effectiveness. Recent modernist criticism, insofar as it emphasizes multiplicity and otherness, tends to reproduce the very object it hopes to critique. Our desire to differentiate ourselves from history, from our past, not only implies the dialectic continuity of these two moments, but also, in this particular instance, all the more clearly establishes our ideological kinship with the moderns. In other words, revolutionary modernism already asserts the political necessity of otherness and alterity, as embodied in Woolf's "outsider's society," Marcus Garvey's Back to Africa movement, or the John Reed clubs for the working class. But even the work of High Modernism – and in its most reactionary mode – is notable for its commitment to individualism and alterity. Eliot's celebration of "individual talent" and Pound's advocacy of the "factive personality" posit a rigid dialectic of individualism and totality, fragment and structure. Our work, insofar as it privileges related figures and themes, might only replicate and reinforce this dialectic. The need to be otherwise, to imagine our own critical otherness or to project that otherness on an otherwise forgotten modernist, augments as it obscures the ideological conditions from which that need derives.

This book, then, is partly about the way in which modernism repeats or extends itself into the future, and it explores the larger historical forces that continue to condition this activity. I start from a position similar to that of Gianni Vattimo, for whom modernity is caught or "in fact dominated by the idea that the history of thought is a progressive 'enlightenment' which develops through an ever more complete appropriation and reappropriation of its own foundations." For Vattimo, modernity is circular, reproductive, and perhaps obsessive: "For if we say that we are at a later point than modernity, and if we treat this fact as in some way decisively important, then this presupposes an acceptance of what more specifically characterizes the point of view of modernity itself, namely the idea of history with its two corollary notions of progress and overcoming."[3] This book, however, further explores the ways in which this paradox is bound to the larger forces and structures of economic modernity. The violence by which our history has been repeatedly overturned, the continual production and consumption of cultural difference, the ceaseless labor and endless discourse that shapes our own profession – these phenomena all feed as they affirm the activity of a voracious market. Indeed, even when our oppositional impulse is founded upon a desire to avoid political totality, it nonetheless replicates the economic logic upon which that fascism was based. We have yet to learn that modernism – like the market itself – consistently fails to deliver on its most important promises, thus forcing us to perform the never-ending work of its completion. In this, as Jeffrey M. Perl argues, it assumes "the quality of a self-fulfilling prophecy, left by the modernists to be fulfilled through other selves."[4]

I want to clarify, however, that it is not modernism in general that propels itself into the future, but a specifically "romantic" modernism, with its promise of aesthetic wholeness and its emphasis on expressivity and otherness. It is a romantic modernism, I argue, that is most closely aligned with the totalitarianism of the twentieth century, whether that totality is figured as static purity or constant change. Meanwhile, "classical" modernism, with its emphasis on contingency and limit, has been wrongly dismissed by scholars. This modernism provides a potential critique and alternative to modernity as it continues to be active in our lives; it contains the origins of a more inclusive, dialectical experience that forces us to rethink the work of art as well as the subject and its political engagement. Indeed, just about every major modernist took a stand on this debate, producing critical and creative work that proclaimed either romantic or classical commitments.[5] The vigor and seriousness with which they approached this matter suggests not simply a commitment to a certain kind of aesthetic experience, but also an awareness that the very fate of the modern world was at stake. It is my contention that if we must persist in reproducing the past, particularly in our hostility to it, then it is only by reviving this specific debate that we can understand what that reproduction signifies. It is through these terms that we can begin to reestablish not only the socio-economic origins of various modern practices, but also their late-twentieth-century legacy.

From impressionism to futurism to surrealism and beyond, the avant-garde movements of the twentieth century share a rigidly oppositional logic. Paradoxically, these antagonistic programs are united in their efforts to construct authority against and through the rival claims of each other. For each, the attempt to establish a certain authenticity, a new perspective, a transcendent consciousness, depends upon the presence of some fallen other, some decadent or marked double. Indeed, as argued by critics from Walter Benjamin to Rita Felski, it is this oppositional logic that informs the avant-garde's tendency toward domination and violence.[6] The most casual look at futurist or vorticist activity exposes avant-gardism as a largely imperial attitude, one informed by discourses of cultural, if not racial, superiority and evolutionary progress. Similarly, these movements, along with German expressionism or French cubism, express a masculine agressiveness, an often hostile and repressive attitude toward various cultural markers of the feminine. Ultimately, it is also this oppositional logic and its manifestations that link the avant-garde with totalitarian politics. Avant-gardism and the fascist movements of the early twentieth century are united by their celebration of violent renewal and progress, by their faith in an aesthetic transcendence of the fallen world. They revel in a shared opposition to bourgeois culture and its materialism, and in a shared yearning for redemption and pure, original selfhood.

But, despite this undeniably repulsive violence, the avant-garde continues to confound our understanding of the modern period. As many critics have observed, the avant-garde's often radical commitment to progress and innovation calls into question its often reactionary polemics. Its iconoclastic and dissonant art complicates its support of totalitarian structures and regimes.[7] What needs to be clarified is that these movements, both aesthetic and political, tend to eschew the conventional terms of tyranny – order, control, stasis – for a dialectic of change and stability, revolt and regulation. They find in constant war or upheaval a certain perverse stasis or stability. Indeed, even many High Modernist works support a ceaseless activity of interpretation or production of meaning. Even in what appears to be their systematic denial of closure, they conjure – albeit negatively – the possibility of a rational wholeness or transcendence. Ultimately, then, what appears to define the aesthetic politics of the period, despite the specifics of political affiliation, is a romantic metaphysic that can achieve authority only by way of dissent, the center by way of margins, the self in and through the other. As the romantic artist evokes a creative struggle of work and world, the nation establishes itself through war against another.

Importantly, these violent dialectics move us beyond specific aesthetic and political regimes to a much more pervasive economic influence. Marshall Berman characterizes the modern period by the insatiable activity of its market. "This system," he writes, "requires constant revolutionizing, disturbance, agitation; it needs to be perpetually pushed and pressed in order to maintain its elasticity and resilience, to appropriate and assimilate new energies, to drive itself to new heights of activity and growth." Modernity's progressive movements, he adds, cannot be theorized apart from "a ruling class with vested interests not merely in change but in crisis and chaos. 'Uninterrupted disturbance, everlasting uncertainty and agitation,' instead of subverting this society, actually serve to strengthen it."[8] Modernist aesthetics, particularly as they emerged out of rapidly industrializing nations such as Italy and Germany, offered a positive vision of this activity. Whether it be the hyperproductivity of avant-garde invention, the ceaseless reckoning of part and whole in High Modernism, or even the interpretative dynamism of new criticism, the period as a whole is distinguished by its faith in the activity of production. By locating aesthetic value not in the art object, but in a constant aesthetic creationism, these avant-gardes reinforced the logic of commodification and the violence it demands. The avant-garde aesthetic, as it was diffused throughout the social order, offered ontological stability to a culture driven by market relations. Thus, as I argue in chapter 1, we need to reformulate Walter Benjamin's notion of "aesthetic politics" and its associations. "Aestheticization," as it occurred during this period, refers not to a false semblance of symbolic unity, but to a particular activity of semblance, a constant production and consumption of difference. Similarly, "totalitarianism" should not be defined simply as the incapacity to permit alterity, but must be seen as a rhetoric that privileges a certain kind of alterity as necessary to a socio-economic order already in place.

The history of the continental avant-garde, however, does not necessarily account for the London scene at this time, out of which emerged a radical critique of bourgeois culture and thus an alternative to modernity in general. Early twentieth-century London, as is well known, drew many expatriates into its vortex. The city was bubbling over with a violent energy – new ideas in the air, new politics on the streets, new machines in the factories. Many artists – from Conrad, Wilde, and James to later moderns such as Pound, H. D., and Eliot as well as avant-gardists like F. T. Marinetti, Henri Gaudier-Brzeska, and Jacob Epstein – ventured into this cultural swelter, hoping to harness its progressive dynamism. However, immediately before and during World War I, the years which roughly frame this study, the energy of modern London began to grow stale. The hope of progress, the demand for newness – these urges, particularly in relation to the technological precisionism of modernity, seemed empty or, worse, treacherous. For British thinkers and artists, these years mark the beginning of a great disillusionment, an increasing suspicion that cultural modernity was somehow complicit with the horrors of economic modernity. From this point on, their work was forced to contend, in both style and content, with this insidious revelation.[9] Pound, for example, began to rage against the city's creative destruction; a cheap flood of commodities was eroding any hope of redemption. The age, he cried, demands only "an image / Of its accelerated grimace . . . a mould in plaster, / Made with no loss of time . . ." In the marketplace, "All things are flowing . . . But a tawdry cheapness / Shall outlast our days."[10] Eliot, similarly, foresaw that the violent production of modern life was congealing into habit. London was full of "swarming life . . . Responsive to the momentary need," yet these vital impulses were easily managed by an efficient market, the "formal destiny" of a reified economy.[11]

In other words, London artists found themselves in the peculiar position of needing to be modern after the modern had already occurred. Their art, while seeking to draw upon the energy of the new world, faced its potential appropriation and dissolution within that world.[12] As perceived by this small circle of rebels, creativity may now exhibit an unprecedented state of freedom, but it has never experienced a greater homogenization. Vital expression has been given over to passive identification, and desire for freedom is subsumed by mere imitation. The average man and the aesthete grow indistinguishable; chaos and conformity work together to destroy social integrity. As Wyndham Lewis griped,

> Revolutionary politics, revolutionary art, and, oh, the revolutionary mind, is the dullest thing on earth. When we open a "revolutionary" review, or read a "revolutionary" speech, we yawn our heads off. It is true, there is nothing else. Everything is correctly, monotonously, dishearteningly "revolutionary." What a stupid world! What a stale fuss![13]

Lewis, not without a certain amount of paranoia, recognized that the most radical aesthetic efforts were not immune to the expanding market. The chaotic desires of society, no matter how violent or transgressive, were quickly contained and neutralized by the affective dimensions of advertising, fashion, and consumer demand. Much like the modern work of art, the commodity sold itself by "instantaneous suggestion" and "sensation"; it captures the man in the crowd by a "sequence of ephemerids, roughly organized into what he calls his 'personality.'"[14]

Needless to say, this paradoxical situation stymied the efforts of British artists to establish themselves. Painters and writers struggled to resist the rhetoric of expressive individualism as well as the emptiness of efficient mimesis; their work needed to be an alternative to both romanticism and formalism, to both the avant-garde and the marketplace.[15] For these artists, then, classicism served as the only viable response to democratic capitalism and its romantic affirmation. This aesthetic alternative emphasized the material tensions that define and delimit individuals, classes, and nations. It begins with the chaotic energy of the relative, the romantic spirit, but subject and object exist in a dynamic tension that restricts the tendency of either to spin out of control. Worldly forces restrain and refine each other, constructing an order that is stable and thus knowable, but also open to change and desire. In Hulme's famous formulation, "The classical poet never forgets this finiteness, this limit of man. He remembers always that he is mixed up with earth. He may jump, but he always returns back; he never flies away into the circumambient gas."[16] The classical work of art, then, always bears the traces of its creation, the artistic struggle or agon, and thus regrounds idealism within its particular socio-historical context. The work, in fact, expresses as it reinforces these worldly tensions; its static presence serves to halt, clarify, and possibly redirect the violent production (and reproduction) of the modern world. In this, the classical work of art presents its radical alternative to the auraticized commodities and rigid mechanisms of the modern world. It serves to expose the human presence behind the alienated object or the reified relation, and thus to reopen the latter back into history. Ultimately, the work figures as both culmination and antithesis of its productive moment, as both a rigid monument and ultimate negation of modernity's terrifying order.

Most scholarship on classical modernism correctly foregrounds this art's static and dehumanized qualities. Classical works are characterized as fragments, traces, fossils, shells, and corpses. This scholarship, however, tends to interpret this propensity as simply reactionary, as a form of rigid libidinal binding that protects the subject from that which is considered other. Hal Foster, for example, argues that Lewis's work exemplifies a "protofascist desire to elevate self-alienation into an absolute value . . . as a form of ego armoring."[17] I would like to argue, however, that classical stasis is never necessarily chauvinistic, reactionary, or escapist, but more often than not serves an important critical function. The work's very promise of fulfillment is denied by its own coldness or inaccessibility; it thus both inspires and impedes the spectator's desire for identification or sublimation. British artists valued this intentional *halting* insofar as it could transform blind desire into conscious choice, as it could expose the treacherous identifications of modern culture and reground the subject within the world. As Peter Nicholls recognizes, this anti-vital aesthetic serves to drive "a wedge between art and life." He explains, "Once the habits of identification and assimilation are checked, the way is open to conceive the work as the production of aesthetic otherness which opens a gap or breach within the rhythmic flow of social life" (434, 433). As I hope to establish here, classical modernism is responsive to its own historical moment and its art affects an experience that is at once critical and constructive within that moment. At its best, this art serves not only to critique the signs and images that direct modern activity, but also to model and inspire alternative forms of identity and community.

Wyndham Lewis's BLAST[18] emerged out of the London scene at this time and the Vorticist movement, as it was closely aligned with British classicism, offers the most compelling account of these issues. Indeed, the only way to make sense of the journal is to consider it in its multiple contexts: a defensive aesthetic manifesto, a pre-war nationalist screed, and a bold economic critique. For Lewis, these three spheres – the aesthetic, the national, and the economic – rise and fall together; the terms of one condition and define the others. Thus, in the first section of the journal, a wild collection of blasts and blesses, he depicts London as a decadent city overrun by a rampant cult of the new and exotic. Lewis smugly lists the trends and fads that have weakened the minds of his contemporaries. France has infected them with "SLIPPERS, POODLE TEMPER, BAD MUSIC," while Spain has provided "GYPSY KINGS and ESPADAS"; England itself offers "BRITANNIC AESTHETE, WILD NATURE CRANK," and, of course, "DALY'S MUSICAL COMEDY GAIETY CHORUS GIRL" (*B*, 13, 19, 11). For Lewis, this ceaseless production and consumption of the modern is driven by a chronic romanticism. These various trends are united by a vulgar sentimentality of the self, a widespread faith in the freedom and vitality of the individual. Free trade in economics, liberalism in politics, protestantism in religion, vitalism in philosophy – each serves the rather uncritical notion, derived from Rousseau and the French Revolution, that "LIFE is the important thing!" (*B*, 129). Lewis further aligns this widespread fever with the growing demands of the market. Here, all that is seemingly free and revolutionary feeds a consumer-based economy; all that is excessive and violent serves a single, static order. This becomes apparent at the end of the journal's first section, when Lewis announces, with mixed disgust and awe, that England has been given over to a "violent boredom." "In England," he writes, "there is no vulgarity in revolt. Or, rather, there is no revolt, it is the normal state" (*B*, 42).

The most prophetic passages of BLAST outline this double bind. Lewis laments the impossibility of attaining true individuality in a cultural market that consistently appropriates all difference. Creativity, he claims, is immediately given over to mimetic technologies, by which it becomes common, vulgar, and useful. For Lewis, this tragedy is most painfully acute in the case of the artist, whose attitude is now aped by the average citizen. As he explains, "Vulgarity and the host of cheap artisans compete in earning with the true artist" and thereby destroy the possibility of his "creative genius" (*B*, 15). This loss of aesthetic individualism, however, also ensures the loss of social order. Without true visionaries and a ceaselessly renewed stream of ideas and inventions, society as a whole begins to suffer. In fact, despite its productivity – its "VAST MACHINERY" – England has atrophied as a world power. The nation has been overrun by an "effeminate lout" who can only reproduce himself (*B*, 11). As Lewis suggests, then, the country is threatened by the very principles of free trade it uses to justify its dominance; imperial power is undermined by the guilty liberal ideology it uses to appropriate world resources. Ultimately, modern society, driven by the unchecked energies of the market, negates individualism as well as community, creating a world at once homogenous and anarchic.

Lewis holds tightly to this basic critique and strives to establish a viable alternative. As he recognizes that a greater assertion of individualism against the mass would only reproduce the terms of the whole, he reconceives the individual as he exists within and through the mass. In *BLAST* and elsewhere, Lewis's solution is to undermine the oppositional logic that defines modern identities and assert a constitutive, intersubjective unity. The individual exists only through a process of "egotistical hardening" in the tension that persists, and must be constantly renewed, between himself and his environment (*B*, 134). He is forged, Lewis argues, by shocks and blasts experienced on the urban streets; he is clarified and strengthened by an intense jostling within the mass (*B*, 32). Conversely, it is left to the individual to exert pressure upon and thereby shape the amorphous mass that surrounds him. Lewis privileges chemists, mechanics, and hairdressers in that they use their skills to order and define otherwise unruly material. The artist, too, is valued for his ability to curb "aimless and retrograde growth into CLEAN ARCHED SHAPES and ANGULAR PLOTS" (*B*, 25). His power is that of the machine or turbine, drawing and channeling the flow of energy that surrounds him. As Lewis explains, "The Vorticist is not the Slave of Commotion, but its Master" (*B*, 148). Later in the journal, Pound similarly proclaims that the artist's occupation is that of "DIRECTING a certain fluid force against circumstance, as CONCEIVING instead of merely observing and reflecting" (*B*, 153).

For Lewis, these tensions and contingencies restrict the potential excesses of both the individual and his world. Intellectual solipsism is tempered by physical engagement, whereas a vulgar materialism is challenged by critical thought. This doubleness is clearly reflected in the vorticist aesthetic. For many, Lewis's movement represents a simple hybrid of cubism and futurism. The vortex is a symbol of that which is at once geometric and vitalistic, formal and fluid.[19] Lewis, however, does not necessarily unite these two modes; rather, he allows stasis and vitality to restrain and strengthen each other. In

describing modern tendencies in art, for example, Lewis rails against naturalism for its weakness, passivity, and general failure to define necessary
boundaries. Naturalism, he argues, "is the typical cowardly attitude of those
who have failed with their minds, and are discouraged and unstrung before
the problems of their Spirit; who fall back on their stomachs and the meaner
working of their senses" (*B*, 129). But Lewis also criticizes abstraction, for
being precious, disposable, and disengaged. Picasso's still-lifes, he argues,
"have a splendid air, starting in pure creation, with their invariable and
lofty detachment from any utilitarian end or purpose . . . But they do not
seem to possess the necessary physical stamina to survive." As he explains,
"they lack the one purpose, or even necessity, of a work of Art: namely
Life" (*B*, 139–40). Ultimately, for Lewis, good art maintains a tempered
balance between these two modes: it both resists and incorporates its opposite, life. As he argues, "It is all a matter of the most delicate adjustment
between voracity of Art and digestive quality of Life. The Finest Art is not
pure Abstraction, nor is it unorganized life" (*B*, 134). The successful work,
then, is at once a stable, bounded object and a moment within a larger
dynamic field. It neither fully escapes nor fully reproduces the ideological
forces of its making, but always signals those forces and their potential
transformation.

   For Lewis, identity – whether personal, national, or aesthetic – is neither
stable nor organic, but epidermal. It is elastic and posable, conditioned by a
multitude of relations within the world. In *BLAST*, he presents subjectivity
in the truest sense of the word, as being subject to some other. His figures
and objects never exist in isolation, but find definition and distinction
only in their engagements. In this, Lewis tries to beat the market at its
own game. Superficially, his art seems to celebrate the reified positions
and stances of the modern world. Yet this mechanization suggests never
simply stasis or control. Rather, his best work revels in the self-conscious
activity of construction and reconstruction; it serves to expose the molding
of identity and to model possible alternatives. In other words, Lewis never
adopts mechanical formalism, or even abstract formalism, for its own sake.
Rather, his work is committed to rendering the process of mechanization,
the industrial reification of human experience. In this, it figures at once as an
extension of modernity as well as a means of counteracting that modernity.
On the one hand, each work is only a metonym, a cog in a vast system of
industrial efficiency. On the other, it is a frustrating reflection or metaphor,
an aesthetic wrench halting the smooth productive machinery of the social
order and forcing a reconsideration of its effects.[20] Yet it is only in the
demonstration of art's contingency, in the debunking of its seeming purity

and the exposure of its inherent violence toward the material world, that this sabotage occurs.

The same can be said for Lewis's treatment of social machinery, the ideological organization of mass desire. In the opening pages of *BLAST*, Lewis seems to advance and deny all of the often contradictory positions that define modern life: aestheticism, naturalism, futurism, cubism, individualism, liberalism, toryism, and suffragism. These blustery proclamations and reversals, though, expose the constructed or performative nature of all stances; the ease with which Lewis moves from one attitude to another suggests, in the words of one critic, that he "is not so much defending an aesthetic position as playing with the idea of aesthetic position."[21] Moreover, insofar as Lewis manages to "talk with two tongues," presenting each position against its opposite, he shows that all political posturing depends upon the compromising presence of some antithesis.[22] With this deconstructive performance, he establishes the work as a space of critical consciousness; as he explains in *BLAST*, "We start from opposite statements of a chosen world. Set up violent structure of adolescent clearness between two extremes" (*B*, 30). In the words of Nicholls, this art "celebrates the 'characterless, subtle, protean social self of the modern world' which is made possible by the 'conventional, civilized abstraction of social life.'" The classicist adopts a sort of satirical "mimetism" that must be "grasped (and controlled) as self-conscious play rather than misconstruing it as self-expression" (224).

In this activity, though, Lewis also defends himself against a certain criticism, namely, that his work is guilty of the very idealism that he condemns elsewhere. With his contradictory approach, he systematically denies the possibility of any authority, any claim to establish a self-identical, transcendent position beyond the squabbling of the everyday. In fact, Lewis's greatest reversal is that of his own avant-garde authority. His commentary runs from the dour to the ridiculous, asserting revolutionary politics as it also mocks Marinetti and the transformative power of art. In this, Lewis understands his work as a mode of performance or satire aligned with the British tradition established by Jonathan Swift (*B*, 26). It is all surface or façade, a mocking performance of the various poses of his contemporaries. As Lewis writes later, "Satire is *cold*, and that is good! It is easier to achieve these polished and resistant surfaces of a great *externalist* art in Satire" (*MWA*, 99). This method, insofar as it consistently exposes its appearances as such, figures as a sort of immanent critique. The artist pushes his awkward, excessive figures to their breaking point in order to expose their dependence upon that which they negate; ideal identities are shown to be responsive to, and conditioned by, worldly demands and desires. "It is what is beyond the Façade," Lewis writes, "that alone can be of any interest in such a pantomime" (*MWA*, 103). This satirical mode does not claim to evade ideology, but continuously negates its power. It occasions a rather nervous laughter, the uncomfortable, yet hopeful, recognition that all identities are under construction.

In *Enemy of the Stars*, BLAST's iconoclastic centerpiece, Lewis provides a dramatic example of his critical method.[23] The story begins in self-consciously conventional terms, signaling the themes and tropes of classical tragedy. Lewis delineates his characters as "types"; their struggle is "universal." Arghol, our proud hero, champions aesthetic detachment and pure selfhood. He puts his faith in a free, unencumbered ego and maintains this heroic stance against not only the baser instincts of his body, but the corrupt purposiveness of his cultural milieu. While "EACH FORCE ATTEMPTS TO SHAKE HIM," he stands "CENTRAL AS STONE. POISED MAGNET OF SUBTLE, VAST, SELFISH THINGS" (*B*, 61). Arghol's enemy, his double, is the earth-bound Hanp, an "APPALLING 'GAMIN,' BLACK BOUR-GEOIS ASPIRATIONS UNDERMINGING [sic] BLATANT VIRTUOSITY OF SELF." Hanp is clearly all our Vorticist hero despises: bourgeois petti-ness, rampant reproduction, repressive habit. Hanp's world, meanly pur-posive, cannot bear the arrogance of the individual or, by implication, the hope of true difference. His commitment to the status quo inspires a blind aggression: "His criminal instinct of intemperate bilious heart, put at the service of unknown Humanity, our King, to express its violent royal aversion to Protagonist, statue-mirage of Liberty in the great desert" (*B*, 59).

Lewis, however, quickly asserts that the relationship between these two entities is not simply antagonistic, but symbiotic. Arghol's name, in fact, recalls the binary star upon which their unity is modeled. He is bound to the dark other – the body, the mass – from which he tries to escape. His desire to transcend, his hostility to this other, is precisely what restricts him, and the intensity of his effort can only expose its failure.[24] Despite his efforts, there is "Always a deux!" (*B*, 80). This struggle is further complicated by the energy it necessitates. Arghol can only assert his freedom from purpose with a highly compromising purposiveness. The very will he uses to escape is common, instinctive, and animal; it both propels and hinders self-realization. Thus, the centrifugal force of his desire becomes centripetal and "made him a monster in his own eyes" (*B*, 80). As depicted here, the artist-hero is at once host and parasite. The self is conditioned by that which it rejects, by the very process of rejection, and so it remains impure. As Arghol explains, "The process and condition of life, without any exception, is a grotesque degradation, and 'souillure' of the original solitude of the soul" (*B*, 70).

The relationship between Arghol and Hanp is further confused by the metaphorical identifications that define them. A series of dialectical inversions tends to blur the distinctions between self and other, mind and body. Arghol may despise Hanp, but he does so in terms of his own body; his disgust is at once cultural and physical. "You are," he explains, "an unclean little beast, crept gloomily out of my ego. You are the world, brother, with its family objections to me" (B, 73). Hanp tries to make sense of similarly complex emotions. While he dreams of Arghol's comeuppance, he is also intrigued by the latter's arrogance and extreme disgust. For Lewis, these feelings are circular: Hanp's hatred of the individual is fueled by an even greater envy. The mass's antagonism is entwined with a radical self-hatred: "Perfect tyrannic contempt: but choking respect, curiosity; consciousness of defeat. These two extremes clashed furiously. The contempt claimed it's security and triumph: the other sentiment baffled it" (B, 71). Caught in this vicious cycle, both characters begin to lose stability. In their vicious codependency, their seemingly solid egos begin to blend and blur. Identification becomes introjection and vice versa. Identities rupture and leak into each another. In the text, proper names are quickly replaced by pronouns which are in turn replaced by abstract forms and forces.

Strike his disciple as he had abused him. Suddenly give way. Incurable self taught you a heroism.

The young man brought his own disgust back to him. Full of disgust: therefore disgusting. He felt himself on him. What a cause of downfall! (B, 74)

Here, as mutual disgust reaches its breaking point, the two positions are shown to be merely formal, codeterminate and mutually constitutive.

In fact, while Arghol frequently mouths a rhetoric of purity, he ultimately repudiates the notion of a transcendent subject. He resents the falseness of romanticism, which can only mask the subject's animal nature. He scoffs at the "the lily pollen of Ideal on red badge of your predatory category." "Scrape this off," he tells Hanp, "and you lose your appetite." As importantly, Arghol associates idealism with sterility and, in fact, the loss of identity. For him, solipsism is suicide, detachment is death. "To leave violently," he claims, "is to take header into starry cold." (B, 67). Consequently, Arghol rejects a life in the city, the scene of modern exile, anonymity, and possible self-creation. He returns to the country and willingly submits to the provincial routines and bitter conformity of his relations. For Arghol, the best self exists only in its subjection to the constant buffetings of experience. Identity is forged in the blows dealt out by a hostile environment, under the phenomenal conditions of one's birth:

Accumulate in myself, day after day, dense concentration of pig life. Nothing spent, stored rather in strong stagnation, till rid at last of evaporation and lightness characteristic of men. So burst Death's membrane through, slog beyond, not float in appalling distances. (*B*, 68)

A true Vorticist, Arghol recognizes that he is at "his maximum point of energy when stillest" and in this manner tries to cultivate a violent tension (*B*, 148). He takes his beatings in order to generate a "guilty fire of friction." He drags his "hot palms along the ground," accumulating energy, as his face works like a "calm seismograph of eruptions" (*B*, 67). Arghol, like Lewis, turns "egotistical hardening" into a practical value. He transforms the shocks and barbs of the modern world into his defense, an armor as well as an arsenal. He accepts his radically contingent self, "all nerves, vice and dissatisfaction," as the "necessary" source of consciousness and strength (*B*, 71).[25]

Lewis similarly celebrates the artist's ability to affect this transformation for the greater mass. As we have seen, Arghol's utter hostility ensures Hanp's conscious ambivalence. The artist-hero provides the terms that "focussed disciple's physical repulsion: nausea of humility added" (*B*, 71). But, more specifically, it is Arghol's duplicity, his ability to "talk with two tongues," that creates the tension necessary for change. Arghol, as we have seen, exists midway between the ideal and the worldly, and thus consistently undermines his own values. His activity, insofar as it is at once detached and engaged, disrupts the very hierarchies he represents to his follower. As Hanp explains, it was Arghol's decision to fight back, his all-too human desire to strike out, that drove both men mad with violence:

Sullen indignation of Arghol ACTING, he who had no right to act. Violence in him was indecent; again question of taste.

How loathsome heavy body, so long quit, flinging itself about: face strained with intimate expression of act of love . . .

He gave men one image with one hand, and at the same time a second, its antidotes with the other. (*B*, 80)

This is precisely the oppositional method that Lewis performs throughout *BLAST*. Arghol's ultimate trick, deconstructing his own romantic pretensions, forces a recognition of the subject's utter contingency and bestiality. The artist-hero generates desire through his construction of an ideal identity, but he does so only to show the unbearable falseness of that construction. Thus inspired and denied, Hanp attains self-awareness for the first time. As Lewis explains, "His whole being was laid bare" (*B*, 83). Most importantly, this performance forces Hanp to recognize his participation in the construction of their relationship. The story ends with the latter's realization that he has been a willing dupe, a host to parasitical masters. Hanp asks, "WHOSE energy did [Arghol] use?" It is clear that "Arghol was glutted with others, in coma of energy . . . He had just been feeding on him – Hanp!" (*B*, 81).

Lewis, however, suggests that, in the modern world, this heroic struggle can only end in tragedy, "not with a bang but a whimper." Hanp's knowledge arrives too quickly and too late; the awareness of his power merges with his intense hatred. He stabs Arghol, thus draining him, and the world, of all energy. Without the individual, without his rigorous hostility and the tensions it affects, entropy ensues. Now, there is only flesh, "and all our flesh is the same. Something distant, terrible and eccentric, bathing in the milky snore, had been struck and banished from matter" (*B*, 84–5). Interestingly, this battle and its tragic outcome are mirrored by the work's modulating style. On the first few pages, a crisp, faceted prose serves to halt and intensify the fluid energy of its own syntax. Syntactic and typographical gaps heighten the tension between the auratic stasis of each phrase and the vital pulse of the narrative. As Arghol's energy dissipates, however, Lewis's method devolves into a more conventional narrative mode. While the individual undergoes a process of incorporation, the gemlike fragments of the first few pages slowly melt into formal clauses and complete sentences. The text itself seems to decay, conveying perhaps a greater sense of loss than the story could on its own.[26]

But this change serves a further, perhaps more critical purpose. Lewis is once again playing opposites against one another, for the subtle change from iconoclasm to convention has the effect of heightening our awareness of both. The text foregrounds, in fact, not only the distinctions between these two modes, but also their constructed interdependency. Once again, Lewis proclaims his commitment to a radical aesthetic program as well as his skepticism toward the very notion of commitment. He plays the avant-garde mercenary who can "talk with two tongues," advancing and denying his own claims to essential identity. In fact, from the start, *Enemy of the Stars* is self-consciously presented as a performance. The reader is ushered past a "box office" to a grand arena; "THE ACTION OPENS" on a stage set with gangways, scenery, lighting (the titular "STARS?"), and an operatic chorus (*B*, 55, 61). Arghol and Hanp wear masks throughout, which are "fitted with trumpets of antique theatre" (*B*, 60). In this, Lewis proudly declares that his work is a grand tragedy equivalent to the dramatic work of the ancient Greeks. Arghol is his modern version of the heroic individual, here struck down not by divine fate, but by a cruel socio-economic order. More importantly, though, Lewis is interested in drama insofar as it signals the performative aspects of all identity and thus, for better or for worse, the interdependence of individual and mass. His tale suggests that even the most romantic forms of identity are both contingent and malleable; the tragic fall entails a reversal of heroic selfhood and the recognition a larger, contingent order. Furthermore, by exposing appearance as such, Lewis's audience is made aware of its collusion in this production. This is perhaps most clearly signaled by an opening claim that the story is "VERY WELL ACTED BY YOU AND ME" (*B*, 55). Lewis has agreed to perform the avant-garde impresario, but he asks that we uphold our promise to play the part of the outraged public. The drama, he implies, depends upon our consent. For an audience, this knowledge is at once damning and liberating. Like Hanp, we are forced to recognize our participation and thus our access to the current relations of power. Like Hanp, we are asked to reconsider and perhaps reconstruct the nature of those relations.

Lewis clearly understood his approach as a "'classical' manner of appre-hending," but the idiosyncrasies of his style demand that we more precisely define the classicism that was being revived at this time as well how these revivals were connected to other movements in thought and politics (*MWA*, 103). Certainly, there were as many definitions of "classicism" and "roman-ticism" as there were moderns. Their models were diverse (Greek, African, Italian, Byzantine), as were their applications (aesthetics, philosophy, pol-itics, sociology) and political valences (fascist, royalist, democratic, prole-tarian). Moreover, these definitions arise out of a complex dialectic of force and form within modernism itself, and so they sometime slip in and out of each other without warning. Some self-proclaimed classicists consciously toyed with a certain romanticism (Lewis, Hulme, H.D.); some potential romantics sought stability from a classical tradition (Eliot, Pound, Yeats); others, however, refused to be categorized altogether (Lawrence, Joyce, Woolf). However, despite a complexity of motive and theory, we can say with confidence that the moderns tended to revive and reinflect this debate in ways that consistently spoke to their fears about the expanding market. Certainly, they used these existing categories to defend radically diverse definitions of the work of art, subjectivity, political engagement, and the *polis*. But, as we will find, their thoughts on these matters hinged upon a larger distinction between two different kinds of production, one excessive and violent, the other tempered and conscious. As the moderns saw it, their work – in both form and content – could either persist in a romantic ideology of production and so extend the horrors of modernity into the future or, by way of a classical reserve, grind modern production to a halt and thus clarify alternatives.

We might also recognize that, at certain historical moments, "romanticism" and "classicism" could not be so easily dissociated or even so pragmatically applied. In the early nineteenth century, for example, the two movements shared a common escapism from the industrial world and an affirmative faith in a transcendent signifier.[27] But many moderns sought to redefine this discourse of otherworldly purity as specifically romantic and thus contrasted it to a material tangibility that they called classicism. As they understood it, the former attitude, in its self-affirming unity, could only obscure the contradictions of the market, whereas the latter grounded all ideals within their contingent production. Similarly, we might recognize that, traditionally, romanticism and classicism share a certain agony; they occupy a common landscape of frustrated desire and tragic failure, broken columns and wistful moons. Yet, again, for the moderns, romantic pain was always transcendent; even the denial of the ideal implies, negatively, its abstract persistence. In classicism, however, this struggle never moves beyond the fallen, imperfect world. The classical hero, in fact, revels in the postlapsarian landscape; he constructs a better, if provisional, order amidst its fragments and discontinuities.

Similar distinctions can be used to define the different kinds of "classicism" advocated by the moderns. According to Mark Antliff, classical modernism can be roughly divided into two types, a "reasoned classicism" and a "living classicism." The first, which harks back to the rational conventions of Athenian society, emphasizes the formal construction of order. The latter, founded upon an earlier, ritualized tradition, depicts a world that is at once intensive and affective.[28] Again, we are dealing only with tendencies, but it is clear that the classicism of the High Modernists tended to fall into the former category. In works such as Eliot's *The Waste Land* or Pound's *The Cantos*, the use of the fragment, no matter how dissonant, serves to project some universal or otherwise idealistic order. Here, particularities – either indirectly, in their abstract negation, or directly, in their homologous coordination – find significance only in a formal patterning. At its best, in its negative form, this classicism exposes the unbearable contradictions of history, the failure of democratic capitalism to affect a healthy union of the individual with the community. A persistent irony maintains critical distance against false totalities as well as projects the hope, albeit an ever-receding one, of a better order. Yet, just as often, this classicism tends toward the cancellation of *both* individual experience and concrete community. In these works, the presence of particularity serves to assuage an inevitable sacrifice to totality, and the suggestion of order relieves a subjective impotence. In other words, these works maintain hope in the dissociative activity and damaging paradoxes that inform the market itself. They find a spurious freedom in the alienation that defines modern productive relations and a false security in the reified totality of modern technology. In the words of Michael North, this rational classicism, in its formal effort to redeem the suffering of the modern world, can be seen as "a rearguard action nipping at the heels of a triumphant liberal society."[29]

Other classical works, however, such as those constructed by Hulme, H. D., and Gaudier-Brzeska, offer the fragment as a tangible object of resistance and clarity. This alternative, "living" classicism heightens the incongruous, yet affective elements of time and space; it exposes the necessary tensions within an always changing and somewhat hostile environment. This classicism, particularly as it emphasizes material restraint, undermines those romantic binaries – subject and object, hard and soft, masculine and feminine – that are still used to categorize the modern period and its creations. It consistently exposes the mutuality of the world, the constitutive processes by which identities are shaped and reshaped. Eileen Gregory smartly defines the following oppositions as "a widely accepted, largely unspoken code, an energized discursive field that modern writers could not ignore":

Romantic	*Classic*
soft	hard
wet	dry
hedonistic	disciplined
narcotic light [dreamlight]	daylight
child or adolescent	adult
love of infinite	love of finite
beauty as infinite	beauty known by fixed standard
blurred rendering	exact rendering
escapist, neurotic	realistic
impressionistic, subjective	scientific, objective
insane, unsound, diseased	sane, healthy
oblique, deviant	straight
luxurious	austere
personal	impersonal
democratic	aristocratic
heretical	orthodox
fragmentary	whole
chaotic	ordered
feminine	masculine[30]

As I see it, the more progressive classicists perceived these binaries them-selves as the domain of a particularly romantic attitude. In its form and content, their work suggests the following revision:

Romantic Modernism	Classical Modernism
force/form	tension
hot/cold	friction
hard/soft	posability
past/future	currency
subject/object	the phenomenal
self/other	intersubjectivity
private/public	communal negotiation
spectacle/audience	affect
projecting/receiving	conceiving
creation/mimesis	shaping
whole/fragment	dialectical materialism
idea/thing	embodied consciousness
symbol/icon	index
impression/image	sculpture
aural/visual	tactile
soul/body	skin
masculine/feminine	hermaphroditism/intercourse
god/human	demiurgos
nature/technology	second nature

If romantic modernism privileges the symbolic over and against the material world, classical modernism confounds that binary altogether as it depicts the body as the site of both signification and labor. If romantic modernism privileges form as an ideal unity in opposition to the purposive forces of the everyday, classical modernism always perceives form to be composed of intersecting needs and desires. Perhaps the most revealing point of com-parison is that while romantic modernism approaches the ideal condition of music, as in Eliot's fugue-like *Four Quartets*, Joyce's symphonic "Circe," and, most notoriously, Pound's theory of the "great bass," classical mod-ernism approaches the condition of sculpture, the art of shaping a resistant matter. Here, we find the clearest insistence on material tension: the sculp-tural object exists only within and through the energy of its surroundings, as it in turn shapes that same environment.[31]

   As I argue throughout this book, this logic of force and form adopts, as it updates, a certain tradition of dialectical materialism. Classicism, inso-far as it seeks a middle way between the violence of the avant-garde and the formalism of High Modernism, finds coherence in a progressive phe-nomenology of labor. This classicism acknowledges the expressive desire that underlies any productive effort. It seeks, however, to ground that energy within the world, where it finds clarity and stability. Conversely, this classicism reveals created form as it has been shaped by intentional forces. Form consistently points toward that which is supplemental or other to itself, the socio-historical desires that went into its making. Lewis offers clarity in the contrast he draws between the horrors of modern production and a more humane approach that is attuned to the particulars of its environment. The former, he explains, is governed by a violent egotism that tends to "override" all in its path:

Where men have physically been able to act the giant, and chop through nature, instead of crawling over it, in the manner of Lilliput, and override an accident, instead of accommodating themselves to it, they have not been able to supply the appropriate *mind* for the super-body, that is the trouble.

The other mode is humble, yet affective:

Projecting his torturous, not yet oppressive, geometry, out upon the chaotic super-structures, being methodic where he can, in the teeth of natural disorder, man is seen at his best. He then produces something of intellectual as well as emotional value, which the unadulterated stark geometry of the Machine-Age precludes.[32]

Lewis is typical of this tradition in that he locates productive activity at the boundaries of self and other. Consciousness continually shapes, as it in turn is shaped by, both material conditions and social paradigms. Dialectically, form consistently negates its own stability, disrupts its calm façade of self-identicality. Its presence flickers between the positive and the negative, the reified and the fluid, between the alienated structures of convention and the flux of human desire. At its best, this dynamic reopens the seemingly transcendent to the worldly, affecting a modality at once conscious and free.

In his 1844 manuscripts, Marx applies a similar dialectic to a general theory of labor. For the early Marx, human forces and forms shape one another within a flexible history; phenomenal experience exists somewhere between "subjectivism and objectivism, spiritualism and materialism, activity and suffering." In the best of worlds, he explains, the individual slowly carves his desires and truths into the world, thereby clarifying his existence and its possibilities: "In creating an objective world . . . in working-up organic nature, man proves himself a conscious species-being, i.e., as a being that treats the species as its own essential being, or that treats itself as species being."[33] In the twentieth century, Marx's heirs would begin to clarify the connections between cultural production, particularly aesthetic praxes, and this other, more obvious kind of labour. The work of art, in its structural organization, functions as a metonym for productive activity within the world, extending and challenging its historical coordinates. In this, the work, in its exposed play of fragment and whole, content and style, can be used as either an instrument of critical negation or a positive, constructive hope. Theodor Adorno and the early Georg Lukács, for example, valorize an aesthetic praxis that expresses the impossibility of reconciling subject and object. For them, the successful work is structurally tragic, an organizational failure; in this, it serves as an important defense against false totalities.[34] For others, however, this same dialectic points toward a more constructive attitude; the work's openness suggests a possible negotiation of power. Charles Altieri, for example, privileges a kind of art that makes "manifest the working of forces that at once compose the internal dynamic presence of the art and project beyond that presence in ways that problematize individuality by making visible the dependencies and pressures underlying it." By exposing its appearance as such, the work suggests that power is immanent as well as negotiable. "Self-consciousness," Altieri explains, "emerges as the awareness of the interplay of negative and reconstructive powers."[35]

My discussion, then, is governed by the notion that art can best be understood through a certain phenomenology of labor and that this phenomenology, in turn, must be theorized in terms of history. Moreover, I argue that classicism in particular, even at its most rarefied, most clearly foregrounds this productive history and thus provides a more comprehensive understanding of its trajectory. Perhaps Hannah Arendt's work offers the most positive account of the alternative aesthetic praxis I hope to establish here. For Arendt also, thought exists only in its interaction with the material world, in its material conditioning. The mind's power confronts as it transfigures the world, and conversely, that world remains static until touched by mind. Arendt, however, further suggests that the most valuable result of this interaction is the human artifice, an accumulation of cultural products that includes, but is not limited to, works of art. Arendt celebrates the human artifice because it provides at once the stability and the inspiration by which humans can think freely. As she argues, humans need to make sense to one another; they must produce a common meaningfulness within the world. The artifice, as the conditional embodiment of thought, provides the terms by which a community can peacefully negotiate its needs. It constitutes an "aristocracy of either a political or spiritual nature from which a restoration of the other capacities of man could start anew." Arendt's work asserts the possibility of a stable space, much like the classical *polis*, in which civilization can address itself and its past. This space is not simply conscious or relational, and it is certainly not personally transcendent – it exists only in its material enactment, in the condition of its being actively shaped and transformed. For me, classical modernism partakes in a similar project. This art asserts neither the primacy of the individual nor the finality of history. Rather, in its tangible presence, it provides the terms by which we can rethink our engagement with the world. This art, in its imperfect grace and tragic hope, points toward a community that is at once united and free.[36]

My attempt to defend this classical alternative, however, begs the issue of legacy. We must concede that the modernist faith in classicism, as defined here, ultimately acceded to the call for more restrictive regimes. For Hulme, Lewis, Pound, Yeats, and Eliot, for too many modernists, the story is the same: an early commitment to the tensions that define the individual within his community gives way to increasing demands for social control. For these artists, an initial awareness of contingency leads first to a sense of necessary political engagement and then to the possibility of planned totality. Because identity – individual, cultural, or national – was seen to be so easily manipulated, it was believed that it can and must be manipulated into durable shapes and forms. In Lewis's work, for example, the notion of construction ceased to be playfully critical and turned absolutely dire. His sense of appearance and its affected boundaries informs his later advocacy of a quasi-artistic, yet "centralized consciousness" that could productively channel the energy of the masses. *Art of Being Ruled*, for example, celebrates the artist-politician who can construct and maintain solid caste divisions, "separation not the result of skin-deep 'power,' or of social advantage, but something like a *biological* separating-out of the chaff from the grain" (*AOBR*, 108, 128).

Not surprisingly, for each of the writers mentioned above, this change in attitude can be traced to the first years of World War I. Most of the classicists I discuss – Hulme, Lewis, and Gaudier-Brzeska, in particular – saw battle at the Western Front. Violent experiences in the trenches fueled their hostility to the modern world and its rampant production and consumption. For each, war was a perverse celebration of human vitality and thus directly linked to an expanding bourgeois order. International conflict served to divide and divert the potentially revolutionary communities of the modern world; it augmented the competitive impulse of the market and extended the rapid production and reproduction already underway back home. Their turn toward a more programmatic order of restraint, as such took shape as fascism, is informed by this paranoia and trauma. As they understood it, centralization, directed by an elite group of artist-planners, would help to restrain and remold the increasingly chaotic desires unleashed by the market. Again, Lewis most clearly expresses this mixed fear and reaction: "there seems no reason at present why this period of chaotic wastefulness should not be regarded as drawing to a close. In order to wind it up, further wars and revolutions may occur. But they are not any longer necessary. There is no [sic] even political excuse for them" (*AOBR*, 367). Intriguingly, in light of this response, one might argue that the fate of classical modernism is linked to that of socialism, with which, as suggested above, it originally shared many ideals. After World War I, Europe's flailing labor movements also sought fulfillment in fascism's more aggressive stance, seeking revolution in a more radical anti-liberalism from the right. Left and right, then, dissolved in a shared hostility to bourgeois order, to the detriment of the former and the strength of the latter.

I cannot deny that this history raises serious doubts as to whether classicism of any kind should be advocated at the present time. However, I hope to make clear that there is nothing inherently fascist or totalitarian about classicism (or romanticism, for that matter) and that its significance exists only in terms of its specific uses. Throughout this project, in fact, I have been careful to distinguish between the raw mechanics of modernist devices (image, analogy, stream of consciousness, etc.) and their willful mobilization toward specific political regimes (Catholicism, fascism, socialism, etc.). More importantly, I am not interested in reviving classicism as a unified attitude or system of beliefs, but as a critical adjunct to the experience of modernity, as an inevitable, if unheeded critique of capital's destructive logic. In other words, while some classicists may have looked to the past for inspiration, their work contains an historically specific and politically progressive response to an economy that continues to shape our culture. It is my contention that as long as cultural production depends upon a romantic conflation of sign and essence, as long as it remains captive to the auratic manipulations of capital, it should be dogged by an art that exposes the terms of production. As long as criticism falls under the sway of romantic otherness, as "other modernisms" continue to proliferate across space and time without carefully addressing the history that informs them, it remains necessary to foreground the material conditions that shape all cultural expression. In the end, we will find that classicism confounds the very distinction between modernism and postmodernism and thus provides its own defense. It undermines the modernist fantasy of immediacy as well as the postmodern fantasy of complete mediation, and exposes both as complementary myths of a single, capitalist order. It situates itself between world and word, the body and its representation, and so discloses and disrupts the ideological coordinates that define modernity at large. Hopefully, by emphasizing classicism's performative aspects, its critical thoroughness, and its historical necessity, we can move beyond the self-perpetuating (and self-defeating) discourses of modernity toward a more integrative, constructive kind of work.

With this in mind, I would like to turn to this introduction's epigram. In trying to revive the hidden dialectic of modernist polemics, I have needed to remind myself that my own polemic *must* seem a bit stubborn, unoriginal, old-fashioned even. Throughout, my hope has been that by "standing still," by restraining my own desire to be otherwise, I will make clearer the urges that define both modernism and its critical heritage. That said, I have also tried to remain open (in ways the moderns never were) to the subtle contradictions that define all cultural production, the ways in which a complex society shapes a complex art. In my efforts to redeem a more inclusive experience of modernity, I address both the positive and negative moments that shape each work of art, its tendencies to affirm as well as deny the nightmare of its own history. This book, then, is only roughly divided between "Critique" and "Construction," between two sides of a single phenomenon that is thoroughly modern. In the first two chapters, I take on the chronic romanticism of both the early avant-garde and the High Modernist tradition. Here, I argue that while the energetic avant-garde tends to affirm the productive imperative of the modern economy, High Modernism, in its commitment to formal integrity, tends to consecrate the reified structure of the economy as a whole. The next three chapters trace the emergence and development of a certain classical modernism. They present this aesthetic alternative as it theorizes, in turn, the object world, intersubjective relations, and, finally, political organization. Importantly, these three chapters consider the application of classicism as it moves from an abstract, metaphysical order to a viable political strategy asserted within a wider public sphere. By dramatizing this transition across the great divide, I try to show how this seemingly reactionary aesthetic found amplification in progressive social movements, such as labor and suffrage, and to suggest that these strategies are still available to us today. Like the works on which I focus, the chapters of this book tend to repeat and recycle certain themes in almost ritualistic fashion. I intend, however, that in their subtle modulations, these chapters expose the necessary relations between aesthetics, politics, economics, and theory. It is my belief that it is only by working through these connections, rather than against them, that we have any hope of understanding where we stand today.

PART I
Critique

CHAPTER I

Fascism and/or liberalism: the avant-garde and modern capitalism

INTRODUCTION

Marinetti tore into town, hungry for war and violence. With his loco-
motive jaw and Nietzschean belly, he stormed through cafés and stamped
through museums. He gorged himself on Chelsea and the shops in South
Kensington. He bemired the ancient streets of Westminster and fouled the
Thames. Nothing was spared his incendiary fingertips; no one escaped the
drunken injustice of his eyes. He cursed parliament – that "cow stall!" – and
toasted warmongers. He marched with suffragettes and soiled "very elegant
millionairesses." Ruskin was burned in effigy, Wilde drawn on a cross. He
defied, one by one, the "sacred laws of snobbery" and ate cold meats on
Queen Anne furniture. He rode astride the Dreadnoughts and sang the
music of machines. His wild hymn to progress called for London's destruction. The lymphatic empire would be laid to waste; its "counterfeit men"
and "half women" damned to Sodom. The world itself would be "no more
than an immense tub of red wine in foaming gorges, pouring vehemently
out of gates whose drowned drawbridges shuddered and sounded."[1]

And London fell in love with him. On or about December 1910, a
mad gaiety had gripped the city. A series of popular invasions and faddish
shocks prepared the way for the Italian's entrance. The month of his arrival
alone saw the Russian Ballet, the Japan–British Exhibition, and Halley's
Comet. Bloomsbury was dressing up in Ethiopian garb; restaurants were
renamed *à la française*. Imports were up, exports down. A cult of the outsider, who was at once aristocratic and primitive, made the Italian a super-
star. He filled halls that Shaw had played the night before, danced with
those who danced with Asquith. Crowds gathered around him as if he were
"health itself"[2] and "wildly applauded his outspoken derision of all their
cherished national characteristics and customs."[3] The primitive destruction
of values titillated the British; each new speech, each new painting, was
greeted with gleeful cries of indignation. Importantly, the futurist aesthetic

29

"comforted, stimulated, consoled, edified"[4] – and not despite the fact that it refigured existence in terms of death and violence. London, particularly upper middle-class London and the New Liberals of Cambridge, wanted a war – No, they could not wait for Ypres! – and Marinetti gave them one. Force-fed suffragettes, striking miners, rabid unionists: these were not enough – all hailed the great poet of apocalypse.

Indeed, spectacles of this sort seem to anticipate the real war, the Great War. They attest, in their violence and repetition, to an ideological imperative that both preceded and outlasted the sight of actual bloodshed. In order to understand this imperative, as well as its persistence, we need to focus on modernity's ruling class, the bourgeoisie, and its liberal ideology. As several critics have noted, the former can be characterized by its uneasy attempts to unite conflicting values, such as pride and humility, progress and order. Its liberalism is defined by a related set of paradoxes: it asserts individualism as the foundation of social unity, cultural distinction as the source of national unity. As E. J. Hobsbawm explains,

the bourgeoisie had believed not only in individualism, respectability, and property, but also progress, reform, and a moderate liberalism. In the eternal battle among the upper strata of nineteenth-century societies, between the "parties of movement" or "progress" and the "parties of order," the middle classes had unquestionably stood, in their great majority, for movement, though by no means insensitive to order.[5]

These ideological contradictions, of course, express those of the economy. The complex logic of the bourgeoisie is founded upon the central contradictions of capital production, namely, the formalization of constant change and the ceaseless domestication of the new. Proud humility, organized revolt, repetitive violence – these serve the productive mechanisms of a voracious economy. According to Marshall Berman,

Under pressure, every bourgeois, from the pettiest to the most powerful, is forced to innovate, simply in order to keep himself and his business afloat; anyone who does not actively change on his own will become a victim of changes draconically imposed by those who dominate the market . . . The intense and relentless pressure to revolutionize production is bound to spill over and transform what Marx calls "conditions of production" (or, alternately, "productive relations") as well, and with them, all social conditions and relationships. (94–5)

As I hope to argue here, the violence that marks modern cultural activity, particularly as it culminates in the phenomenon of the avant-garde, derives from the violence inherent to modern production.

As mentioned in my introduction, the avant-garde attacked the purposelessness of autonomous art only to valorize the constant activity of its creation. It reconceived romantic transcendence as a dissociative impera- tive, and thus aligned aesthetics with the productivism of a larger economic praxis. Manifestos, collages, spontaneous writing, found objects – these forms eschew the principles of aesthetic unity for the process of aesthetic mediation. In their willful creation or manipulation of value, as well as in their unending production and consumption of materials, they mime as they glorify the logic of commodification. As should be made clear, the avant-garde's *dissociative* imperative and its *productive* imperative are one and the same. The avant-garde performs the continual production of difference and thus affirms a market that must ceaselessly and efficiently overcome itself with new products. As Russell A. Berman explains, "bour- geois culture undergoes a process of bureaucratization, its forms grow rigid and perfunctory, and the avant-garde emerges with a project of charismatic renewal . . . it promises to carry out the bourgeois project in general more successfully by jettisoning one particular feature, aesthetic autonomy."[6] Similarly, Andrew Hewitt defines the avant-garde by its efforts "on the one hand, to revolutionize the *forces* of production and to resist, on the other, the revolutionary potential of the social *relations* of production." As a cultural phenomenon, the avant-garde can be credited with refiguring the "process of externalized destruction . . . and consequently of enjoying destruction itself as an aesthetic event."[7]

The avant-garde, in other words, reflects as it responds to a specifi- cally modern world and its hyperproductive economy. More importantly, though, the historical avant-garde emerged at those moments when bour- geois culture failed to sustain its own promises, when the inherent contra- dictions of the market became unsustainable. Its valorization of aesthetic activity served to reintegrate and thus annul potentially dissonant forces – whether individual or communal – in terms of their productivity. Thus, I plan to show here that the avant-garde most rigorously asserted its demands in underdeveloped nations, such as Italy, and slowly declining nations, such as England. The movements that emerged in these countries shared a com- mon rhetoric that validates and extends the market at different stages of its history: futurism imagined a new world given over to intense productive activity, in which automatons labor in "violent spasms of action and cre- ation," while Bloomsbury sought to maintain the status quo by insisting that "everyone should be an artist" and arguing for social reforms by which "beauty could be generated without effort."[8]

Admittedly, this argument demands a radical revision of the ways in which we typically theorize early twentieth-century history. As the above comments suggest, futurism found its most direct British counterpart not, as others have argued, in the iconoclastic vorticist movement, but in the bourgeois attitudes and affirmations of Bloomsbury. Similarly, the material violence of Italian fascism found a subtle homology in the individualistic and progressive values of British liberalism. While these pairings may seem willfully provocative, they come into focus once the abstract notion of "aesthetic politics" is grounded in its specific history. These movements differently inflect the necessary relations between modern art and modern politics, but only because they are expressive of the geographical and temporal mutations of a single economic trajectory. In other words, by tracing the interactions between these movements as well as between these movements and their specific audiences, I intend to dramatize the affirmative dialogue between a flexible aesthetic strategy and a changing economic order. I hope to show how the paradoxes of avant-garde activity shift in response to a shifting market that is itself torn between competition and nationhood, invention and rationalization, chaos and order. As I have had to remind myself, though, this approach can only be successful if it adopts a dialecticism of its own. On the one hand, I consider the ways in which the avant-garde shares, positively, in modernity's push for a better world and preserves certain critical spaces from which that world can be reasonably established. On the other, I cannot ignore how the avant-garde serves an affirmative purpose, offering only a *semblance* of political progress and worldly consciousness to the undeniably horrific experience of modernity.

I   WE ABHOR OUR FUTURIST MASTERS

Why London? And why declaim the "Futurist Speech to the English" at the Lyceum Club for Women? Of course, Marinetti warred in order to war and if real enemies could not be found, he "would have to invent" them (54). Where better to invoke an international spell of riot than that great capital city in which pride and prudery still reigned? Marinetti's writings, however, also attest to a rather embarrassing love for this particular corner of Europe. Yes, the city was "conventional and puerile," and he damned its "habitual and hypocritical formality" (72, 68). But behind the standard futurist rant lies a great respect for what he saw as a "strong, virile, and anti-sentimental" city.[9] Marinetti knew that "the Futurist genius of England" had well surpassed that of Italy. From the Dreadnoughts on the Thames to the monstrous Aswan Dam, the empire hummed with electric divinity. He unabashedly praised its leaders for their "potent individualism" and "unbridled passion for every kind of struggle." In fact, London, despite its provincialism, was the model for an "industrial, commercial, and military Venice" (65–7).

But the city served his rhetoric of strength and progress in more complex ways. What Marinetti truly and shamefully loved about London, beyond his love of the steel and the coal and the timetables, was its typically bourgeois culture of contradiction and the ceaseless struggle it implied. For Marinetti, the English were "the most contradictory people on earth," torn between sense and sensibility, sweetness and light, revolution and custom (61). Their "potent individualism" and "broad love of liberty" were directly countered by an "indomitable bellicose patriotism" and "national pride" (59). Here was a master race whose "obsessive mania is to be always *chic*," but, for love of the *chic* "renounce passionate action, violence of heart, exclamations, shouts, and even tears" (60). In his London speeches, Marinetti explained to the English that "To contradict oneself is to live and you know how to contradict yourselves bravely" (64). The futurist acknowledged with glee his listeners' arrogant pride and utter self-loathing: "No one admits to being a *bourgeois* in England: everyone despises his neighbor and calls *him* a bourgeois" (60). Ultimately, Marinetti saw in London an ideology of productive struggle that catered to his hopes better than anything he might find in the fetid swamps of Italy – perhaps better than war itself. He went in order to despise and be despised, to experience the city in which "the pleasure of being booed" had become a way of life. Approached in this manner, futurism takes on a structural character not usually associated with its political stance, but one perhaps truer to its original aims. As we will find, the futurist, in his self-proclaimed avant-gardism, was as bourgeois as his neighbor.

In Marinetti's early work, the struggle of the Heroic Will serves to organize these contradictions. Each manifesto presents itself as a Nietzschean tale of disgust and grandeur, of the will to overcome the past and forge the perfection of the future. Marinetti's superman is celebrated for his efforts to transcend the decadent world; he is driven by a romantic imperative to surpass the claims of the vulgar mass. His defiance is fueled by an "Immense pride"; he stands like a "proud beacon . . . against an army of hostile stars" (47). In "Let's Murder the Moonshine," the futurist hero flees from the city of Paralysis to "the flanks of Gorisankar, summit of the world!" He stomps across the decadent landscape on his way to "the windows of the ideal" (53).

As the reader quickly realizes, however, this hero is never very successful in his quest for transcendence. His struggle lies horizontally and sometimes forces him to backtrack and reverse his position; he never attains anything more than "keen maneuver" (60). In this, Marinetti asserts, as Nietzsche did before him, that perfection exists dynamically rather than essentially. Impossibility is achieved, or at least implied, only in a constant "rivalry":

All surpluses are at play in every human spirit. Rivalry strives for the impossible, purifying itself in an atmosphere of danger and speed. Every intelligence grows lucid, every instinct is brought to its greatest splendor, they clash with each other for a surplus of pleasure. Because they easily find enough to eat, men can perfect their lives in numberless antagonistic exertions. (114)

As throughout Marinetti's early work, struggle attests to an inseverable communion or identification, an obsessive attention to that which emasculates the Will and thwarts transcendence. What is perhaps too obvious about futurism is that despite its idealist rhetoric, it is extremely mired in that abject world from which it seeks to escape. Despite Marinetti's celebration of airplanes and supermen, his work constantly blurs the boundary between the transcendent and the fallen. The movement of the Heroic Will is dialectical at best. For every act of differentiation one finds in the manifestos, there is an equal and opposite gesture of decadent synthesis at work.

At its best, in its earliest forms, futurism revels in these paradoxes; in its ceaseless struggle, it both conjures and dismantles the possibility of an ideal. Undeniably, the avant-garde thrust, no matter how violent, can be seen as a protest against the corrupt terms of the modern world, a recognition that perfection could never be achieved within that world. More importantly, though, this thrust consistently undermines its own claims to authority; the willfully transcendent stance exposes its own constructedness and thus carries along with it an irreducible excess or residue. In other words, in this oppositioning, the avant-garde thrust remains dependent upon its others, on women, lower classes, other races, history itself, and thus on desires that can push it beyond itself. Take, for example, the following scene from the "Founding" manifesto, in which Marinetti's racing car, unable to bear its own power, swerves into a rank ditch:

Oh Maternal Ditch, almost full of muddy water! Fair factory drain! I gulped down your nourishing sludge; and I remembered the blessed black breast of my Sudanese nurse . . . When I came up – torn, filthy, and stinking – from under the capsized car, I felt the white-hot iron of joy deliciously pass through my heart! (48–9)

Paradoxically, a corrupt feminism is embraced as the very source of futurist power and clarity. Here, as elsewhere, a decadent synthesis inspires further acts of differentiation; through an always ironic "pride," matter moves toward greater division and greater unity, greater desire and consciousness (47). This logic similarly informs Marinetti's theory of historical evolution.

The Heroic Will never advances into the future with the reckless abandon ascribed to it. No matter how fast the futurist rages through the streets of Florence, he can never give himself "utterly to the Unknown." At another point in the "Founding" manifesto, Marinetti's automobile is blocked by two creaky bicyclists in its path. Here, the past outraces the future, forcing the prophet to acknowledge his origins:

I spun my car around with the frenzy of a dog trying to bite its tail, and there, suddenly, were two cyclists coming toward me, shaking their fists, like two equally convincing but nevertheless contradictory arguments. Their stupid dilemma was blocking my way – damn! Ouch! . . . I stopped short and to my disgust rolled over into a ditch with my wheels in the air. (48)

Similarly, in "Let's Murder the Moonshine," the industrial work of the futurists uncovers the "carnal Moon, the Moon of lovely thighs." This emasculating light halts production with "sweet drowsiness" and "long gurgles of pleasure." And yet, by this very brilliance, the madmen are able to erect powerful turbines so that "three hundred electric moons canceled with their rays of blinding mineral lightness the ancient green queen of loves" (59). An endless process this is, a constant historical slippage in which progress uncovers a decadent past that, in turn, and potentially with less blindness, inspires further progress.

This struggle of the will forms the vortex out of which all futurist contradictions spin – revolution and order, anarchy and nationalism, spirit and science. Marinetti's early work consistently plays with these dialectics and their multiple configurations, always advancing what appears to be an anti-futurist discourse of aesthetic impurity and historical contingency. In fact, this early version of the avant-garde only indirectly, negatively, affirms the possibility of totality. Futurism seems to exert its power through that which lies outside of the social totality. Order exists conditionally, in a state of progressive tension with a persistent "surplus." This logic, indeed, recalls the finest Hegelian tradition and allows the modernist to maneuver between the twin threats of nineteenth-century thinking, romantic solipsism, and positivist closure. By envisioning the Heroic Will as the force of social progress, Marinetti upholds individual vitality as well as communal order. The futurist dialectic conquers "the seemingly inconquerable hostility that separates out human flesh from the metal of motors" (95, 97).

But as much as one might like to trace an ironic resistance to fascism in this early futurism, in the failure to establish transcendent, transhistorical values, one need not look far to see that Marinetti quickly ousts such a possibility. Marinetti's celebration of struggle and competition, of accumulation and progress, points again and again to the logic of capital. The act of dissociation, here repeated with a desperate insistence, is at once an affirmation of class distinction and a glorified form of labor. Indeed, behind the dizzying rhetoric of futurism lies the traditional trappings of class warfare. As suggested by a 1908 photograph in which Marinetti proudly poses in a sparkling automobile before a massive factory, futurism is little more than a radical affirmation of conspicuous consumption and the exploitation it feeds on (Figure 1). Marinetti, in fact, had little remorse in announcing that futurism was driven by "a purely financial consciousness."[10] The movement, he argued, promised "mountains of goods and a shrewd, wealthy, busy crowd of industrialists and businessmen!" (56). In "Let's Murder the Moonshine," the revelers seek neither freedom nor autonomy; their immediate goal is the construction of a great military railroad for which they need to "Rob the strongboxes heaped with gold!" (57). Moreover, if Marinetti initially presents identity – individual, national, or otherwise – as a willed act dependent upon some other, he eventually abandons that model for one based upon rigid, essentialized distinctions. His dialectical playfulness quickly grows rigid and static; the dance of the Heroic Will is economically reconfigured and thus made sterile. The first manifesto, in fact, already argues that "A racing car whose hood is adorned with great pipes . . . is more Beautiful than the *Victory of Samothrace*" (49). "Let's Murder the Moonshine" compares the moon's brilliance to that generated by gigantic wheels, turbines, and magnetic pulses (59). In these instances, identity is still presented as relation, but now Marinetti – through a language of economic efficiency – tries to master the dialectic. An initially complex "synthesis" gives way to a controlled oppositioning of static forms.

In fact, Marinetti eventually abandons the struggling hero altogether for the more predictable activity of the productive machine. For the futurist, technology efficiently conjoins the progressive and the controlled, and thus offers a purer expression of the bourgeois dialectic. In the following description, the dissociative principle is "no longer human"; technology spiritually transfigures inherently messy productive relations:

My Futurist senses perceived this splendor for the first time on the bridge of a dreadnought. The ship's speed, its trajectories of fire from the height of the quarterdeck in the cool ventilation of warlike probabilities, the strange vitality of order sent down from the admiral and suddenly become autonomous, human no longer, in the whims, impatiences, and illnesses of steel and copper. (98–9)

As Hal Foster nicely states, the futurist machine serves the dual purpose of "binding and unbinding." It aids the futurist in the "aesthetic management"

Figure 1   F. T. Marinetti in a car, *c.* 1908, location unknown.

of desires that are both transgressive and totalitarian.[11] Ultimately, though, these machines are also rejected, so that the futurist utopia contains nothing but the pure, shimmering activity of abstract figures: "The mathematical signs $+ - \times$ serve to achieve marvelous synthesis and share . . . in expressing the geometric and mechanical splendor" (110). With this faith in the "mathematically spiritual," Marinetti purifies his work of any alterity.[12] Perhaps the difference is one of degree rather than kind, but this last formulation of the futurist aesthetic makes clear that an early "anarchy of perfections" has been transformed into a much more frightening perfection of anarchies (114).

Traditionally, criticism has suggested that the futurist integration of art and life is based on an erasure of linguistic mediation and a concurrent emancipation of intuition and physical sensation.[13] I would argue, however, that art and life lose their distinction in this work as both approach a state of complete and constant mediation. The futurist does not attempt to turn art back toward life, but to turn all life into art. Marinetti's work offers a utopian vision in which literature has entered "directly into the universe and become one body with it." For the futurist, vital art is that which "pours out, beyond the body, into the infinity of space and time" (97). This movement toward total mediation represents a collapse of the sign into the signifier and the ontologization of expression. Reality is transfigured as the ceaseless production of new value; meaning is given over to a faddism of signs. More specifically, romantic reverie is reconceived as symbolic tyranny: the ego *must* engage in these formal processes, for identity exists solely in formal, symbolic distinctions. Psychology only fouls a movement that should be purely mechanical:

On the day when man will be able to externalize his will and make it into a huge invisible arm, Dream and Desire, which are empty words today, will master and reign over space and time.

This nonhuman and mechanical being, constructed for an omnipresent velocity, will be naturally cruel, omniscient, and combative. (99)

"Mechanical splendor" lies in the full extension of this process, when all experience has been reduced to its constant production and consumption. Only in this activity is any significance – individual, national, or historical – possible. As I now hope to show, this subtext points toward that which remains hidden in fascism itself, that its construction is both a reaction to and apotheosis of bourgeois capitalism. In other words, the fascist critique of the modern, bourgeois world replicates and affirms the latter's internal logic.

Fascism has most often been defined as an intense mechanization of public and private life, the aesthetic hardening of an otherwise disorganized socius. Its emphasis on order, hygiene, and efficiency serves to counter the decadent flux of the modern world, whether such is signified by democratic politics, the expansion of the market, labor unrest, or the rise of feminism. Conversely, though, fascism has also been defined by its cult of violence and war, its productive madness, its romantic vitalism and rather mystical energy. Its anarchic will to power breaks down the gridlock of modern rationalism, protective tariffs, and political reformism. We can perhaps reconcile these conflicting theories by observing that fascism is itself a contradictory order that serves to objectify flow and thus mimics the organized chaos of the marketplace. More precisely, fascism can be interpreted as an attempt to glorify the suffering of the bourgeois ego and to affirm the potentially disruptive contradictions of capital. As a desperate political expedient for a disadvantaged country, it tried to master the market and shape it into a national order that is both total and progressive.

Zeev Sternhell's recent work also points Italian fascism back to its bourgeois liberal roots and deftly analyzes totalitarianism as an affirmative transformation of the capitalist order:

If Fascism wished to reap all the benefits of the modern age, to exploit all the technical achievements of capitalism, if it never questioned the idea that market forces and private property were part of the natural order of things, it had a horror of the so-called bourgeois values, or, as Nietzsche called them, modern values: universalism, individualism, progress, natural rights, and equality. Thus, Fascism adopted the economic aspect of liberalism, but completely denied its philosophical principles and the intellectual and moral heritage of modernity.[14]

It is, however, not simply the case that fascism discarded the revolutionary content of bourgeois culture and maintained its economic structure. Rather, fascism reconceived bourgeois individualism within a rhetoric of national pride and sacrifice; the supposedly free will of the individual was subsumed under an ideal of collective destiny. More specifically, bourgeois competition was expanded as the mechanism by which the nation as a whole would be strengthened. Private property was transposed first to larger collective entities, the syndicates, and then to a corporate nation. In the end, the violent dialectics of differentiation, at once progressive and productive, informed a strict order of economic progress and an all-consuming nationalism. According to Simonetta Falasca-Zamponi,

Fascism's idea of corporativism rose as a phoenix from the ashes of national syndicalism's vision of labor relations – a vision that affirmed capitalism and the harmonic collaboration of classes as positive elements for the fulfillment of national interest. In accordance with such a vision, the Fascists upheld the role of capital and private property within the new society they wanted to organize.[15]

With its ideological context slightly reconfigured, the competitive capitalist ego was remolded in terms of a bellicose patriotism. The formation of a group of elites, a strong cadre of producers, became the advance guard of social regeneration. Once again, revolution and totality, romanticism and reification conjoin to define the modern experience.

Fascist leaders, in fact, were not ashamed of their bourgeois liberal roots. As Arturo Labriola, the founder of Italian syndicalism, acknowledged, "A class liberalism! That's what syndicalism is! It combats legal privileges for the other class and for itself, and it is only from the struggle and free play of organized economic forces that it expects the emergence of new historical formations." Enrico Leone also hoped that fascism would create a "society of free producers"; he argued that "social harmony can be attained only through the free functioning of the law of individual egoism."[16] For these thinkers, as for Mussolini himself, the new government would evolve out of the best aspects of the former order: it would preserve productive efficiency, it would maintain an emphasis on competition and struggle, and, perhaps most importantly, it would continue to exploit the romanticism of the individual will.[17] The first of these principles, however, would be taken over by machinery, where it would evolve freely. As in Marinetti's work, labor and invention were meant to attain a level of efficiency beyond the limitations and contingencies of the human body. The second principle, competition, would become openly violent as well as increasingly exoteric. The struggles that threaten to undermine capitalism from within were augmented and affirmed by international warfare and the subjugation of minority groups. Finally, the romanticism of the individual would be transposed to a national level. In fascism, romantic nationalism became a versatile expedient that could be used to deny as well as justify exploitation. The abstraction of the nation served to direct and divert any potential social revolution either back into production or against the enemy.

Thus, we come to an issue that we cannot stress enough: the affirmative relationship between twentieth-century violence and capitalism. The modern economy finds its greatest expression on the battlefield, where production and consumption reach exorbitant levels, where the human will is confirmed in its power over the material world, and where glorified sacrifice is possible at every turn. As I argue in chapter 4, the front was literally static, barely moving to one side or the other, yet it was the site of hyper-production and consumption. Order and vitality met in the ceaseless exchange of both human and non-human matter. One finds this logic made clear in Marinetti's "The Birth of a Futurist Aesthetic":

In Japan they carry on the strangest of trades: the sale of coal made from human bones. All their powderworks are engaged in producing a new explosive substance, more lethal than any yet known. This terrible new mixture has as its principle element coal made from human bones with the property of violently absorbing gases and liquids. For this reason countless Japanese merchants are thoroughly exploring the corpse-stuffed Manchurian battlefields. In great excitement they make huge excavations, and enormous piles of skeletons multiply in every direction on those broad bellicose horizons. One hundred *tsin* (7 kilograms) of human bones bring in 92 *kopeks*.

The Japanese merchants who direct this absolutely Futurist commerce buy no skulls. It seems they lack the necessary qualities. Instead the merchants buy great mounds of other bones to send to Japan, and the Benikou station from a distance look to travelers on the Trans-Siberian Railway like a gigantic grayish white pyramid: skeletons of heroes who do not hesitate to be crushed in mortars by *their own sons, their relatives, or their fellow citizens*, to be brutally vomited out by Japanese artillery against hostile enemies.

Glory to the indomitable ashes of man, that come to life in Cannons! My friends, let us applaud this noble example of synthetic violence. (90)

Here, we find all of the familiar qualities of futurist theory at work: the mechanization of subjective experience, the repetitive production and consumption of matter, and the construction of a strong social order through the aggressive pride of the individual. But Marinetti no longer conceals the facts that the war is run by merchants and that its heroes die for the economy. Rather, through the rhetoric of heroism and sacrifice, war proudly grants autonomy and purpose to both the suffering laborer and a treacherous social order. This violence, torn as it is between chaos and efficiency, affirms the complete dissociation of sensibility that threatened, if it had not already consumed, the individual and his society. In fact, the body here undergoes torture as testament to the order and vitality that is not always apparent in the commodified world itself. As Andrew Hewitt explains:

In the same way that the commodity is only a fetish of capitalism, which must itself be understood as a *system* of exchange, so the body (and elsewhere, the psychologized subject in general) is simply a fetish of the vital and productive/destructive forces that pass through it. The body represents and gives form to those forces and yet traduces in that representation by imposing the stasis of embodiment. [In this scene, the] static (bodily) reification of life forces is swept aside by a *new*, explosive commodity (even more powerful in death than in life . . . The Japanese merchants reject the stasis that is the body by burning it, exchanging it, and thereby reinvigorating it. (50–1)

As we will find, it is only with reference to this sustained violence that we can make sense of fascism's emergence and appeal, its ability to adopt and adapt the disaster of an inherently contradictory capitalism. It was only by exaggerating the productive violence, the controlled anarchy of the marketplace, that the movement thrived. Mussolini, in fact, only grew to power by way of the claim that "life is struggle, sacrifice, conquest, a continuous overcoming of one's self." Fascism, he urged, "is a continuous elaboration and transformation: it undergoes a work of unceasing revision, the only means to make an element of life and not a dead remain."[18] As Falasca-Zamponi eloquently explains,

Through reference to war, Mussolini solved the contradiction between his dynamic conception of violence and his view of internal social relations. Politically, Fascism could not tolerate violence within Italy, because the regime's goal was to control the country totally. Aesthetically, conflicts could not exist within the Italian borders, because homogeneity was a necessary element in the development of a beautiful Fascist state. At the same time, however, Fascism's masterpiece could not be achieved by merely accepting and maintaining harmony. Aesthetics' sublime heights were only to be reached through a continuous battle against laws and limits. (40)

The most important point here is that the battle must be "continuous." In fascism's glorification of violence, of endless technological warfare, the capitalist order was affirmed and extended.

2   THE ITALIAN INTRUDER

We are much closer to London than one might think. By the time of Marinetti's arrival, England was considered the "workshop of the world," a model of both progressive politics and industrial might. The total efficiency of this workshop, which simultaneously comforted and frightened the British, was forged upon contradictions similar to those we have been exploring: namely, the rational organization of change and the ceaseless production of otherness. As I show here, then, Marinetti offered Londoners a singularly affirmative vision of their own culture. As an outsider, his presence suggested a possible release from order; it provided Londoners with a much needed spectacle of liberation. But, at the same time, the Italian intruder became a rallying point for national unity; his futurist antics ultimately inspired an intensely conservative backlash. With this encounter, we can more clearly define the ideological aspects of a relatively stable market. The London crowd, with its contradictory love and disgust of the outsider, its vulgar fetishizing of his art, its faith in productive progress, exemplifies the tendencies of the age and their ability to sustain themselves, whether through violence or, in the work of Bloomsbury, a false peace.

British liberalism, particularly as it was theorized in the late nineteenth and early twentieth century, is riddled with paradoxes. Almost every definitional attempt that dates from this period is marked by contradictions that border on the absurd. Take, for example, Edward Freeman's account from the 1885 volume, *Why I Am a Liberal: Being Definitions and Confessions of Faith by the* BEST MINDS *of the* LIBERAL PARTY. His definition is typical insofar as it struggles to reconcile progress with tradition, individualism with nationalism, reason with faith:

THE MAIN WORK OF LIBERALISM HAS BEEN TO PRESERVE THE EARLIEST PRINCIPLES OF OUR POLITICAL LIFE . . . to change boldly where change has been needed, but to change on the old lines. THE OLDEST INSTITUTIONS ARE THE FREEST.[19]

This statement can be interpreted as an appeal to different populations within British society or as an effect of the historical transition from a more rigid social hierarchy to the subtly shifting terrain of democracy. Its paradoxes, however, also point us toward economics; the attempt to reconcile individualism with totality expresses the contradictions of a growing market. More than anything else, individualism here is a capital imperative; competition as well as progressive industrialization are seen to strengthen the nation as a whole. Samuel Smiles's incredibly popular book *Self-Help* more explicitly preached the virtues of the self-made man: "industry, frugality, temperance, and honesty." Here, entrepreneurial success is self-justifying, but it is also the foundation of national greatness. Smiles, in his anti-interventionism, argues that only free trade can establish national greatness:

For the nation is only the aggregate of individual conditions, and civilization itself is but a question of personal improvement.
   National progress is the sum of individual industry, energy, and uprightness, as national decay is of individual idleness, selfishness, and vice.[20]

John Stuart Mill, in his classic text *On Liberty*, pushes this paradox to its limit, arguing that it is not simply individualism, but eccentricity that defines a healthy nation. "Eccentricity," he writes, "has always abounded when and where strength of character has abounded; and the amount of eccentricity in a society has generally been proportional to the amount of genius, mental vigor, and moral courage it contained." Again, this argument points toward a justification of free trade at its most menacingly Darwinian:

Whoever succeeds in an overcrowded profession, or in a competitive examination; whoever is preferred to another in any contest for an object which both desire, reaps benefit from the loss of other . . . But it is, by common admission, better for the general interest of mankind, that persons should pursue their object undeterred by this sort of consequences.[21]

   This individualism – as a moral and a productive imperative – continued to occupy the Edwardian mind. The rhetoric of Smiles and Mill, not to mention Matthew Arnold, conditioned public and private activity throughout the pre-war period. Each good Brit felt the responsibility to put forward his "best self" over and against the "everyday self," for only thus would the country be "united, impersonal, at harmony."[22] Thus, Samuel Hynes defines the period as a curious hybrid, both homogenous and disorganized; its ruling class tended toward complete "ossification" as well as "disorganized multitudinousness."[23] Similarly, Jonathan Rose exposes the coordination of a popular cult of life with a dour code of efficiency. As his work explains, bourgeois Edwardians were drawn to vitalism as well as technology, orgiastic religions and rational planning.[24] Both critics argue that despite these conflicting tendencies, the culture of the period was unified. The bourgeoisie had mastered its contradictory needs, both encouraging and regulating the potentially destructive phenomenon of the day. The age is remarkable for its effective management of the inevitable disruptions generated by capitalism, such as newness, competition, progress, and exploitation. It met potentially threatening, but utterly necessary, phenomena by following the simple maxim that "REFORMATION IS THE SUREST PREVENTATIVE OF REVOLUTION."[25]

During this period, in fact, the most revolutionary initiatives originated from within the middle class and thus appeared in diluted form. For example, the period saw the rise of science and engineering, not to mention a whole slew of inventions in medicine, artillery, communications, and industry. New technological forms, however, were immediately professionalized, pressed into the service of capital and tempered by a rhetoric of efficiency. Government subsidies and state-supported universities served to monitor and direct these potentially liberating resources into the appropriate channels.[26] Similarly, middle-class dilettantes promoted the importation and display of radical experiments in the arts. Their cultured imprimatur, however, tended to domesticate the radical nature of these works, often under the rubric "decorative," and thus tempered audience responses. As Hynes recognizes, "English Post-Impressionism was less a movement than a social group, and one might argue that it became acceptable precisely for that reason . . . Post-Impressionism entered England more readily because it was introduced politely through the intellectual middle-class" (335).

Middle-class influence, however, was most treacherous in the realm of economics. In this case, though, while liberal reformism was essential to tempering mass unrest, Fabian gradualism was the true betrayer of the proletariat. Fabianism, as has been well documented, favored slow reform and efficient change, arguing that only upper-class administration and increased government control could resolve the inequalities of capital. Here, the need to coordinate order and revolt could not be clearer. If productivity is itself potentially dangerous, insofar as it exacerbates the contradictions that define capitalist society, it was during this period that it most needed to be strictly managed. Tellingly, the Fabians advocated a form of corporativism strikingly similar to that of fascism. Their commitment to administrative activity was founded upon a desire to bind the forces of the nation, organizing and augmenting the productive energy of all classes. In George Bernard Shaw's account, the Fabian believed in "State Organization, Efficient Government,

Industrial Civil Service, [and] Regulation of all private enterprise in the common interest." As Rose explains, "The fact is that for the majority of Fabians efficiency took priority over equality, and proletarian democracy was less attractive than government by their own class of professionals."[27]

All of these innovations, of course, were sanctioned by parliament. At its height, the Liberal Party was able to affect a tenuous balance between self-righteous individualism and organized reform. Here was a party that remained in power mostly through the support of dissident groups – labor, suffragettes, the Ulster Nationalists – but often resorted to slogans such as "Business as Usual" and "Wait and See." In fact, the Liberal Party rose to power with only one policy – free trade – and for this developed its propaganda. But insofar as freedom was a necessity, its greatest expression would be found, contradictorily, in the rigorous reform of a free market. In fact, Gladstone, in one of his more direct speeches, explicitly aligned the "spirit of organized monopoly" with the nation itself.[28]

However, as these phrases suggest, bourgeois thinking and the Liberal Party both faced the threat of becoming programmatic and stale – change became impossible when revolution was the norm. By the end of the first decade, these regulatory strategies demanded intensification. After December 1910, a more violent abandonment can be discerned, in the change in Georgian attire, the painting of the Café Royal, and the construction of the London Coliseum. According to Malcolm Bradbury, London sought turbulence with a new energy that was only a bit "more empirical, meliorative and liberal" than that of the avant-garde ("London 1890–1920," 179). As in all times of great standardization, these spectacles provided a much-needed sense of cultural freedom and release. "Little England" seemed to resist the threat of complete assimilation with an increasingly violent iconoclasm and an obsessive cult of the outsider. In this, Marinetti can only be given credit for having arrived at the right time. The crowds of pre-war London offered the perfect outlet for his faddish aesthetic. According to Richard Cork, "Almost overnight, anything new and shocking was saddled with the arbitrary nickname of 'Futurist': men's pyjamas, lampshades, cravats, silk purses, quilts and bathing suits, not to mention interior decorating schemes and backdrops at the theatre."[29] In fact, amidst the trendy tumult, Marinetti himself would quickly become passé. *The Times* (*The Times*?!) eventually called futurism "academic" and "commonplace." And Roger Fry (Roger Fry!) accused Marinetti of not having a "complete and absolute originality."[30]

But these critical commonplaces obscure the true nature of modern spectacle, and perhaps that of modern imperialism as well. As Marinetti was well aware, the British were torn between a "potent individualism" and a "belli-cose patriotism" (59). As much as they welcomed cracks in the cultural dam, they also sought to contain the continental flood within the category of the Foreign. London's infatuation with all things futurist extended beyond a liberal's love of personal freedom, for it also served to uphold a strong sense of national identity. Cultural autonomy was rigorously constructed against the "foreign invader," in opposition to his "anarchical extravagances."[31] This thinking is made clear by a London reviewer who argued that "All great capitals have those whom the stress of life has maimed; our hospitals can show even the victims of strange imported maladies from abroad; yet London is not leprous or plague-stricken."[32] As we find throughout the period, this language bespeaks a need to preserve rather than rid the country of infectious matter. An oppositional logic, in which autonomy is established over and against the Other, informs national activity across Europe. Marinetti, of course, knew his audience well. He was well aware that his presence offered the British a smug sense of autonomy. In fact, he invites such logic in the opening of his London speech: "To give you an idea of what we are, I will tell you first what we think of you" (67).

As I have been trying to argue, then, the bourgeois spectator was torn between an intense hatred toward the other and a desire to be that Other: autonomy was forged *against* as well as *through* the image of the intruder. Of course, one need not look far to see the dialectical implications of these identifications and differentiations. The possibilities of release and control seemed progressive, organized, endless; such contradictions could be carried out forever. This phenomenon, though, reveals a much deeper unity between the British public sphere and its entertaining invader. The experience as a whole exposes modern identity as a publicly enacted drama of continual self-mastery and self-violence. It lends, in fact, full support to Marinetti's claim that "No one admits to being a *bourgeois* in England: everyone despises his neighbor and calls *him* a bourgeois" (60). In other words, the bourgeois individual must continually place himself over and against his neighbors, and so against himself. He must, in an activity at once symbolic and productive, put on display his disgust with himself. All Marxist hopes aside, this type of progress, a progressive self-loathing, typifies the age and its economy. As we will find again and again, England was no exception to this violence. It too sought order by way of revolution, unity through ceaseless differentiation. The empire constructed itself through a daily process of self-destruction.

Ultimately, England opened itself to what Churchill called a "festival of disorder" – strike riots, window-smashing, and gun-running. Each played its part to preserve an order in which personal, political, and commercial violence had become routine. On any given day on which Marinetti declaimed, *The Times*'s headlines offered one violent spectacle after another. On 19 March 1912, for example, one could find the following list of national threats: *German Armaments and Finances – The Macedonian Revolutionaries – Escaped Convicts Shot – Lessons of the Coal Strike – Englishwoman Tried for Murder in India – Boiler Explosion in the United States – Aerial Quick-Firing Gun – Uric Acid Suffering – Organized Terrorism in Galway*. This issue's Parliament Report offered *Submarines – The Navy Estimate – The Coal Strike – Sentences on Suffragettes – Destroyer Flotillas*. Of course, in these pages, you can find your occasional *Dickens Exhibition*, but such idylls are always overshadowed by thrilling reports of the latest *Fatal Balloon Accident*.[33] As Hynes suggests, these headlines carried the nation right up to the frontlines; the "cracks and fissures" that defined Edwardian culture erupted fully in August 1914 (357–8). For Rose, too, the war "was the inevitable end of the Edwardian cult of life. The word had always implied adventure, intense and passionate experience, and in 1914 the greatest adventure of all was to die fighting for England" (113).

George Dangerfield, in *The Strange Death of Liberal England*, more decisively places liberalism at the heart of the British war effort. As he explains, the liberals "had reached a point where they could no longer advance"; the "contradiction could not be born forever; a man cannot be proud and prostrate." Their solution – "running very fast and in any direction" – led them directly to war.[34] Hobsbawm seconds this conclusion on a larger scale, arguing that "As bourgeois Europe moved in growing material comfort towards its catastrophe, we observe the curious phenomenon of a bourgeoisie, or at least a significant part of its youth and its intellectuals, which plunged willingly, even enthusiastically, into the abyss" (190). It is important to note, then, that the great unrest of the second decade represents not a proud revolt against tradition or conformity, or even a mass suicide, but a profound need to affirm and restore what seemed to be a crumbling bourgeois culture and a receding hope of progress. Ultimately, the dual promise of order and vitality ceased to exist except in terms of physical combat. Europe needed more money, more resources, and more blood to keep the ideological wheels spinning.

3   "THE RAT PLAGUE OF LONDON"

The first post-impressionist show, organized by Roger Fry and endorsed by his Bloomsbury coterie, also helped to stir up strife. The work of Cézanne,

Gauguin, and Matisse, already passé by European standards, easily shocked a public that wanted to be shocked. The show gave rise to a slew of rumors that portrayed the artists as foreign desperados and political anarchists. The art critic for *The Morning Post* duly noted that the opening of the exhibit fell on Guy Fawkes day: "A date more favorable than the Fifth of November for revealing the existence of a wide-spread plot to destroy the whole fabric of European painting could hardly have been chosen."[35] But despite reports of raised voices and uncontrollable tittering, these works challenged the public in decisively non-physical ways. The aesthetic advanced its own sort of destructiveness, but such was confined to various "states of mind" and their artistic representations. The members of Bloomsbury *attacked*, if one must use such terms, a particularly bourgeois sensibility, means-end rationality and its attendant aesthetic, the representational.[36] As I hope to show here, though, this iconoclasm retains the very social values it had hoped to change. The members of Bloomsbury, while driven by an admirably progressive hope, used the category of the aesthetic to promote an explicitly bourgeois ideology. Through their art, they domesticated the violence of futurism and freed the totalizing power of capitalism from the onus of war.

G. E. Moore's dreamy philosophy, which posited the existence of simple, autonomous truths, underlies most of Bloomsbury's aesthetic and political activity. His *Principia Ethica* describes the restorative power of certain purposeless mental states as they exist beyond the realm of practical activity: "By far," he contended, "the most valuable things, which we know or can imagine, are certain states of consciousness, which may be roughly described as the pleasures of human intercourse and the enjoyment of beautiful objects."[37] One can, in fact, commend the Bloomsbury group for its insistence that the cultivation of certain sensual experiences was socially valuable. A liberal faith in the freedom of expression allowed them to unite, in not uninteresting ways, their commitment to aesthetic innovation with their political activism. The celebration of "things in themselves" proceeded from an inherent need to stake out alternative spaces within a world of increasing standardization; a certain aesthetic distance from practical activity offered resistance to the spread of the bourgeois mentality.[38] As Woolf famously argued, she was "working for our common ends – justice and equality and liberty for all men and women," but only "outside your society, not within."[39]

In general, though, the group's idealist turn produced little enthusiasm for public affairs. As Fry would claim, "I know I have no right to detach myself so completely from the fate of my kind, but I have never been able to believe in political values."[40] Woolf echoes this sentiment, praising the artist who "rides his mind at a gallop across country in pursuit of an idea," but is "wholly incapable of dealing successfully with the material world."[41] In other words, in Bloomsbury, Moore's philosophy all too easily excused a social status that already granted luxurious "states of consciousness." In fact, in this district, one finds bourgeois "contradictions" in their purest form: here, the artist admittedly "despises his neighbor and calls *him* a bourgeois." The group's writings offer ample support for this claim. Take, for example, the conclusions of Woolf's essay "Middlebrow":

I ask nothing better than that all reviewers, for ever, and everywhere, should call me highbrow. I will do my best to oblige them. If they like to add Bloomsbury, W. C. I, that is the correct postal address, and my telephone number is in the Directory. But if your reviewer, or any other reviewer, dares hint that I live in South Kensington, I will sue him for libel. If any human being, man, woman, dog, cat or half-crushed worm dare calls me "middlebrow" I will take my pen and stab him, dead.

Woolf's ironic tone barely masks her condescension. She seeks a very public recognition of a position that is both aesthetically and economically distinct. Elsewhere in the essay, she condemns the middlebrow to South Kensington, the land of "betwixt and between," where he spends his life "obscuring, dulling, tarnishing, and coarsening." She curses him for his mediocrity and middlebred intelligence – his middlethoughts, middlevalues, and middlesex. He is blamed for seeking neither art nor life, but "both mixed indistinguishably, and rather nastily, with money, fame, power, or prestige" ("Middlebrow," 150–4). Lytton Strachey expresses a similar disdain when he laments the "ineradicable Victorian instinct for action and utility" and condemns "those clever, cautious, mediocre intelligences who make one thank Heaven one was at Cambridge." He claims that this "inveterate lack of ideals and imagination seems really unredeemed; when one has peeled off the brown paper wrappings of phrases and compromises, one finds – just nothing at all."[42] Again, the self-irony with which these writers approach the matter does little to mask an inherent disgust towards a purposive, lower-class world. More often than not, this mode bespeaks only a desire to distance themselves from the need to address what they can only see as a dirty public sphere.[43]

Even when confronting social ills, Bloomsbury's activism was more reformist than revolutionary. In Maynard Keynes's economic interventionism, Leonard Woolf's participation in the Cooperative Movement, and Virginia Woolf's support of the Women's Cooperative Guild, we find efforts that might have improved, but did not necessarily challenge the status quo. Their work, in fact, even at its most conscientious, tended to preserve rather than dismantle social distinctions of nation, gender, and, importantly, class. Fry, we will see, supports the age's productivist ideology, but he wants to maintain an occupational division between the "humbler" crafts and an "organization for leisure." "In the process of time," he writes, "one might hope to see a sharp line of division between work of this kind and such purely expressive and non-utilitarian design as we call ornament" (*VD*, 77). Similarly, in works such as *To the Lighthouse* and *Three Guineas*, Woolf defends a division of labor in which the lowbrows of the world alleviate the material burdens of the highbrows, whose ultimate goal is visionary. For Woolf, work should be efficiently distributed in order to sustain a permanent leisure class; "Culture," she writes, "would thus be stimulated" (*Guineas*, 111).

Thus, with its cult of spiritual alterity and its dissociative aesthetic, Bloomsbury advances the dialectical logic that defines its class. Raymond Williams, in fact, goes so far as to characterize the group as a thinly disguised instrument of bourgeois domination. Bloomsbury's would-be iconoclasm, he argues, figures within a continuous revolt that underlies bourgeois culture as a whole, a constant revolt which is "at once against its dominant ideas and values and still willingly, in all immediate ways, part of it." The group can be seen simply as a new version of the Pre-Raphaelites or the Godwin Circle; its revolutionary angst only rephrases, in order to renew, the terms of its class supremacy:

in their effective moment, for all their difficulties, they were not only a break from their class – the irreverent and rebellious young – but a means toward the necessary next stage of development of that class itself. Indeed this happens again and again with bourgeois fraction . . . It is a revolt against class but for the class, and it is really no surprise that its emphases of style, suitably mediated, should become the popular bourgeois art of the next historical period.

For Williams, this kind of revolt, with its emphasis on "style," is actually a form of "adaptation," a "recruitment of others," which allows the ruling class to persist under evolving historical circumstance.[44] As I will further argue, though, Bloomsbury, with its emphasis on civilized individualism and leisurely experience, did not merely uphold the terms of its own supremacy, but also established a new way of foreclosing the possibility of any positive social change. Its elitist aestheticism, with its emphasis on "style" and "expression," suggests a more complete disavowal of the potentially disruptive contingencies of the material world and thus a more complete affirmation of the contradictions that define the market.

Thus, I will now turn to Fry's writings on post-impressionism as they provided the structural and thematic foundations of Bloomsbury aesthetics.
As I will argue, while Fry's movement bears a clear structural resemblance
to futurism, it can be distinguished by the very different social reality it
addresses. Whereas futurism found its most complete expression in material aggression and thus sought to align Italy with the violent aspects of
modern production, post-impressionism establishes the "imaginative life"
as the site of both individualism and order and thus affirms the smooth,
seemingly peaceful machinations of advanced capital. In other words, post-
impressionism also advocates a dissociative logic, and it too reproduces the
social contradictions and exploitative fissures of the modern economy. But,
in its celebration of the imagination as the site of dissociation, it allows
the ideological operations of the market to bypass the material world altogether. Ultimately, it exists as a swifter, more efficient productivism that
serves a society already fully engaged in the logic of commodification. Its
liberal framework provides it with a much more effective rhetoric than was
ever found in fascism.

In his critical essays, particularly the seminal "An Essay in Aesthetics,"
Fry's defense of progressive art is everywhere inflected with class fears and
market demands. Drawing upon Moore's aesthetics, which in turn draw
upon Kant's, Fry first condemns the limitations of modern vision as conditioned by the practical exigencies of the marketplace:

The needs of our actual life are so imperative, that the sense of vision becomes
highly specialised in their service. With an admirable economy we learn to see only
so much as is needed for our purposes; but this is in fact very little, just enough to
recognize and identify each object or person; that done, they go into an entry in
our mental catalogue and are no more really seen. In actual life the normal person
really only reads the labels as it were on the objects around him and troubles no
further. (*VD*, 18)

According to Fry, modern vision, insofar as it is governed by "appropriate
action" and "economy," can only obscure the "fullness and completeness
of spiritual life" (*VD*, 14). This vision – as it is enforced by the market –
ultimately dulls the imagination and thus preserves a complacent status
quo:

the level of our imaginative life [has become] incomparably lower; we are satisfied
there with a grossness, a sheer barbarity and squalor which would have shocked
the thirteenth century profoundly. Let us admit the moral gain gladly, but do we
not also feel a loss; do we not feel that the average business man would be in every
way a more admirable, more respectable being if his imaginative life were not so
squalid and incoherent? (*VD*, 16)

Fry focuses this critique on representational art, which, he claims, can only reinforce the limited attitudes of bourgeois culture. For Fry, this art figures as a "purveyor to the conveniences of the middle class." Its "perpetual economising" leaves the viewer caught in a brutally closed world.[45] Moreover, representational art infuses its limitations with an affirmative rhetoric of moral industry. This art justifies its means in terms of a "standard of resultant action" and thus insidiously equates "spirituality" with a brute pragmatism (*VD*, 19). Tellingly, throughout Fry's essay, he critiques the bourgeois artist's efforts to narrate dangerous encounters with various wild animals, first a wild boar, then a bear, and, later, a tiger (*VD*, 17, 28, 103). Woolf, in her biography of Fry, suggest that these voracious figures are emblematic of Fry's great fear of the masses and mass opinion:

"The Herd" is the phrase which dominates [Fry's] letters at this time – the herd with "its immense suggestibility more than ever at the mercy of unscrupulous politicians." The herd has taken the place of the adversary; the herd is the adversary, swollen immensely in size and increased in brute power. The herd on the one side, the individual on the other – hatred of one, belief in the other – that is the rhythm, to use his favourite word, that vibrates beneath the surface. (*Fry*, 232)[46]

With this anxiety, Fry's critique of conventional perception, like that conveyed throughout avant-garde and High Modernist work, exposes itself as founded upon the very class logic it hoped to transcend.

Fry's alternative, of course, is based on a belief in the power of unworldly, intuitive contemplation. He turns to the individual imagination as the site of pure, purposeless vision, one that abandons "useful action" and embraces "emotion in and for itself" (*VD*, 19). "All art," he writes, "depends upon cutting off the practical responses to sensation of ordinary life, thereby setting free a pure and as it were disembodied functioning of the spirit" (*VD*, 242). Interestingly, his first model for this visionary power, long before it was Benjamin's, is the cinematograph. For Fry, this modern device, by which the spectator's perception is nearly emptied of desire, offers possibilities for a renewed, more precise sensibility:

with regards to the visions of the cinematograph, one notices that whatever emotions are aroused by them, though they are likely to be weaker than those of ordinary life, are presented more clearly to the consciousness. If the scene presented be one of an accident, our pity and horror, though weak, since we know that no one is really hurt, are felt quite purely, since they cannot, as they would in life, pass at once into actions of assistance . . . we become true spectators, not selecting what we will see but seeing everything equally. (*VD*, 15)

Fry, though, who serves first and foremost the individual, seeks more than precision, which is as far as the collective space of the cinema will take him. "Pure vision" must offer "freedom" as well as "sincerity" and thus occurs only within the autonomous space of the individual's "imaginative life." Here, reality is fully removed from "necessary eternal conditions" and therefore attains not only objectivity, but liberation. This "sense of vision" is valued for its doubleness, in that it allows one to witness life in its "fullness and completeness." In fact, the whole of Fry's career translates into a tireless exploration of the ways in which this visionary ideal offers both "order and variety," "fullness and completeness," or, in Dangerfield's estimation of bourgeois needs, "security and individualism."

With this call for "order and variety," Fry struggles to rid idealism of its solipsistic messiness and, conversely, to redeem reason of its finality. Yet, increasingly in his work, this demand for dissociation seems only to reinforce these extremes in more oppressive ways, as, first, a willed blindness and, later, a forced distortion of the material world. Tellingly, throughout his essays, Fry is hard-pressed to locate the intrinsic value of the imagination. Its glories seem to exist solely in opposition to the qualities of actual life. The "desirability of the imaginative life," in fact, "is the direct result of that first fundamental difference" (*VD*, 17). The aesthetic promise of "freedom and sincerity" exists, if at all, within the act of differentiation itself (*VD*, 15–17). In this, Fry suggests that aesthetic value rests not within the frame of vision, but as that frame itself. It derives solely from the act of differentiation, through the creation of an objective boundary that divides and organizes various modes of perception. This logic also informs Fry's celebration of artistic expressionism. Certainly, at this time, many critics championed art as "the expression of the emotions" and focused their criticism on the success or failure of the artist to achieve such (*VD*, 19). Fry, however, argues that it is *only* in its individual expression that the "imaginative life" has any value. Only the isolated voice or vision – one clearly differentiated from the common horde – can convey "consciousness of purpose" (*VD*, 21). This claim reveals its bad faith in its paradoxical redress to the masses. Echoing one of the central tenets of liberal economics, Fry argues that individual activity can serve as the foundation of communal order. Only when art functions as an "expression of the emotions," does it express the "feelings and sentiments of humanity" (*RFR*, 103).[47]

A similar logic informs Fry's defense of abstract art, but here it grows more explicitly oppressive. As expected, Fry argues that the absence of representational demands permits a transhistorical and non-naturalistic expression of reality. Abstraction figures as an "expression" of the imagination for it "presents a life freed from the binding necessities of our actual existence" (*VD*, 15). He continues to argue, though, that this art provides disinterested contemplation only through its enforced unity. "Unity of some kind," he argues, "is necessary for our restful contemplation of the work of art as a whole, since it lacks unity we can not contemplate it in its entirety, but we shall pass outside it to other things" (*VD*, 15, 22). Here, Fry praises art for its resistance to the decadent leakage of representational art. He insists that it be "as remote from actual life and its practical utilities as the most useless mathematical theory" (*VD*, 211). With this remark, the critic's valued purposelessness begins to seem a bit purposeful and thus highly problematic. He appears to advocate a vision that is intentionally blind, at once excessively subjective and utterly rationalized.

Fry, in fact, suggests that abstract art should preserve "a minimum of naturalism," but only in order to expose the artist's willful manipulation of that nature (*RFR*, 102). He condemns a "receptive, passive attitude" and celebrates art that reveals the manner in which it harnesses and transfigures reality (*RFR*, 82). The artist, he claims, has a moral responsibility to "*mis*represent and distort the visual world" (*RFR*, 101). He or she must "arrange the sensuous presentment of objects . . . with an order and appropriateness altogether beyond what Nature herself provides" (*VD*, 26). If this strategy was meant to expose the horrors of modern rationalization, one might excuse its implied violence. But, ultimately, Fry's defense of "expression" transfers all positive value from the object of mediation to the process of mediation itself. Art's significance – its promise of "purposeful order and variety" – lies solely within the activity of its production. Only the eccentric work of art, in its radical break from the commonplace, suggests both individualism and order. Productivity attests to an "infinitely various" reality and thus renews the "essential conditions of our physical existence" (*VD*, 26, 24). Here, what once seemed to be a valorization of pure, objective vision turns into its complete opposite: constant, willful manipulation. The very rigidity and blindness that Fry criticizes in representational art eventually finds its way into his own theory. In fact, he later claims that certain "fundamental laws" may help modern society attain "what distinguishes some of the greatest periods of artistic production, an anonymous art" (*RFR*, 101).

This spiritual transvaluation of an otherwise violent productivity mirrors what we explored in futurism. Fry, like Marinetti, seems to aspire to a "mechanical splendor," a complete reification of human activity. But this static totality, one established in terms of multiple constructed differences, does not fully account for the manner in which Fry's aesthetic spreads its logic. Since the autonomy of the art object exists only as long as it can claim difference from actual life, it immediately ceases to hold any aesthetic value once it establishes that relational position. Significance is simultaneously produced and consumed and thus exists only in its continuous renewal. Order must be upheld by the ceaseless production of "shocks," each both reviving and confirming all that has occurred before. Fry acknowledges this imperative in his description of the primitive artist and the reception of his art:

The development of primitive art . . . is the gradual absorption of each newly observed detail into an already established system of design. Each new detail is hailed with delight by the public. But there comes a point when the accumulations of an increasing skill in mere representation begin to destroy the expressiveness of the design, and then, though a large section of the public continues to applaud, the artist grows uneasy. (*RFR*, 84)

One notices at the end of this passage a sour sense of conscience and perhaps remorse. Fry here seems to accept his public's suspicion, but he continues to demand the complete and constant mediation of life: "What, indeed, could be more desirable than that all the world should have the power to express themselves harmoniously and beautifully – in short, that everyone should be an artist" (*RFR*, 88). Fry calls for more artists, greater production, new markets to exploit: "If by some miracle beauty could be generated, without effort, the whole world would be the richer" (*RFR*, 89). Ultimately, the promise of "order and variety" demands nothing less than the constant subjugation of experience and complete "sacrifice of sensual beauty" (*VD*, 21).

In Fry's work, as in Marinetti's, expression ceases to exist, as, perhaps, does the expressed. The constant construction of difference erases all difference, the ceaseless production of meaning renders all meaningless. Aesthetic activity reduces experience to a succession of mere forms which the artist-producer assumes and casts off in its turn. Like Marinetti, Fry does little more than adapt the principles of nineteenth-century aestheticism to the productive imperative of bourgeois culture. His work spiritually transfigures capitalist modes of production, restoring an auratic resonance to that which destroys all aura. Thus, the immaterial becomes material and mediation becomes immediate. Nature grows unnatural, history ahistorical. The individual becomes perfect, plastic, and alien, his expression mute. He is "comforted, stimulated, consoled, edified" by the perversion of experience and thus by his own death. And art? Fry celebrates abstract art for its ability to express that which was previously inexpressible in universal terms.

But he refuses to recognize that this inexpressibility stems not from any human failing, but from the growing inhumanity of the order in which he participates.

But while both Marinetti and Fry increasingly advocate a mechanical violence, their ideas function within entirely different spheres. Fry's theory of the "imaginative life" clearly sets up the same dialectic that we find in futurism, but it never even addresses that world from which Marinetti seeks transcendence. History, progress, the great globe itself – these have no place in Fry's abstract aesthetics. Difference responds only to difference, language only to language. His work presents a soul-shaking sight of a culture already carried away by the power of abstract commodity relations. Whereas the futurist still seeks to prove the material power of such relations, Fry exhibits an unwavering faith. The latter has no need of war in order to be convinced of the market's spiritual design.

Dmitri Mirsky has criticized the Bloomsbury intelligentsia on similar grounds. He argues that the definitive feature of their work is an immaterial productivity in which the capitalist order is spiritually rendered:

The basic trait of Bloomsbury is a mixture of philosophic rationalism, political rationalism, aestheticism, and a cult of individuality. Their radicalism is definitely bourgeois, a product not even of Shaw's new progressivism or the Fabian, but of the old bourgeois radicalism and utilitarianism . . . Bloomsbury idealism can be defined as a thin-skinned humanism for enlightened and sensitive members of the capitalist class who do not desire the outer world to be such as might be prone to cause them any displeasing impression.

Mirsky adds that Bloomsbury's defense of abstraction redeems the suffering caused by the marketplace and thus denies any hope of a materialist politics that could seriously challenge the power of the marketplace:

This is devised in order to master the particular suffering and dissolve it away. The suffering is wrapped up in self-contained rhythms and sublimated from the world of reality to a world of aesthetics. [Woolf's] lulling rhythms are a fine example of the narcotic function which art takes on in the hands of liberal aesthete, who turn it into a new and more perfect form of dope, though of course one not intended for the people.[48]

For me, Fry's thought represents that to which Marinetti's aspires; his work represents the ultimate affirmation of commodity culture, its moment of complete mediation. The British critic is a truly "multiplied man," who has managed to "reduce his heart to its true distributive function."[49] His stint as leader of the British avant-garde was short-lived only because the public soon followed him. As Woolf was to exclaim, "The pictures are the same; it is the public that has changed" (*Fry*, 153).

4 "OH, THE WORK!"

Woolf's theories of aesthetic production are equally vexing, but in a way that helps us to clarify potential alternatives. Her work – in its desperate defense of the aesthetic, its anxious redoubling between the material and the abstract, and its fraught engagement with the working class – foregrounds the ways in which a more progressive aesthetic politics meets with the market's intense demands. As we will find, everywhere in her work an earnest, rigorous materialism collides with class fears and bourgeois values; in the end, what promises to be an alternative to the creative destruction of modernity ends up affirming a violent productivism and a strict division of labor.

Undeniably, in Woolf's writing, a disruptive materialism guards against the romantic flights of her contemporaries; the solid world of experience impinges upon the bourgeois subject, disrupting its willful idealism. Similarly, she portrays the work of art as a confluence of forces, some material, some discursive, each finding expression only in their contingency. In *A Room of One's Own*, for example, the aesthetic object is bravely defined as "a spider's web, attached ever so lightly perhaps, but still attached to life at all four corners . . . these webs are not spun in mid-air, but are the work of suffering human beings, and are attached to grossly material things, like health and money, and the houses we live in."[50] Woolf's work, in fact, is best when it strives to restore this more integral unity of imagination and experience. Her most substantial "moments of being" entail a dynamic interaction by which the mind can begin to negotiate its way in the world without blindness or violence. Jesse Matz, in his astute account of literary impressionism, best describes this phenomenological thrust:

Consciousness here makes its object – but without therefore reducing that object to unreality. The making is reciprocal, and experience of the object is one with its essence; material description has the utter vitality of tumbling laborious processes, and the "ideal" mind finds itself happily well rooted . . . this unified mode of perception does best justice at once to the real world and to the life of consciousness.[51]

With this phenomenology, Woolf partakes in the classical tradition I explore later. Her subjects seem to exist, and find clarity, only in a larger contingent field; difference is a constructive, positive force that works through, rather than against, the limited forms of its environment. Expression and

experience find coherence only in their dynamic reciprocity, an always
open-ended modality.

Yet militating against this confluence is precisely the logic by which Woolf
hopes to achieve it. When most heavily invested in the theories of Moore
and Fry, Woolf tends to assert this unity *against* the supposed corruption of
the masses. She places the fullness of the imagination above the purposive,
"middling" ways of the modern world. She adamantly privileges "privacy,"
"leisure," and "indifference" as the preconditions for artistic truth and
rejects any kind of worldly "tampering" of visionary genius. In "Mr. Bennett
and Mrs. Brown," for example, Woolf seeks an art that is "self-contained,"
"eternal," and "infinite." Echoing Fry, she argues against any art that seeps
outside of itself, into the worldly. Here, in fact, she appears to be more
disconcerted by Arnold Bennett's materialist themes (house property, rent,
and wages) than the clunkiness of his prose. Rather nastily, she condemns
the novels of the Georgians because "in order to complete them it seems
necessary to do something – to join a society, or, more desperately, to write
a cheque" (70–82).

If Woolf seeks a more substantial union of imagination and experience,
this act of dissociation immediately denies the latter, or at least a vital part of
it. Matz calls this Woolf's "trick of otherness": the novelist seeks an experience that is "so alien – so minimal, and so meaningless – that investigation of
it can enable her to bracket off conventional experiences and conventional
ideas" (186). The great danger in this solution is the way in which it overlaps with other social tendencies and fears. More often then not, Woolf's
dissociations draw upon binaries that are readily mapped, both positively
and negatively, onto social contradictions. Again and again, she divides
her abstract antitheses along social faultlines, aligning, for example, the
fluid imagination with specifically female characters or equating a certain
aggressive purposiveness with, alternately, Georgian novelists, lower-class
servants, and male soldiers. It is, of course, one thing when the search for
dialectical unity allows her to define and then embrace a certain feminist
perspective, as it does in *Mrs. Dalloway* and *A Room of One's Own*, but
another when it allows her to affirm stereotypes of a brute lower class, as it
does in *To the Lighthouse* or "Middlebrow."

Nowhere, in fact, is this crisis more painfully, more beautifully, drama-
tized than in Woolf's *To the Lighthouse*.[52] At its most basic level, Woolf's
novel yearns for that integral order described above, one in which mind
and matter move each other toward greater, perhaps communal, truths. To
this end, in the first section of the book, Woolf advances a dialectic that
is at once conscious and productive. Mr. Ramsay sets out alone, rugged

and uncompromising, to pursue the finality of hard reason. In his proud defiance, in his mock-masculine modernity, "he would find some crag of rock, and there, his eyes fixed on the storm, trying to the end to pierce the darkness, he would die standing" (35). Conversely, Mrs. Ramsay extends her sympathy to all, casting forth vital connections by which an ideal community can be established. She, too, faces her own despair; in this imaginative extensivity, a certain solipsism, if not existential despair, vexes all her musings (16). With a schematicism that could almost be graphed, Woolf allows these extremes to find redemption in each other. The masculine insistence on rational analysis provides a stable framework by which feminine sympathy can flourish. The decisively heterosexual dialectic is, in fact, resolved at the moment of intercourse, a necessary intermingling that is at once creative and conscious:

Mrs. Ramsay, who had been sitting loosely, folding her son in her arm, braced herself, and, half turning, seemed to raise herself with an effort, and at once to pour into the air a rain of energy, a column of spray, looking at the same time animated and alive as if all her energies were being fused into force, burning and illuminating . . . and into this delicious fecundity, this fountain and spray of life, the fatal sterility of the male plunged itself, like a beak of brass, barren and bare. (37)

Thus, reason and sympathy work together to forge an integral community, both in the family and beyond it. In the novel's famous dinner-party scene, a certain formalism (appropriate lighting, proper seating arrangement, decent conservation) conjoins with an intuitive sympathy (Lily for Tansley, Minta for Mr. Ramsay, Mrs. Ramsay for them all) to create a gloriously mutable order. Here, caught amidst this "moment of being," Lily realizes that "there is a coherence in things, a stability . . . in the face of the flowing, the fleeting, the spectral" (105).

This dynamic also informs the novel's self-reflective aesthetic musing. To Woolf's credit, she does all she can to ground Fry's rarefied theories. One scene, for example, follows closely the recipe for "significant form" that Fry offers at the end of "An Essay in Aesthetics." It takes place, however, firmly within the natural world, or, more specifically, at the coast, a literal boundary of force and form. Here, Woolf grounds vision within the material world, as she allows that world to be redeemed by vision:

They [Lily and Bankes] came there every evening drawn by some need. It was as if the water floated off and set sailing thoughts which had grown stagnant on dry land, and gave to their bodies even some sort of physical relief. First, the pulse of colour flooded the bay with blue, and the heart expanded with it and the body swam, only the next instant to be checked and chilled by the prickly blackness on the ruffled waves. (20)

Lily's vocation as a painter further suggests Fry's influence, but the specific terms of her creative activity expresses none of Fry's easy expressionism. Consistently, her work is depicted as a painful struggle with multiple constraints – formal, social, economic, and material. At one point, these pressures threaten to sweep away not only creative vision, but consciousness altogether:

Always (it was in her nature, or in her sex, she did not know which) before she exchanged the fluidity of life for the concentration of painting she had a few moments of nakedness when she seemed like an unborn soul, a soul reft of body, hesitating on some windy pinnacle and exposed without protection to all the blasts of doubt. (158)

Lily's power as an artist derives from her ability to negotiate these all too material pressures with imaginative vision. The artist, always a hermaphrodite, needs to be in two places at once, both within the violent flux of life, subject to its blows, as well as on a promontory, freely finding patterns within the turmoil below. She must become one with her object, with the intentional world, so that she can lift it into art; she must attain not simply "knowledge," but "intimacy," a knowing that is also a willing (51).

We must recognize, however, that over the course of Woolf's novel, this dialectical unity becomes increasingly difficult to uphold and, during the war, destroyed altogether. Ultimately, with the demise of the late Victorian community, Woolf seems forced to relocate, and thus contain, her ideal within the isolated art object. Mrs. Ramsay may be dead, but her sympathetic effort lives on in Lily's resurrectionary art – both figuratively, as Lily seeks wholeness within the work, and literally, as she is painting a picture of Mrs. Ramsay. This transition, though, is also a retreat, a withdrawal from materiality and into the imaginative. Lily, unable to bear the pain of death, the contingency of life itself, seeks an inward solace; history finds resolution, or redemption, in romantic reverie. In fact, it is only with the end of desire, the end of worldly purpose, that Lily is allowed to resurrect the wholeness that was Mrs. Ramsay. Or, rather, we might say that the painful desire is discharged, rendered null, in the semblance of a better world:

And now slowly the pain of the want, and the bitter anger (to be called back, just as she thought she would never feel sorrow for Mrs. Ramsay again. Had she missed her among the coffee cups at breakfast? Not in the least) lessened; and of their anguish left, as antidote, a relief that was balm in itself, and also, but more mysteriously, a sense of some one there, of Mrs. Ramsay, relieved for a moment of the weight that the world had put on her. (181)

Ultimately, Lily's creative ecstasy is founded upon the act of dissociation; it takes place in an isolation at once social and historical. Moreover, the resultant work "relieves" the world of any potentially disruptive desire – it absorbs, in other words, any potential revolution.

Importantly, though, this ecstasy cannot fully disavow the economy that supports it, and so the latter is presented as a self-sustaining hierarchy of creative labor. Opposed to Mrs. Ramsay's intuitive art of the everyday and Lily's visionary struggle at her easel, Mrs. McNab lurches into the novel as "a force working; something not highly conscious." She clearly lacks the grace of an "imaginative life," but she serves well enough to "stay the corruption and the rot." McNab, in fact, can appear in the novel only when her more fully human counterparts are absent. Physically, she is confined to the scullery beyond the drawing room, "the depths of darkness" (130–1; 139). Structurally, she is condemned to the section of the novel that Woolf described as void of "the most difficult abstract piece of writing – I have to give an empty house, no people's characters, the passage of time, all eyeless and featureless with nothing to cling to."[53] In other words, McNab is granted access only for her ability to serve the upper classes – literally, as a servant, and figuratively, as a sign of distinction. She performs a task at once material and ideological, a distinction both productive and conservative. The logic here is similar to that expressed in Woolf's famous definitions of high brows and the low brows. The "high brow," she writes, "is the man or woman of thoroughbred intelligence who rides his mind at a gallop across country in pursuit of an idea." He may have no idea how to conduct the important business of "real life," but he helps us to see beyond our limited perspectives toward the ideal. The low brow, conversely, is "a man or woman of thoroughbred vitality who rides his body in pursuit of a living at a gallop across life." He may be blind to beauty and the "imaginative life," yet he helps run the world, ceaselessly toiling, like McNab ("Middlebrow," 196–7). In this, Woolf belies the fears that shape her dialectical art. High brows need low brows, but they need them to be different; social order rests upon the division of labor.

As mentioned, for Woolf, the act of dissociation is necessary for dialectical unity to be achieved. In fact, as we saw in Marinetti and Fry, distinction must be continually maintained alongside the activity of reconciliation. One might expect Woolf to use this dynamic to create interesting, progressive tensions between the individual and the community. But, throughout all her work, it seems to be distorted by larger, implacable cultural forces. In *To the Lighthouse*, Woolf's feminism allows her to rescue Mrs. Ramsay, to lift her out of the muck and into the frame of the painting; feminine sympathy is necessary for the establishment of a positive community. Yet, her class politics leave Mrs. McNab leering within the blindly natural; humble work is necessary, but negatively, both as something that allows distinction and as something to be avoided. Ultimately, Lily's dissociative labor is replicated by the structure of the novel as a whole, in which the leisure-based interaction of the upper-middle class is bracketed off, quite literally, from the history – the manual labor – that makes that leisure possible. In both instances, Woolf champions the activity of the imagination over the activity of the body, the organic work of self-expression over the ceaseless repetition of physical toil. Ultimately, though, there is no reward other than this work itself: McNab never experiences the fruits of her own labor, Lily never displays her painting. In fact, there is no affirmation other than that provided by work: McNab in the kitchen enables Lily at her easel, Lily at her easel grants significance to McNab in the kitchen. "Oh the work!" – in the end, the only protest left is Mrs. McNab's dumb cry of pain (139).

5   WHITHER DEMOCRACY?

Ultimately, this discussion of productive and dissociative imperatives, which, as mentioned, are really one and the same, raises questions about the modern political spectrum, for the intensity with which so many different groups expressed their difference seems to confound the very idea of political categorization. I have already mentioned Bloomsbury's commitment to a moral individualism and its resistance to moral convention. Much of Fry's work attests to these principles and a concomitant desire to democratize art. He repeatedly proclaimed intentions to make "the sculptor's and painter's endeavour once more coterminous with the whole range of human inspiration and desire" (*RFR*, 110). Post-impressionism was an art that "one's maid . . . might by a mere haphazard gift of Providence surpass one in" (*VD*, 204). Woolf, too, confirms that "Anyone's sensation – his cook's, his housemaid's – was worth having. Learning did not matter; it was the reality that was all important" (*Fry*, 153). But this belief in the liberating power of art was countered in Bloomsbury by an unyielding elitism. While the "imaginative life" was not associated with any single class, only a grateful few actually possessed its power. Despite his maid, Fry claimed that "A person so entirely preoccupied with the purely formal meaning of a work . . . is extremely rare" (*VD*, 209). In other words, Bloomsbury's "sense of vision" both embraced and resisted the entire social order. These thinkers and artists, precisely because they defined themselves as outsiders, saw themselves as the embodiment of a larger society composed of out- siders. They believed that the distance they maintained from "actual life" not only provided them with an objective perspective, but allowed them to posit that perspective as normative. In their moral individualism, they found totality; like their fascist counterparts, they made elitism popular. Thus, in their dissociative activity, in their simultaneous disgust and iden- tification with the masses, these artists exemplify a single ideological order that extends across the political spectrum.

In other words, the postures of the avant-garde suggest a phenomenon in which contemporary political distinctions are necessary, but empty. As critics such as Michael North and Seamus Deane have argued, by the begin- ning of the twentieth century, bourgeois demands for differentiation had reduced political reality to a succession of mere forms.[54] Even the Tories, in fact, presented themselves as the one true source of alterity; they, too, sought to translate their increasing alienation from current social realities into a certain cultural capital. They somewhat smugly stood back and observed as New Liberalism, New Money and New Art compromised the national order, and gleefully declared their irrelevance when, on 10 August 1911, they gave up the House of Lords and its power of veto. Ironically, the politi- cal right most proudly defined their estrangement by way of a rigorous antagonism to what appeared as decadent, leftist art. Critics consistently presented post-impressionism as a threat to national culture; in the words of one writer, supporters of the new movement "should be treated like the rat plague in Suffolk."[55] Artists and organizers were accused of primitive regression, madness, egotism, anarchism, communism, disease, contami- nation, and unmanliness. One hardworking critic managed, by way of the shady psychologism of the day, to suggest all of these qualities at once:

Morbid and suffering egotism is the spring of all anarchy in conduct, in art, as in criticism, but do not let us blame the impressionists for those who were unable to follow them or accuse France of decay owing to a few bad and mad painters. All great capitals have those whom the stress of life has maimed; our hospitals can show even the victims of strange imported maladies from abroad; yet London is not leprous or plague-stricken. Mr. Ross is again wrong in suggesting that the "Grafton Decorations" should be burnt; they might interest the doctors of the body and the students of the sickness of the soul.[56]

As before, the desire to preserve the object of disdain is telling here. For what the nature of this criticism suggests is that the right also negotiates its position of authority by virtue of its distance from society's bourgeois stink. One important critic of the day argued that post-impressionism, like futurism, was the epitome of democratic wastefulness for it "made no violent breach with the past either in excessive futility or in extravagant originality."[57] As I have tried to suggest, this desire for a "breach," for absolute difference, cannot be divorced from the logic of the market. It is the ideological property of any group that wants to assert its authority in a world in which personal, political, and aesthetic ideals are constantly being produced and consumed. Left? Right? Capitalist culture simultaneously erects and erases all such differences.

Ultimately, in early twentieth-century London, a ceaseless domestication of extremes served to maintain a single political order. True alterity became almost impossible to claim as it almost always upheld a dynamic social totality. We might even say, contra Dangerfield, that bourgeois liberalism did not "die" out during the modern period, but pervaded society as a whole, making its naming superfluous. One might even argue that the early twentieth-century division of the Liberal Party into opposed Conservative and Labour factions was merely an expression of the former's internal paradoxes: these newly empowered parties merely reinflected different aspects of that controlled competition already evident in liberalism.[58] This is also perhaps why contemporary theorists of modernity, whose work typifies a larger celebration of alterity, have consistently ignored the London scene: they refuse to see that its relative calm and order derives not from a rigid traditionalism, but from the reification of revolt. Writing in 1913, one London critic proudly claimed that "violent materialism will fail to find a permanent footing" in London. He reasoned that his country maintains an "ordered vitality which is the basis of art and existence alike."[59] Yes, the truly oppressive discourse in London at this time derived not from the country's traditionalism or moral conventionality, but from capitalism, the New Liberal commitment to "freedom, free trade, progress, and the seventh commandment." Bloomsbury, too, was a conservative force not because of its refusal to participate in politics, but because of its participation in a widespread aestheticization of market processes. It secured its (class) position not through the celebration of traditional values and structures, but through their constant upheaval. Ultimately, today's scholarship needs to understand how the most effective rhetoric of revolution and progress in London came from the middle classes. This phenomenon complicates not only the modern political spectrum, but our own attempts to position ourselves within or even outside of it.

6   THEORIES OF THE AVANT-GARDE

The similarities between fascism and liberalism, particularly as they mani-fest themselves in the logic of capital, find their most complete analysis in the work of the Frankfurt School. For Walter Benjamin, fascism is founded upon an inevitable crisis in bourgeois culture; totalitarianism is both an extension and revision of bourgeois society as it faces calamity. In "The-ories of German Fascism: On the Collection of Essays *War and Warrior*, edited by Ernst Jünger," Benjamin argues that the greatest effect of World War I was its destruction of humanist values. The war, he claims, proved that bourgeois ideology no longer provided a suitable foundation for social order. An excessive faith in reason led only to a dehumanizing technol-ogy, while violent competition compromised both individual and national identity.[60] The early fascists, however, responded to this crisis not by aban-doning these values, but by celebrating the ego in increasingly irrational forms. In their anxiety, they tended to ape, in extreme form, the ideological postures of the bourgeoisie. As Benjamin explains, "the virtues of hardness, reserve, and implacability they celebrate are in fact less those of the soldier than those of the proven class militant" ("TGF," 127). Ultimately, in fas-cism, the competitive activity of the bourgeois, now drained of its spiritual content, became a nervous, rigid "stance." In this extreme romanticism of the self, dissociation replaced critical thought, and reproduction obscured material reality ("TGF," 125). The fascist, like his capitalist counterpart, worked to construct an auratic unity of being, an ideal wholeness that is blind to the world it destroys.[61]

Benjamin's work on fascism, however, is most famous for its discussion of "aesthetic politics." Much, of course, has been made of this phrase, and for many literary scholars it has become a way of placing their subject within an urgent social dynamic. Often, however, "aestheticization" is reduced to a somewhat non-historical theory of aesthetic totality or wholeness. For example, Susan Buck-Morss argues that fascist aesthetics is a form of anaesthetics or "sensory alienation." Her definition rests upon only one aspect of fascist culture, the artist-politician's hostility toward the sensual world and his efforts to shape and organize the masses at will.[62] Falasca-Zamponi similarly argues that the fascist leader "claims full autonomy to his creative will and substitutes his artistic vision for the disenchanted world of democratic governments. Guided by a romantically aesthetic approach to politics, Mussolini conceived the world as a canvas upon which to create a work of art, a masterpiece completely neglectful of human values" (13).

While these theories correctly define fascism's egoistic will to power, they do not explain how fascist violence may be enjoyable as a sensual experience, why, in the words of Benjamin, the modern subject "can experience its own destruction as an aesthetic pleasure of the first order."[63] In Benjamin's formulation, fascism seeks to affirm a specific crisis in capital and thus, with war, it reconceives a specifically bourgeois art, namely, aestheticism. "The most rabidly decadent origins of this new theory of war," he writes, "are emblazoned on their foreheads: it is nothing other than the uninhibited translation of the principles of *l'art pour l'art* to war itself" ("TGF," 122). In one sense, Benjamin argues that just as aestheticism once served to absorb and contain subjective desires, so fascism generates war as a way of managing potentially revolutionary energies. "Fascism," he writes, "sees its salvation in giving these masses not their right, but instead a chance to express themselves. The masses have a right to change property relations; fascism seeks to give them an expression while preserving property" ("WOA," 241).[64] More importantly, though, for Benjamin, fascist warfare provides affirmation for a subject no longer convinced of its wholeness; it retranslates aestheticism as an expression of subjective wholeness into an expression of subjective dissolution. In other words, by the early twentieth century, the romance of the complete, entrepreneurial individual had been rendered obsolete by the corporate market. War thus emerges as a form of affirmation responsive to the newly exploited subject; egoism for its own sake is transmuted into a rhetoric of vitality and sacrifice, of "forceful spiritual convulsion" ("TGF," 126). It is ultimately only in this reworking and reapplication of aestheticism that fascism can be considered a form of "aesthetic politics." In the violent, yet efficient consumption and production of the self, the painful relations of the capitalist world are more acceptably "expressed" ("WOA," 241).

Herbert Marcuse similarly defines fascism as an aesthetic affirmation of the bourgeois subject. In "The Struggle Against Liberalism in the Totalitarian View of the State," he argues that the fascist celebration of violence is not simply military, but economic: "The new weltanschauung reviles the 'merchant' and celebrates the 'gifted economic leader,' thereby only hiding that it leaves the economic functions of the bourgeois untouched" (11–12). In this context, Marcuse also shows that aestheticism has been forced to undergo a transformation in order to remain affirmative. For Marcuse, nineteenth-century aestheticism, particularly as it romanticized the human soul, served to isolate and thus control potentially revolutionary desires:

By affirmative culture is meant that culture of the bourgeois epoch which led in the course of its own development to the segregation from civilization of the mental and spiritual world as an independent realm of values that is also considered superior to civilization. Its decisive characteristic is the assertion of a universally obligatory, eternally better, and more valuable world that must be unconditionally affirmed: a world essentially different from the factual world of the daily struggle for existence, yet realizable by every individual "from within," without any transformation of the state of fact.[65]

This seemingly transcendent realm, as it is both detached and obligatory, temporarily satisfies those needs that remain unfulfilled under capitalism. It serves to deflect and diffuse the energy that could erupt against the social order. As Marcuse explains, "the spiritualization of sensuality demands of the latter what it cannot achieve: withdrawal from change and fluctuation and absorption into the unity and invisibility of the person" ("ACC," 112).

Importantly, though, Marcuse further argues that, under pressure from the market, aestheticism has been forced to transfer value from the static art object to the dynamic activity of art's creation and reception. The promise of aesthetic pleasure has been reapplied to the violent processes of production and consumption that defines modern life. Thus, the fantasy of individual wholeness becomes an active, mobilizing force within the world:

Without distinction of sex or birth, regardless of their position in the process of production, individuals must subordinate themselves to cultural values. They must absorb them into their lives and let their existence be permeated and transfigured by them. ("ACC," 94)

The public, in other words, is trained to desire an aesthetic experience that is always just out of reach. The search for fulfillment becomes the only source of fulfillment, and thus ensures the persistence of a painful labor and a ceaseless consumption. Marcuse writes,

Insofar as such culture aims at the enrichment, beautification, and security of the totalitarian state, it is marked by its social function of organizing the whole society in the interest of a few economically powerful groups and their hangers-on. Hence its attributes of humility, sacrifice, poverty, and dutifulness on the one hand, and extreme will to power, impulse to expansion, and technical and military perfection on the other . . . The idealist cult of inwardness and the heroic cult of the state serve a fundamentally identical social order to which the individual is now completely sacrificed. ("ACC," 129)

Here, capitalism is fully exposed as the missing link between liberalist and fascist ideologies. The suffering caused by the market is obscured and excused by the ever-receding promise of aesthetic fullness. The public is a willing dupe to the constantly renewed allure of wholeness, the always eventual attainment of the perfect commodity, whether individual or national.

It was perhaps only in the late twentieth century that the avant-garde's complex relation to this process became clear. In 1984, Peter Bürger writes,

> In bourgeois society, art has a contradictory role: it projects the image of a better order and to that extent protests against the bad order that prevails. But by realizing the image of a better order in fiction, which is semblance (*Schein*) only, it relieves the existing society of the pressure of those forces that make for change. They are assigned to confinement in an ideal sphere. Where art accomplishes this, it is "affirmative" in Marcuse's sense of the term. If the two-fold character of art in bourgeois society consists in the fact that the distance from the social production and reproduction process contains an element of freedom and an element of the noncommittal and an absence of any consequences, it can be seen that the avant-gardistes' attempt to reintegrate life into the life process is itself a profoundly contradictory endeavor.[66]

For Bürger, the avant-garde affects neither a complete sublation of social energy nor a full reintegration of art back into life's praxis. Rather, it launches the undeniable tension between work and world into action, propels that antagonism into the future, so that it remains constant and productive. As Bürger's account suggests, the modern subject no longer looks to art as an expression of wholeness. Or rather, the modern subject, his or her sensibilities completely shattered by the market, no longer responds to art as an expression of wholeness. Conditioned by those same economic changes, the work of art has become preoccupied with its own production and consumption. Art's content has become art's activity, and so the promises of order and variety now rest upon a continuous labor. The fact that avant-gardism is constructed in terms that seem antagonistic to affirmation – individualism, innovation, and violence – should not obscure the nature of its work, but should make clear the miserable experience that it seeks to affirm. With the avant-garde, the violence of modern life appears scientifically perfect and ceaselessly renewed, the dissociation of sensibility both liberating and organized. This art spiritually transfigures a specifically capitalist logic, reconceiving technology as spirit, competition as consciousness, and alienation as freedom.

CHAPTER 2

"No end, but addition": T. S. Eliot and the tragic economy of High Modernism

I BURIAL OF THE DEAD (UNDER HEAPS OF CLUTTER)

Son of man, you have been borne unto a world of clutter. Deep and wide is the waste, the heaps upon heaps of junk. Look not to nature, a place unfit for habitation. Nature is chaos, refuse,

> Rocks, moss, stonecrop, iron, merds.[1]

Nor is there refuge in the civilized world. The city is a dumping-ground, mired in sin and the debris of history. Its rivers and streets are glutted, unclean with

> . . . empty bottles, sandwich papers,
> silk handkerchiefs, cardboard boxes, cigarette ends . . .
> (58)

It is in vain that you seek peace in the city, yet vain also that you turn homeward. The house is no haven: the waste without is the waste within, inescapable:

. . . the cups, the marmalade, the tea . . . the porcelain . . . the sunsets and the dooryards and the sprinkled streets . . . the novels . . . the teacups . . . the skirts that trail along the floor . . . (14–15)

Look, there in the bureau! – the neuropathic debris collects!:

> Old letters, programmes, unpaid bills
> Photographs, tennis shoes, and more,
> Ties, postal cards . . .[2]

No, do not turn inward! Your own romantic soul is corrupt. Fanned by desire, enflamed by guilt, memory throws up a thousand images of despair:

> . . . sunless dry geraniums
> and dust in crevices,
> Smells of chestnut in the streets,

69

And female smells in shuttered rooms
And cigarettes in corridors
And cocktail smells in bars.   (27)

Oh, list! Destitute are the ways of man. Pride? Sloth? Lust? No, our crime is overproduction – killing and breeding without end! We have tilled the soil of our most bestial desires, and now must reap the desiccated fruits of sin. How can we set our lands in order? Who will speak for us now? Who will clean up this mess!?

T. S. Eliot, who can rage like thunder and whimper like a possum, comes to us with the weight of the age on his shoulders. His poetry, vexed by pain and fear, reminds us that the modern crisis is also a spiritual one; his brutal sermon exposes the deep relations between a corrupt history and a corrupt ethics. At the heart of his work, though, lies a rigorous critique of economic modernity, linking material causes and ideological effects, locating the ruins of capital in everything from sex to art to science and religion. Indeed, Eliot's work responds directly to the standardized chaos described in the last chapter; if there is one argument that unites the many facets of his poetry – its style, its chauvinism, its spiritual fervor – it is that "over-production, excessive wealth, [and] an irrelevance and lack of relation of production to consumption" is directly linked to a wider ethical weakening of "restraint."[3] As I argue here, this is not simply a curmudgeonly attack on modernity, but a nuanced theory of productive technologies, the cultural institutions that support them, and the possibility of locating alternative modes of thought and being. Yet, importantly, Eliot's art – in both theory and practice – is riddled with contradictions. His poetry, as it attempts to neutralize and contain the horrors of modernity, seems to locate coherence and faith in the affective structures of the market itself.

Eliot's work is perhaps best characterized by its anti-modernism, its idealization of past cultures and their organically restrictive orders. Tradition, the Church, Nature itself – these institutions once provided the means of structuring and restraining the human tendency toward excess. As authoritative norms, they served to limit and direct desire, to curb excess and maintain balance between passion and intellect, the individual and his culture, the particular and the abstract. Conversely, Eliot laments his own historical moment as bereft of any organizing principles, as an age of "dissociation." An absurd faith in the integrity of the individual, coupled with advances in industrial technology, have led to complete chaos; everywhere, limits are abandoned and superseded – the gentle order is obscured by piles of waste. Eliot's poetry, of course, is typical of the High Modernist tradition in that it yearns for a power strong enough to oppose these productive excesses and restore balance. Like Pound's *Cantos* or Yeats's *The Tower*, it expresses faith in an authoritative voice, one that can affect, by way of identification, the solidification of the rabble.

Yet Eliot's work is also typical in that, even at its most dogmatic, it expresses a certain preoccupation with that which always exceeds or undermines aesthetic control. In fact, his poetry – in both content and structure – seems to be founded upon the very waste it descries; his success as an artist stems from an innate facility for slumming and a ceaseless activity of recycling. In his early poetry, for example, Eliot roots around desolate alleys and vacant lots, finding "charm" and "repose" in scenes of squalor. In his later, more acclaimed creations he picks through Western culture for scraps of beauty to shore against the ruin (*Hare*, 15). His relation to the material world is similarly conflicted. Most often, he recoils from the "world of contact"; he depicts nature as a hated place of trial, a corrupt landscape that needs to be transcended (*Hare*, 68). Yet, this world also often fulfills his need for restrictive patterns. Eliot turns again and again to fertility myths that are based on natural cycles, and he repeatedly uses an elemental logic to structure his poems. Moreover, it is precisely the vexed contingency of nature that inspires the poet with thoughts of divinity. In "First Debate between the Body and Soul," he maintains that worldly "sensations" inspire knowledge of the ideal; "the dull precipitates of fact / the emphatic mud of physical sense" lead to an experience of truth both "simple and profound" (*Hare*, 65).

Tellingly, Eliot's work consistently disrupts its own patterns, sullies its own beauty. It teases us with unity, whether mythic, religious, or symbolic, but only to foreground that which is irreducible, irresolvable. Throughout, totality and fragment confound each other; if any reconciliation is provided, it is only in their mutual negation. In *The Waste Land*, for example, the thunder speaks with a patriarchal boom, but its word – "Da" – is presented as always already adulterated by its interpreters (66–7). *Four Quartets* imagines the "still point of the turning world," but the "Garlic and sapphires in the mud / Clot the bedded axle-tree" (*Quartets*, 15–16). Indeed, if images of purity are rare, so are heroes and heroic deeds. Pound can look to the factive personality of Malatesta, and Joyce finds a suitable role model in the fabulous craftsmanship of Dedalus; Eliot, however, consistently fails to identify a substantial regenerative power. While his poetry hints at Hamlets and Grail Knights, it foregrounds the experiences of lesser types: alienated clerks, humiliated sinners, and withered old men. These contradictions are perhaps most dramatically expressed in Eliot's frustrated effort to position himself in the modernist debate between classicism and romanticism. The poet everywhere advocates a classical order that can curb and sublimate the excesses of modern humanism; again and again, though, he finds himself caught between dogmatism and relativity, between a profound skepticism toward divine authority and his disgust with the material world.

In this chapter, I contend that Eliot's inability to reconcile these conflicted impulses forces him to adopt the paradoxical logic of the marketplace as a viable mode of social organization. His work, while seeming to preserve a certain critical distance in relation to modernity, finds solace in mimicry of the ideologies and structural principles that sustain the modern economy at large. Importantly, Eliot reconceives the individual as divine, his own cruel master, and thus assents to the ethical codes of the bourgeois order. He adopts and adapts the spiritual logic of fall and redemption in terms of a worldly loss and profit; rational self-scrutiny and self-sacrifice become the preconditions for personal and communal greatness. More treacherously, Eliot tries to resolve his fears in a subtle dialectic of negation, one in which the alienated fragments of a fallen world invert themselves into an imaginative unity. In this, he more completely mimics the paradoxical ideologies that support the market; he redeems an historical suffering and alienation as the only proof of a universal redemption. Ultimately, while religion and economics overlap throughout Western literature, Eliot's solution, with its particular emphasis on rational reckoning, cannot be explained apart from his specific historical moment. If the poet wrestles with his own demands, it is because the contradictions in his soul mirror those of modern capital. In his poetry as in the economy, order exists only in a reified production and consumption of the self and the community as a whole.

In this regard, two little-explored influences demand careful attention: Eliot's Protestant heritage and his career as a banker. As is well known, Eliot sought a more heroic religious tradition than that he inherited from his Unitarian ancestors. He yearned throughout his life for a more ecstatic religious experience, the terrifying iconography and restrictive dogmas of a purer, communal creed. Yet Eliot could never quite escape his Protestant origins, which extend back to his mother (a religious poet herself) to his grandfather William Greenleaf Eliot (the founder of American Unitarianism) and his prominent ancestor Andrew Eliott (a Calvinist pilgrim). His work – in its respect for silent suffering, its devout observance of ritual and pattern, its commitment to a preordained calling and position in the world – consistently foregrounds this tradition. His poetry returns again and again to the image of the isolated penitent, quietly trying to remake his world according to a divine plan. Certainly, there are many ways to distinguish between (Anglo-) Catholicism and the Protestant tradition. Here, however, we must have recourse to Eliot's own definitions:

> There are only 2 things – Puritanism and Catholicism. You are one or the other. You either believe in the reality of *sin* or you don't – *that* is the important moral distinction – not whether you are good or bad. Puritanism does not believe in sin: it merely believes that certain things must be done.[4]

Throughout his work, Eliot defines Catholicism by its formal principles, as a static, otherworldly order of contrasted states. Conversely, he sees Protestantism as a kind of activity, a dynamic of fall and redemption, a praxis that "must be done." While Eliot vehemently defends the iconography and dogmatism of the former, he depends upon Protestant ideology as a way of directing his life and poetry. As I hope to show, it is this active, pragmatic faith, grounded in rationalized labor and sacrifice, that allows him to affirm the modern order.[5]

Eliot's ancestors, however, were not only good Protestants, but also good businessmen; his father and grandfather were both known for their ability to turn a profit in the New Land. This, too, Eliot inherited, as evidenced by his nearly decade-long success at Lloyds Bank. A respect for "honest" toil kept him at his post, even in the face of several offers from the literary establishment. As Eliot explained, he took comfort in the fact that "part of my time is spent on a definite paid job which I believe to be useful."[6] Eliot's search for a personal discipline found an easy answer in the standardized routines of the bank (as it would later in the sacraments of the Church). As Peter Ackroyd writes, "if he enjoyed manipulating the little figures of symbolic logic, how much greater enjoyment was to be had in handling the larger figures of finance" (78). Most importantly, though, Eliot was genuinely interested in the "science of money," and his ability to reconcile accounts led not only to several significant promotions, but a consistent poiesis.[7] As I will argue here, Eliot's work at the bank – in both content and structure – provided a way of transmuting the emotional wreckage of modern life into the formal economy of the marketplace. His repentant soul was drawn to the rational activity of tabulating account balances, which, in turn, became the model for an aesthetic activity that "trims down emotions to fit the business world."[8]

This chapter, then, explores Eliot's work as it voices the deep, poetic homologies that exist between the Protestant ethic and the economics of the modern world. Drawing upon the theories of Max Weber, I explore the ways in which High Modernism – in both form and content – is dictated by the affective logic of capital. Here, salvation and damnation are reconceived in economic terms; poetic order is achieved by way of rationalization, the dead reckoning of balance and excess. As we will find, the modern poem is forever engaged in the process of reconciling that which resists order. In the account book as in the poem, the activity of reckoning depends upon the presence of waste – symbolic redemption proceeds from some place of contingent messiness.[9] As importantly, this discussion also points toward a reformulation of the relation between avant-garde productivism and High Modernism's tendency toward auratic, spatial structures. The affirmative aspects of the avant-garde – its commitment to aesthetic dissociationism, violent expressivity, technological production – are also present in Eliot's work. One sees, however, in the shift from aesthetic dynamism to aesthetic structure, an affirmation that is much more rigid in its assertion. If the energetic avant-garde defends the productive imperative of the economy, High Modernist form affirms the rationalized structure of the economy as a whole. As we will find, Eliot's search for a beneficial order leads to a poetic bureaucracy, an abstract, pseudo-reconciliation of material difference and communal unity. His aesthetic replicates the affective terms of the economy at large, redeeming its alienation as individualism and its reification as objective truth. To borrow from Weber, Eliot's poetry, like the capitalist economy it mimics, presents itself as "an immense cosmos into which the individual is born, and which presents itself to him, at least as an individual, as an unalterable order of things in which he must live. It forces the individual, insofar as he is involved in the system of market relationships, to conform to capitalistic rules of action."[10]

2   THE SLOUGH OF ROMANTICISM

Of all of Eliot's masters, Harvard professor Irving Babbitt was perhaps the most severely influential. Babbitt's writings on classicism provided the poet with his most trenchant critique of modern excess and thus shaped the latter's politics as well as his poetry. For Babbitt, this critique resolutely began with Rousseau, an "extremist and foe of compromise," whose sin was being "profoundly convinced of the loveliness of his own soul."[11] Rousseau, in his romantic celebration of the "private and personal self," had released the individual "not merely from outer formalistic constraint, but from all constraint whatsoever" (*RR*, 6, 67). According to Babbitt, these delusions had ushered in a decadent age in which "Whirl is king, having driven out Zeus."[12] The individual was not now free, but more thoroughly enslaved by his most vulgar impulses and desires. Society, in turn, was infected with a "cunning" individualism and thus sacrificed to "endless change and relativity" (*RR*, 6). The results could be seen in all areas of thought: liberalism in politics, relativism in philosophy, positivism in science, romanticism in the arts. In each, a once rigid hierarchy had been completely undermined: "The whole vocabulary that is properly applicable only to the super-sensuous realm is then transferred to the region of the subrational" (*RR*, 284). As I hope to show here, for Babbitt and his disciple, this decadence inspired demands for absolute order, for a return to the phallocentric law of Zeus. Their "classicism" was a plea for consciousness, tradition, and stasis, a recognition of the individual's "permanent self that is felt in its relation to his ordinary self as a power of control."[13] However, by the time these two would-be reformers understood the nature of this crisis, this classicism had to be severely qualified and thus highly compromised.

For Babbitt, naturalism is the evil, but not the normalizing or mediatory naturalism of the Renaissance. Naturalism is problematic insofar as it privileges vitality and pure process. In its bastardized form, naturalism promotes an uncritical acceptance of the spontaneously given, the ceaseless production and consumption of difference. With this definition, Babbitt attempts to relate the corrupt branches of modern thought. The positivist and the relativist are united in their common revolt from order; both abandon the guidance of eternal form for the purity of supposedly liberated forces. The positivist exhibits a harmful faith in physical determination and natural change. His work is marked by a failure to valuate what the senses perceive: "Since everything is a matter of process, how are we to know that all this process is really progress or improvement?" (*SC*, 68–70). The relativist similarly values the "spontaneous product of the popular imagination" (*RR*, 21). As Babbitt claims, "With the elimination of the ethical element from the soul of art the result is an imagination that is free to wander wild with the emancipated emotions" (*RR*, 165). For Babbitt, relativism idealizes man ruled by his internal passions, while positivism leaves him victim to forces from without. In both cases, the desire for freedom affects a base subjugation. Mind and body, convinced of their great freedom, are enslaved by the most haphazard circumstances and desires. As Eliot echoes, "Romanticism stands for *excess* in any direction. It splits up into two directions: escape from the world of fact, and devotion to brute fact" (*Facsimile*, 43).

The value of this critique lies in its recognition of a collusion between romantic excess and mechanical reason. These classicists outline a frightening dialectic in which an unchecked vitality or individualism results in radical sameness:

Bergson's assertion that "life is a perpetual gushing forth of novelties" is in itself only a dangerous half-truth of this kind . . . As the French have it, the more life changes the more it is the same thing. (*RR*, 6)

In retreat from external guidance, the subject is driven by an all too purposive egoism. His "efficient megalomania" takes an horrifically instinctive form and thereby produces a widespread commonness (*RR*, 277–8). According to Babbitt, the "epicurean" and the "average man" have grown indistinguishable; chaos and conformity work together to destroy civilization (*SC*, 62). Democracy, in fact, has become "purely expansive," concerned with the quantity rather than the quality of individual freedom. It spreads its so-called freedom through a rigorous "efficiency," the "worship of mere machinery" (*SC*, 58).

Eliot, too, recognizes that modern life is riddled with contradictions, but his critique is more specifically focused on the issue of appropriation. The individual has been given a certain measure of freedom, but without standards, without external guidance, he is easily misled and exploited. From Prufrock to Tiresius to the Puritan settlers of *Four Quartets*, Eliot's personae are caught between their unbidden urges and a conventional formalism. Each is a "throbbing" machine, measuring out desire through the habituated rhythms of modern life. The demand for release all too easily finds expression in the efficient mechanisms of the marketplace. Romantic individualism has coupled with industrial technology to produce an horrific conformity. "One thinks," Eliot writes, "of all the hands / That are raising dingy shades / In a thousand furnished rooms" (22). The city may be full of "swarming life . . . responsive to the momentary need," yet it moves toward an horrifically "formal destiny."[14] As Eliot summarizes in a later essay, "Out of Liberalism itself come philosophies that deny it." Out of democracy comes "regimentation and conformity . . . the puritanism of a hygienic morality in the interest of efficiency; uniformity of opinion through propaganda, and art only encouraged when it flatters the official doctrines of the time" (*Prose*, 285–8).

However, in response to this paradoxical treachery, the classicists were only able to qualify, and thus weaken, their position. The double extremism of modern society caused them to promote a healthy balance of individualism and order, to temper their conservative demands with a "spirit that refuses to take things on authority" (*RR*, 5). This qualification becomes clearest in their efforts to historicize the dialectic of romanticism and classicism. Babbitt begins his whirlwind account of historical change with the Renaissance, describing its excessive celebration of wit and its obsessive "pursuit of the singular and the novel." He then describes the Neoclassical period as a "recoil," a reaction against this imaginative indulgence and a will-ful restraint upon metaphysical abstraction. This correctness, however, also became "a sort of tyranny" and thus inevitably inspired a counter-revolution that even more forcefully reasserted the power of the imagination. Today, he argues, the two movements exist together, but without balance, at "war with one another" (*RR*, 22–5). The critic laments not romanticism per se, but the "divorce between reason and intuition." This separation has allowed both to spin wildly out of control; imagination is no longer kept in check by reason or reason by imagination (*RR*, 36).

Eliot argues similarly in "The Metaphysical Poets." He turns first to the positive example of the sixteenth century, a period in which verse was distinguished by "a fidelity of thought and feeling." The poets of this age, particularly those of the metaphysical school, displayed a "direct sensuous apprehension of thought, or a recreation of thought into feeling." Eliot, offering his now famous theory of the "dissociation of sensibility," detects a qualitative change in the mind of the seventeenth-century poet. Like Babbitt, he laments the fact that thought and feeling have gone their sepa-rate ways. The former has grown more artificial and refined, while the latter has never been more crude. Modern poets consistently fail to "modify the spirit"; their verse lacks the ability to transform "an observation into a state of mind" (*Prose*, 62–6). On the one hand, Eliot wants to rein in unchecked feelings with certain objective forms. On the other, he hopes that these powerful feelings can help to recharge a now brittle language. He seeks a unity of faculties that works to clarify and refine both, a mind that could conceive of possibilities as well as judge them.

In this attempt to balance extremes, the classical reaction begins to fall apart. Babbitt and Eliot, in their double fear of closure and chaos, produce solutions that are at once, conversely, relative and final. Babbitt, of course, was always a humanist at heart. He seeks solace only in what he describes as a more "critical humanism" (*RR*, 287). Much like Matthew Arnold before him, he demands submission to nothing more substantial than a "perma-nent self that is felt in its relation to his ordinary self as a power of control" (*RR*, 27).[15] In fact, Babbitt finds solace in the very imagination he critiques elsewhere. Only the creative activity of culture, he argues, can maintain a balance between the vital and the static:

To look to a true center is . . . according to the classicist, to grasp the abiding human element through all the change in which it is implicated, and this calls for the highest use of the imagination. The abiding human element exists, even though it cannot be exhausted by dogmas and creeds, is not subject to rules and refuses to be locked up in formulae. (*RR*, 295)

In this extreme relativism, one wonders how recognition or even judgment is possible. If all restraints are self-created, they must always be negotiable. For Babbitt, totality exists, if it all, as an ideal norm between disparate practices. "Absolute values" are simply "mediatory values," the result of "probability" and "habit" (*RR*, 27).[16] Ultimately, Babbitt sounds less like a stern reactionary and more like a practical liberal. His classicist demands for order and restraint are a bit soft; his ideal man is simply "moderate and sensible and decent" (*RR*, 13). The law we are to follow is a local "law of measure"; our "supreme value" is, sadly enough, "decorum" (*RR*, 26–7, 287).

Despite his calls for "measure," Babbitt slowly sinks into the slough of romanticism. He has repudiated outer control for inner control and so remains unable to produce anything greater than that which needs to be saved. Eliot seems to have predicted this failure, and his critique of Babbitt helps to clarify his own potentially more rigorous alternative:

What is the higher will to *will*, if there is nothing either "anterior, exterior, or superior" to the individual? If this will is to have anything on which to operate, it must be in relation to external objects and to objective values. (*Prose*, 281–2)

Quite simply, for Eliot, the issue is spiritual and its solution is religious. "Man is man," he writes, "because he can recognize spiritual realities, not because he can invent them."[17] With this, Eliot expresses a lifelong disgust with the Protestant dissolution of proper religious feeling. He laments a tepid, inconsequential faith that teaches us "to see goodness as practical and to take the line of self-interest in a code of rewards and punishments" (Gordon, *Imperfect Life*, 113). Thus, he also argues for the necessity of the terrifying, supernatural dogmas of earlier religious practices; he defends submission to a purely external order of otherwordly values. Only Christianity's "single spiritual core and dogmatic creed" could provide the proper imaginative appeal. Discipline depends upon "the revelation of the supernatural," upon "the 'outer' restraints of an orthodox religion" (*Prose*, 229). However, as I hope to show, Eliot's ethics are also tainted by a humanistic orientation and a moral relativism. His frightening dogmatism rests upon ideal relations between individual perspectives. His polemic is distinct from Babbitt's only insofar as it further clarifies and hardens the lines between disparate practices.

From the first defense of poetic meter to the last avowal of Christianity, Eliot's work is saturated with the dialectics of relativity and stasis. In 1917, he argues that the very life of verse is a "contrast between fixity and flux . . . constant evasion and recognition of regularity." He praises poetry in which

innovation enhances regularity and regularity clarifies the presence of innovation: "Freedom," he explains, "is only truly freedom when it appears
against the background of artificial limitation" (*Prose*, 33–5). "Tradition
and the Individual Talent" offers the most concise account of this dialectic
and Eliot's sense of its double value. The essay begins with a now famous
description of traditional order and its demands upon the individual. On
the one hand, "Tradition" exists prior to the individual, as an objective
force. Its immensity asserts an infinite number of "difficulties and responsibilities" upon the poet. But this influence is in turn subject to the will of
the particular poet, to the terms and intensity of his relative position. For
Eliot, the value of the system lies in its flexibility. Each revision guarantees
the security of the whole as well as the freedom of its particular parts. In
fact, Eliot might argue for "self-sacrifice," "humility," and the "extinction of
personality," but he ultimately assigns value to the "most individual parts"
of a poet's work. Only "the really new," in fact, guarantees both the validity
of the present and the security of all that has come before. The most individual parts of a poet's work are "those in which the dead poets, his ancestors,
assert their immortality most vigorously" (*Prose*, 38–40). Ultimately, literary history is a system in "relation to which, and only in relation to which,
individual works of literary art, and the works of individual artists, have
their significance" (*Prose*, 68). The key word here is "relation," for only
the relation between particulars establishes "a sense of the timeless as well
as of the temporal and of the timeless and the temporal together" (*Prose*,
39). Eliot wants to objectify the subjective differences between subjects, to
compose a spatial order out of temporal, relative changes in sensibility. In
this, he offers up an affirmative version of an all too familiar world, one
that is always static and always open, total as well as anarchic.

Most importantly, Eliot's attempt to balance extremes leads him to the
power of rationalization. He seeks to clean up the messiness of the subjective
by submitting it to a process of reductive abstraction and then quantifi-
able relation. In the second half of "Tradition and the Individual Talent,"
he argues that healthy tradition is established through the depersonalization
of emotion. He carefully outlines a process of mental "transmutation" by
which the artist's passions, in all their complex purposiveness, are made conscious, distinct, and hard (*Prose*, 41). Eliot locates the possibilities of both
order and renewal within a ceaseless activity of "conformity." He demands
a constant objectification of subjectivity, a continual application of the
rational rule of equivalency in "which two things are measured by each
other" (*Prose*, 38–9). This process, he claims, occurs throughout time in the
work of all great poets. Tradition exists in a series of sacrifices to an order

that is always complete, yet always changing; the world forever moves both toward and within a static consciousness. As we will find, Eliot's definition of this supposedly "organic" whole is typical of his tendency to rationalize, rather than transform, the terms of modern individualism (*Prose*, 68). Whereas Babbitt emphasizes the conservative average of bourgeois thought, Eliot reifies the entire structure. As Michael North explains, Eliot's order is nothing more than a "rearguard action nipping at the heels of a triumphant liberal society" (114).

Eliot's later, most dogmatic claims, in fact, are based on these same rationalized relations. His most restrictive orders, whether national or religious, mysteriously arise out of all too relative desires. Any "definite ethical and spiritual standpoint," he admits, is simply the result of "divers and contradictory personalities." Truth is fully "peculiar to ourselves"; the individual does not "recognize," but "invents" spiritual values (*Prose*, 102–4). Indeed, Eliot's ideal communities are only semi-abstract, existing as mediations of their local entities. His beloved Britain, for example, is "only actual in diverse local manifestations"[18]; the Christian community is the product of a tenuous "control and balance" (*Prose*, 288). Eliot, in fact, confesses that "The *absolute* value is that each area should have its characteristic culture, which should also harmonize with, and enrich, the cultures of the neighbouring areas" (*Notes*, 53). Furthermore, Eliot's justification of a ruling class is founded upon its ability to abstract and rationalize subjective identity. Its position of dominance is determined only by a greater "consciousness" of human relations. As Eliot contends, "we should not consider the upper levels as possessing *more* culture than the lower, but as representing a more conscious culture and a greater specialization of culture" (*Notes*, 47). As it appears, Eliot's final faith is based on the false promises of a bourgeois order, in which a series of empty, mechanical relations assuage the painful isolation of the individual. Order is simultaneously created, perceived, and upheld by an aggregate of alienated dreamers. Absolute truth and ethical value are based on the fantasy of a common denominator.

As I hope to show, Eliot's work consistently affirms this paradoxical order. In his attempt to reconcile and temper the extremes of the modern world, the poet reproduces them in more invidious forms. He seeks both individual freedom and cultural authority, but finds solace in a confusion of human and spiritual orders. He demands absolute submission, but to institutions that are quasi-human in form and content – tradition, the church, England. In this, his claims appear both more subjective and more final; he advances his personal faith with a frightening dogmatism. Indeed, it is perhaps this confusion that lies behind his interest in myth and dogma; with these, Eliot is promoting nothing more than the necessity of "admitted fictions."[19] But what most urgently needs to be addressed is how this confusion of the human and divine inevitably involves a submission to rationalization. In Eliot's thought, divinity is not simply recast in the self, but in the self as dictated by efficient reason. The human power concealed behind divine power is reinvested in instrumentality; the individual recalls his power from god only to submit it to the industrial apparatus. Eliot's return to the human is problematic not simply because it is romantic or relativistic, but because it returns by way of an oppressive rationalization. Instead of thinking through the contingency of the material world as a possible source of graceful order, he turns against it with all the fervor of angry god.

3 POSSUM ON THE PULPIT

Why does Eliot both demand and flinch from supernatural authority? His criticism consistently espouses the necessity of spiritual order, his poetry everywhere affirms the organizational power of myth, and, above all, his conversion to Anglicanism attests to his faith in otherworldly values, and yet he is unable to affirm anything more than a tough humanism or, worse, a rigid rationalization. As I hope to show here, Eliot's work gives voice to an historical trajectory in which changes in religion are intimately linked to changes in the market. Like many of his contemporaries, the poet was tormented by a spiritual ethos he had long since discarded for humanism, leaving him convinced that he himself is loathsome, yet unable to locate anything other than himself as the source of redemption. His poetry – from "The Love Song of J. Alfred Prufrock" to *Four Quartets* – remains caught between his disgust toward a fallen world that he cannot escape and his desire for an authority that he no longer trusts. As Lyndall Gordon aptly characterizes the dilemma, "If civilization is 'unreal' and God sends no 'sign', where do we find a reliable authority?" "Here is the heart of Eliot's *aboulie*," she writes, "a horrified glimpse of innate depravity and the related fear that few have the stature to transcend it" (177). What needs to be addressed here are the ways in which this despair, caused by the demystifying power of industrial efficiency, finds solace in a newly mystified version of that efficiency. Eliot's poetry needs to be re-evaluated for its attempt to redeem the experience of modernity by reproducing its most corrupt aspects.

Eliot comes closest to defining this confounded spiritual state in a semi-autobiographical account of his compatriot Henry Adams. Eliot describes Adams as the victim of a "Puritan inheritance" that has laid upon him "the heavy burden of self-improvement." Adams does not simply want "to do something great," he is miserably "dogged by the shadow of self-conscious incompetence." According to Eliot, this insatiable desire expresses itself negatively, in a dissatisfaction with all forms of authority. "Working with and against his conscience," Eliot writes, "was the Boston doubt . . . a scepticism which is a product, or a cause, or a concomitant, of Unitarianism; it is not destructive, but it is dissolvent." Here, Eliot identifies his own religious inheritance as the source of a chronic restlessness. Adams-Eliot is caught in a specifically Protestant bind in which he "yearns for unity," but lacks all "conviction." He is driven into a neurotic frenzy, haunting history and culture for some glimmer of grace. He seeks solace "with the wings of a beautiful but ineffectual conscience beating vainly in a vacuum jar."[20] This restlessness helps to explain some of the most frustrating aspects of Eliot's own work. The ceaseless adoption of new masks or personae, the perfunctory use of symbolic structures that are then just as perfunctorily discarded, the painful self-mockery – each is fueled by a chronic suspicion of all authority, a refusal to yield and an inability to accept. As Eliot himself explained, "I am one whom this sense of the void tends to drive towards asceticism or sensuality."[21]

Eliot's self-characterization finds a provocative echo in Weber's theory of the Protestant spirit, which defines this practical ethos as the ideological bulwark of capitalism itself. In Weber's account, the earliest Protestants saw God as subject to no law or intervention; his was a mute sublimity, self-sufficient and obscure. He may occasionally provide glimpses of truth, rare moments of ecstasy, but "everything else, including the meaning of our individual destiny, is hidden in dark mystery." According to Weber, the "extreme inhumanity" of this doctrine produced within the individual a "feeling of unprecedented inner loneliness." As God's law was final, unimpeachable, no saint, no priest, no friend could help – to repent was useless, to query was sin (60). But, on a practical level, this withdrawal inspired a somewhat contrary effect. According to Weber, God did not simply die; rather, his power was usurped, uneasily adopted by the sinners who betrayed him. The missing authority was recast in the individual, who was now caught in "a restless and systematic struggle with life," with himself (64). In other words, self-loathing and self-love mingle in a hierarchical confusion – the self is forced to depend on a self it has learned to despise. The individual's fundamental antagonism toward the sensual world, coupled with a nagging desire to master one's fate, led to a ceaseless labor of redemption. External conformity to God, which was lax at best, was replaced by a much more rigorous, yet always skeptical self-submission (99).

In the previous chapter, we saw how this anxious dialectic organized competitive bourgeois neighbors in relation to each other. Weber's account, however, helps us to understand its specific productive power. As he explains, in the Enlightenment world, the more ecstatic forms of religious experience were no longer possible. Catholic grace, the magical redemption of absolution, was scoffed at as primitive and irrational. The Protestant, however, could not sit idly by while his fate was decided elsewhere; his anxious skepticism found relief only in an intense worldly activity. Election might be aided by a continual labor and its objective result; any hope of salvation needed to be augmented "by real, and not merely apparent, good works." Here, divine creation overlaps with mortal labor; the glory of the former is mimed by a regime of "systematic self-control." The fallen cannot rest; they must develop a "consistent method for conduct" and thus renovate "the whole meaning of life at every moment and in every action" (69, 71). For Weber, this transformation in praxis proved decisive. Protestantism supported not just individualism, but an efficient individualism, a micromanagement of conscience that was easily transposed onto the economic arena. The process of self-fashioning found fulfillment in sensible investment, the manipulation of pecuniary loss and profit. Thus, the relation of a sinner to his God was ultimately understood as "that of customer and shopkeeper. One who has once got into debt may well, by the product of all his virtuous acts, succeed in paying off the accumulated interest but never the principle." The self was reinterpreted as a "religious account-book in which sins, temptations, and progress made in grace were entered and tabulated" (76–7).[22]

The connection between Weber's theory and Eliot's work is most clearly expressed in the Protestant concept of a "calling." As Weber explains, for Luther and his followers, success in a calling, no matter how material it may be, revealed the individual's commitment to the divine plan and, conversely, God's commitment to that individual. Indeed, it is only by the work performed in the name of a calling that a soul can attain "the highest good towards which this religion strove, the certainty of salvation" (69). But it was the necessary efficiency and the continual activity of the calling that revolutionized the individual. Constant self-scrutiny, a ceaseless reckoning of success and failure, became the order of the day (44). Paradoxically, this aspect of the concept of the calling at once asserts and confounds the essential unity of the individual. The Protestant attitude fuels a schizophrenic activity of self-scrutiny and self-transcendence. The self emerges here in a state of self-alienation, confounded by an imperative to improve itself. Its neat particularity was countered by an unbearable dissociation, an irreducible excess that always needed to be reconciled. In fact, we might even say that the self emerges here as a particular property, a piece of capital that must be efficiently cultivated. It existed as an objective investment for which only a "methodically rationalized ethical conduct" could reduce waste and maximize profits (77, 114).[23]

Eliot's account of his own calling attests to a belief that one's given task carries a supreme ethical responsibility. For Eliot, this task materializes as an effort not simply to master the self, but to transform the "excesses" of emotion into a neatly organized, highly rational structure. The poet's work entails a hygienic efficiency by which all that confounds the clear conscience is brought into line with symbolic norms and standards. In his essay "Hamlet," for example, Eliot argues that Shakespeare's play is an "artistic failure" for its emotional wastefulness. The prince, he explains, is "dominated by an emotion which is inexpressible, because it is in *excess* of the facts as they appear . . . It is thus a feeling which he cannot understand; he cannot objectify it, and it therefore remains to poison life and obstruct action." Similarly, Shakespeare himself has failed to transform his own crude emotional material into a suitable symbolic order. The emotional problem "proved too much for him"; intense feelings never found their objective equivalents and thus sully the play's effects (*Prose*, 48–9).

In the same essay, this logic informs Eliot's definition of the "objective correlative." Here, the desire for authority finds expression in a process of self-rationalization:

The only way of expressing emotion in the form of art is by finding an "objective correlative"; in other words, a set of objects, a situation, a chain of events which shall be the formula of that *particular* emotion. (*Prose*, 47–9)

As we have seen, "Tradition and the Individual Talent" offers a similarly "impersonal theory of poetry." In this essay, Eliot more completely defines the poet as a split subject, ceaselessly reworking his emotions into crystalline forms. "The more perfect the artist," he writes, "the more completely separate in him will be the man who suffers and the mind which creates; the more perfectly will the mind digest and transmute the passions which are its materials." Tellingly, Eliot compares this process to a laboratory experiment in which hazy gases are combined to create a single, concentrated acid. All that is messy about the poetic experience – and, by implication, all that is messy about the self – must submit to rational process; the poet works in the "neutral" lab of the mind, methodically forming "new compounds" out of his own emotions (*Prose*, 40–1). In "The Function of Criticism," Eliot explicitly refers to Luther's discourse of "calling and election" to define this process. He first laments a lack of authoritative norms that might aid in the process of evaluating creative and spiritual matters. We have been left to our own devices, he argues, and now must engage in a "frightful toil" of figuring things out on our own. He then outlines a "dry technique" by which the unknown is "made into something precise, tractable, under control." By a careful process of "comparison and analysis" – not to mention a constant labor of "sifting, combining, constructing, expunging, correcting, testing" – the "most nebulous" feelings are "clarified and reduced to a state of fact" (*Prose*, 73–5).

This ethos, of course, finds its most provocative expression in Eliot's poetry. According to Manju Jain, Eliot attained success in his work only once he learned to manipulate the terms of Laforguian "dédoublement":

The term dédoublement refers to the process of the "undoubling" or the splitting of the self into subject and object – into the self thinking and the self observing itself think and act . . . This division or splitting of the self is the result of acute self-consciousness which paralyzes the will and the power to act and feel.[24]

The poet, however, did not need to look so far afield for ways of turning self-struggle into poetic form. His formal irony takes its cue from his Protestant faith in self-analysis, a ceaseless scrutiny of one's own transgressions. Indeed, Eliot's voice is everywhere doubled with the sermonizing style of his Unitarian forebears. His verbal tics and mannerism – bibliolatry, authoritative commands, apocalyptic imagery, and incantatory rhythms – derive from the pulpit. His structural principles – the spiritual quest, the chronicle of transgression, the ironic revelation – were adopted from the Bible. In fact, Eliot's best poems, such as *The Waste Land* and *Four Quartets*, mainly cohere as catalogues of sins and salvations, road maps from personal damnation to personal salvation. In these, the self's turmoil is observed, judged, and rationalized into coherent imagery. In these, Eliot mimes a preacher's skill of conveying inner crisis as a struggle of objective forces. In one article, tellingly titled "The Preacher as Artist," Eliot characterizes the best sermons as those which convey an "Eye, curiously, patiently watching himself as a man." His beloved Donne is described as an intense "Egoist" who had a talent for turning his "introspective faculty" into a graceful "tale."[25] Similarly, in a lecture on lyricism, Eliot celebrates the poet who can talk to himself in the voices of different characters. He praises a kind of self-ventriloquism whereby emotions are objectified and thus made coherent. The successful poet contemplates his own emotional struggles as if they were external to him, as part of larger symbolic order.[26] In all of these descriptions, self-scrutiny meets with self-objectification; the good poet resembles the good Protestant, attentive to an inner life that needs to be reconciled with a larger, divine order.

We will return to this process of externalization in chapter 4, for now it will suffice to show that the anxiety that attends this self-scrutiny is most apparent in what Eliot himself noticed to be his poetry's "confusion of pronouns" ("Voices," 100). In his early monologues, for example, pronominal slippage is the direct result of the individual's struggles to translate conflicting internal forces into a coherent antithesis of self and other.[27] The very first line of "The Love Song of J. Alfred Prufrock" moves from the muddled unity of "us" to a groundless distinction between "you and I." This referential confusion clearly implicates the reader, but it also provocatively points toward subjective boundaries that are not easily maintained. Similarly, in "Portrait of a Lady," the narrator addresses a "you" who is not exactly the lady he fails to address during their intimate encounters. Here, the speaker is more directly caught up in a forced misidentification; the narrator refuses to recognize the superficialities of the lady as his own. Both of these instances, though, express a chronic difficulty of reconciling the self with the self-as-authority. Paradoxically, an already uneasy narrative voice must depend upon itself as the voice of judgment. Prufrock's "you" is both an internal entity as well as an external authority to which he feels compelled to appeal. Similarly, in "Portrait of a Lady," the narrator first addresses "you" with a certain condescension, but at the end of the poem, he submits a guilty defense before it. Both personae cast about for an authority that they do not fully trust; both put forth assertions that later, in bad faith, they retract.

In "The Love Song of J. Alfred Prufrock," Eliot considers the effects of this crisis in their most tangible form, upon the individual body. Here, he provides his most trenchant critique of his uneasy faith, but nonetheless fails to provide a suitable alternative. The title of the poem alone suggests deep fissures: the romantic theme of the "Love Song" is juxtaposed with the financier's signature; the objective hardness implied by "Proof" and "Rock" is countered by the sentimental daintiness of "Prude" and "Frock." These contrasts, of course, continue throughout the poem. Social contradictions of class and gender provide the objective correlatives for the protagonist's confounded psyche. The "tedious argument" that follows is splayed across spaces, bodies, and minds; in each case, tension flares between desires for emotional or sexual release and a commitment to a formal order of clearly defined boundaries. Importantly, then, Prufrock is not simply an outcast; rather, he lacks suitable means to reconcile his inner desires with the conventional forms of his everyday world. Like the poet who animates his needs, this figure exists in a state of skeptical limbo; he can "connect / Nothing with nothing" (62). Furthermore, Eliot suggests that Prufrock confronts his world in a profound state of fatherlessness. Prufrock lacks appropriate models of identification by which he may master his experience. Indeed, he scrambles after masculine figures of authority – Michelangelo, Hamlet, John the Prophet – but these men have been rendered unsuitable for identification. Each is exposed as corrupt, impure; Michelangelo hangs castrated on the wall, the prophet has literally lost his head. The important point here is that Prufrock, as a direct result of this paternal crisis – this Protestant crisis – must be his own authority. The subjective split the poem records is not simply psychological, but religious – Prufrock is forced to master his own existence, to regulate and direct his own desires toward suitable ends. Of course, he fails miserably – the sinner in him does not trust the sentence that the god in him has passed. His life is nothing more than the "tedious argument," unanswerable questions, insecure assertions, and, ultimately, painful misgivings. His procrastination is grounded in extreme uncertainty; time is filled by "a hundred indecisions . . . a hundred visions and revisions . . ." (12).

Prufrock also expresses a typically Protestant attitude in his continuous labor of self-cultivation, his ceaseless effort to restore the inconsequential details of his personal experience to a larger meaningful order. Ian Watt, in his excellent account of Protestant individualism and British fiction, sees this activity as central to the characterization of the Protestant hero:

[These heroes] all have an intensely active conception of life as a continuous moral and social struggle; they all see every event in ordinary life as proposing an intrinsically moral issue on which reason and conscience must be exerted to the full before right action is possible; they all seek by introspection and observation to build their own personal scheme of moral certainty.[28]

In Watt's account, it is a specifically Protestant tradition that makes an everyday hero like Prufrock possible. This ideology is essentially democratic in nature: each individual has a place in god's plan, the struggle of any soul is important before god's eyes. Watt's theory also explains Prufrock's obsession with his life's tedium. Protestant ideology implies an equality of experience; even the most inconsequential details of a life must be queried for divine resonance (Watt, *Rise* 77). For Prufrock, there is nothing to distinguish the eating of a peach from an "overwhelming question" that can "disturb the universe" – both must be made meaningful. Ultimately, the apparent incommensurabilities of the poem are not necessarily mock-heroic, and Prufrock is not necessarily an ironic hero. For the Protestant, everyday struggle is spiritual struggle; the "taking of a toast and tea" is a "possible moment of greatness" (12, 14). Another way of saying this is that the Protestant subject depicted here *is* both ordinary and divine; his dédoublement is a result of his having to be his own authority. Prufrock both acts and judges that action; his mundane experiences are filtered through the judgment of an Old Testament God.

If Eliot here laments this dilemma, it is not simply because of its painful uncertainty. More importantly, Prufrock's crisis leaves him susceptible to manipulation. In the absence of a beneficial order, in the absence of appropriate identifications, he is victimized by his contemporaries. Here, Eliot's depiction most clearly touches upon the Freudian, as Prufrock's conscience is largely a cultural construction, composed of other voices and images. His speech is littered with all too human figures of authority, suspect voices from a multitude of sources – religious, national, scientific, artistic. Eliot perhaps would like to see this phenomenon in a positive way, as it signals the possibility of a communal consciousness. Here, however, it is depicted pessimistically, as a treacherous appropriation, for Prufrock has no way of judging what he hears. The authority of the masses, the least common denominator of modern identity, intrudes violently upon his deliberations. His monologue is peppered with frighteningly disembodied judgments of the most superficial kind: "[They will say: 'How his hair is growing thin!']" and "[They will say: 'But how his arms and legs are thin!']" (12).

Above and beyond these recognizably false commands lies a more horrific domination by rationalization. Hoping to master a fate that cannot be mastered, unable to trust any earthly authority, Prufrock submits to the rigid formalism of an instrumental life. Like his creator, he seeks to transmute the complex business of material existence into "objective correlatives" that can be easily negotiated. His search for a coherent system of meaning leads him to reduce all particularity into abstract markers and thus stable formula. He finds some kind of perfection, and at least stability, in quantification; he measures experience with coffee spoons, neatly cataloguing his "evenings, mornings, afternoons." Indeed, throughout the poem, organic meaning is shunned in favor of formal units; society, experience, and the body itself are broken down into lifeless units. Prufrock knows eyes, hands, and arms, but not in their material particularity, and not in relation to any integral whole; these are merely cogs in a much larger experiential apparatus, necessary components of an efficient life. When he is finally confronted with irreducible contingency, the frightening carnality of "light brown hair," he must begin the process of rationalization all over again (13).

Ultimately, in this activity, the tragic economy of heroic individualism is reduced to the sad economy of modern efficiency. The potentially regenerative power of the hero, whose brave sacrifice renews the social order, is replaced by a meek business of self-restraint and accumulation. Hamlet, the Catholic prince, is given over to Polonius, the Protestant steward. The latter is simply "one that will do," no more than "Deferential, glad to be of use / Politic, cautious, and meticulous." He may not be able to "squeeze the universe into a ball," but he is an efficient investor who can "swell a progress, start a scene or two" (15). Prufrock ultimately turns his back on the complexity of the self, the tensions of the material world. He concludes his monologue by imprisoning his desires in Weber's "iron cage" of rational efficiency. It is, in fact, in this regard that the poem's crustacean imagery makes sense. Prufrock devolves into the crab, whose tough exoskeleton and efficient "scuttling" masks a sad heart. Indeed, the crab is nothing more than his claws, a purposeful pair of hands (14).

Yet "The Love Song of J. Alfred Prufrock" does not end comfortably. Eliot's protagonist fails to find a suitable authority; rationality is not completely grasped, and powerful emotions continue to lurk beneath the surface:

> We have lingered in the chambers of the sea
> By sea-girls wreathed with seaweed red and brown
> Till human voices wake us, and we drown.   (16)

In this, Eliot seems to refuse to reconcile the contradictions of his age and thereby preserves a certain critical space between reification and romanticism. In fact, his poem thus seems to suggest that the Protestant condition is not entirely a negative one. The end of religious idealism gives rise to a radical uneasiness within the subject, but it is precisely this anxious state that entails a certain critical consciousness. The modern individual, caught between a god he mistrusts and a world he despises, is in a unique position to renegotiate the terms of his existence. Slavoj Žižek, in his discussion of *die Versagung*, comes to a similar conclusion. For Žižek, the modern subject has renounced his identification with god the father; more precisely, he has sacrificed his earlier sacrifice to that father. Without this secure identification and thus without a secure identity, the ego now experiences a pathological condition of "subjective destitution." "We renounce," Žižek writes, "the symbolic alliance which defines the very kernel of our being – the abyss, the void in which we find ourselves thereby, is what we call 'modern-age subjectivity.'" At this historical moment, at the extreme end of self-negation, the subject seems to gain a certain openness in his attitude toward the world. The destitution of modernity affects a split between identity and ethics, allowing the latter to assume a more flexible character. The individual who is unable to identify with a powerful authority finds himself free to adopt and adapt alternative value systems. The subjective void that appears here is "simply the void of freedom" and "the possibility of a new life opens up."[29]

At his best, then, Eliot willingly relinquishes ecstatic identification in order to preserve this critical condition. He chooses to live in excess of the ideal, unequal to the sublime, and thus hopes to maintain a certain difference out of which thought may rise. However, increasingly in his work, the poet's fears force him to abandon this openness. The Protestant crisis, in which the self must double as its own authority, pushes him toward a rigid totality. Eliot's fascination with "original sin" proves essential here. For him, original sin is at once the cause of banishment from paradise and the source of knowledge. Our corrupt inheritance makes innocence impossible, yet it also provides us with consciousness and freedom of will. Eliot sometimes revels in this state, however painful, as it provides a necessary difference out of which criticism and creation may arise. Yet, at the same time, for Eliot, original sin is a constant goad to self-improvement; the mortal soul, corrupt to the core, must ceaselessly strive for purity. In Eliot's work, the sinner has fallen away from perfection and remains in arrears; he must toil to balance his account with the Lord. In this, the "necessary dogma" of original sin becomes the affirmation of ceaseless toil and rationalization; it recasts the self as capital that must be put to profit in a larger economic order ("Second Thoughts," 437–8). As Watt explains, "'original sin' is really the dynamic tendency of capitalism itself, whose aim is never merely to maintain the *status quo*, but to transform it incessantly" (65).

If "The Love Song of J. Alfred Prufrock" gives voice to a soul that resists reification, *Four Quartets* – written decades later – depicts that soul long after its capitulation. Here, the poet seems to have fully accepted his fallen state, his incommensurability with the godhead, as well as the humble, penitential labor that this state entails. He thus revives the efforts of his Puritan ancestors to redeem the self and its unruly passions, to create a perfect life on earth in accordance with divine plan. The poem begins with a fall that is simultaneously a fall into sin and a fall into temporality. We are given a glimpse of divine order, of children's laughter in the garden, but only to be whisked away into the unredeemable present, a world of alienation and doubt, a "place of disaffection" (17). The vision of Eden remains to haunt us, to direct our efforts, but we have been left to toil "in the aspect of time . . . in the form of limitation . . ." (20). Eliot, of course, urges us to be happy in our fall, thankful for this difference. Imperfection, in fact, is a grace that pushes us to work God's will. "Adam's curse" is our salvation; labor is our purgation – indeed, it is only in this loss that we gain (29). We are not saints, Eliot argues, and our lives are not filled with ecstatic visions of "the timeless / With time." Our religious experience must remain common, humble, and arduous; we have only "hints and guesses" of the divine will, while our lives must be disciplined by "prayer observance, discipline, thought and action" (44–5).

Here, Eliot no longer hides the ceaselessness of this effort, or its rationalization. The spiritual struggle is explicitly interpreted through the logic of capital. Innerworldly asceticism finds its counterpart in the logic of rational investment. Born in debt and always accumulating interest, the self works in hopes of reconciling his account with the Lord. The poem, in fact, consciously conflates its religious themes with an economic primer of terms such as "value," "valuation," "competition," "gain and loss," "business," "commerce," and "costing." Eliot, at times, playfully toys with these relations, as when he rhymes "unpayable haul" with the "prayable / Prayer of the one annunciation" (38). Elsewhere, he uses the analogy to distinguish between the worldly and the spiritual. He claims, for example, that the repentant seek "neither gain nor loss"; "For us, there is only the trying. The rest is not our business" (32). In each of these instances, though, the poet encourages a mutual affirmation. Even at its most ironic, the poem draws together the deep structural relations between spiritual and economic reckoning. Throughout, the Protestant experience of the self overlaps with the entrepreneurial experience, thereby reinforcing each other.

These relations are most dangerously asserted in Eliot's depiction of penance as a ceaseless process of reckoning. Eliot's poem presents the fall as a condition of not simply alienation, but excess. The sinner is born into a world that everywhere falls away from the balanced "completion" of the divine word; here, there is only a "partial ecstasy" and "partial horror," divergences from the "resolution" of the whole (16). Existence is a process of accumulation, an increase of sin and a decrease of grace: "There is no end, but addition: the trailing / consequence of further days and hours . . ." (37). Tellingly, in the economy of the poem, negation always precedes fulfillment and fulfillment culminates in negation. Alterity feeds and affirms the efficient order; that which is deemed "waste" serves as crude material for a rational activity of purgation and purification. Indeed, at times it is difficult to distinguish between the degradation of sin and the movement toward grace; in Eliot's expressive lists, purgation is accumulation and addition is subtraction. Take, for example, the following account, in which a tallying of that which is lost swells into presence:

Oh dark dark dark. They all go into the dark,
The vacant interstellar spaces, the vacant into the vacant,
The captains, merchant bankers, eminent men of letters,
The generous patrons of art, the statesmen and the rulers,
Distinguished civil servants, chairmen of many committees,
Industrial lords and petty contractors, all go into the dark,
And dark the Sun and Moon, and the Almanach de Gotha
And the Stock Exchange Gazette, the Directory of Directors,
And cold the sense and lost the motive of action.   (27)

This logic finds resonance in Eliot's turn to the *via negativa*, his commitment to the negation of worldly pleasure as the precondition for positive transcendence. For Eliot, as for Augustine, Ignatius, and countless other saints before him, the moment of purgation brings forth divine abundance; the loss of self is a spiritual profit. In this, the poet draws upon theology's most marketable formulation, redefining grace as a rational activity of possession and dispossession:

In order to arrive at what you do not know
      You must go by a way which is the way of ignorance.
In order to possess what you do not possess
      You must go by way of dispossession.   (29)

Here, as everywhere, *via negativa* is transformed into *via economica*.

What concerns us most is the way in which this logic of negation proffers a pseudo-reconciliation of conflicting demands for difference and order. In the account-book of the soul, like that of the bank, excess attests to the particular as well as the whole. Credits and debits are revealed in time, but their significance exists in relation to some zero sum. Here, as throughout Eliot's work, personal experiences are limited to their own moment, yet in relation to each other they conjure up a divine order. As he explains, "Except for the point, the still point / There would be no dance, and there is only the dance" (16–17). Indeed, Eliot's balance teeters precariously in a state of utter imbalance, between two debts that mirror, but do not annul each other. Eliot depicts the "still point" as "Neither flesh nor fleshless . . . Neither from nor towards . . . Neither arrest nor movement . . . Neither ascent nor decline . . ." (15). There is no "Zero summer," no spiritual perfection, but only "the dance" (49). Indeed, his very syntax is twisted by negations and thus always exceeding toward its ideal:

We can*not* think of a time that is oceanless
Or of an ocean *not* littered with wastage
Or of a future that is *not* liable
Like the past, to have *no* destination.
                     (38; emphasis added)

In the context of this negative activity, the constant reconciliation of an excess that cannot be reconciled, the poem's enigmatic epigram begins to take on another meaning. If "the way up is the way down," it is only because debits *and* credits, excesses of any kind, exist in relation to some ideal reckoning (10).

With this logic, one might argue, Eliot avoids both insignificance and totality, relativism and idealism. Yet, in privileging an economy of negation, he also reconceives suffering and oppression as their affirmative opposites, freedom and order. In other words, Eliot assuages the pain of temporal experience as necessary to a state of grace, and redeems subjugation as self-chosen. He transforms the nightmare of history, the immediacy and finality of exploitation, into an order that is unimpeachably divine. This sleight of hand is most clearly exposed in his effort to reconcile temporality with the timeless. The mortal experience of time, he argues, is painfully limited, blind at once to the cause of our suffering and its ultimate purpose; yet these moments, no matter how incoherent on their own, together fulfill God's significant plan. As Eliot writes, "Time past and time future / Allow but a little consciousness," and yet, "Only through time time is conquered" (16). Elsewhere, he explains, "History may be servitude, / History may be freedom," but "history is a pattern / Of timeless moments" that exists "beyond desire" (55, 58). This is the logic of Protestantism, in which worldly labor serves to fulfill a divine plan. However, it is also the logic of industrial capital, in which individual activity is conducted according to the universal dictates of efficiency. In the account book, particular moments of expenditure are tallied in relation to a timeless balance; in the marketplace, real value is rendered according to abstract rules of equivalency. More violently, in the factory, the worker submits his particular pain to a monstrous apparatus that only appears reasonable.

Despite its emphasis on critical distance, on an irreducible excess, *Four Quartets* replicates and reaffirms the structure of the economy at large. In its glorification of significant toil, in its justification of alienation, and, most importantly, in its rationalization of contingency, the poem imaginatively resolves the crises of the modern age. Without irony, Eliot concludes the poem by claiming to speak for the "defeated" (57). Pain and suffering, political revolt, historical atrocities (even fire-bombing by Nazis!) – these are simply negations of negations. This pain, this passion will be resolved, annulled, in the great beyond:

> These men, and those who opposed them
> And those whom they opposed
> Accept the constitution of silence
> And are folded in a single party.   (56)

In the end, our pain is our only salvation – "the fire and the rose are one" (59). Here, Weber's critique seems most significant, for it suggests that Protestantism affirms exploitative practices from the perspective of the laborer as well as the entrepreneur. Through the logic of the calling, which preaches ceaseless toil and mute submission before a hidden God, the pain and alienation of the modern economic order is ratified. The "power of religious asceticism," he writes, creates "sober, conscientious, and unusually industrious workmen, who cl[i]ng to their work as to a life purpose willed by God." In conjunction, the notion of predestination helps to inure the worker to inequality and to divert potentially revolutionary desire. In the eyes of the Protestant laborer, "the unequal distribution of goods of this world was a special dispensation of Divine Providence, which in these differences, as in particular grace, pursued secret ends unknown to men" (120).

4 DEAD RECKONING

As Eliot's most sustained successful critique of modernity, *The Waste Land* also reveals the extent of his capitulation. Here, the poet's desire to reshape the modern world gets the best of him; his prejudices and fears push him toward even greater dogmas of self-sacrifice. In the face of social perversion and mass destruction, "Human voices" become too painful to bear, and so they are submitted to the rigid laws of efficient reason. Eliot, like the Sybil he alludes to at the beginning of *The Waste Land*, locks himself in the "iron cage" of rationalization, containing and neutralizing any cultural dissidence within a static order. He advances a poetic formalism that, in its abstract reckoning, represses the excesses of his contemporaries; aesthetic structure performs a totalizing activity that makes subjugation appear both necessary and inevitable. As I hope to show, then, *The Waste Land* is affirmative in its very *form*; it mimics the *affective structure* of the market as a whole. Its reader remains caught between an acute particularity and an incoherent totality, and so accepts a meager semblance of rational order. Abandoned by God, yet disgusted with the fallen landscape, he willingly submits to a sprawling poetic bureaucracy.

The Waste Land is most powerful in its depiction of a society that has lost its integral, animating soul. Eliot's voice finds strength and clarity in his account of a hypermodern world void of natural and national blood-ties. London, the "Unreal City," has been overrun by passions out of touch with the material contingencies that might otherwise serve to shape them. The first few verses, for example, show that diurnal and annual cycles have been abandoned; geographical borders and racial lines have also been superseded. Marie, for example, reads when she should be sleeping and travels to avoid climatic change; she is mistaken for a Russian, yet comes from Lithuania and claims to be a German (51). This dislocation most disastrously leads to excesses and perversions in the productive process. By abandoning nature, or the ancient fertility rites based upon natural cycles, the modern world has lost the ability to produce in moderation. Intercourse is either violent, comic, or simply impossible – its produce deformed, withered, or dead. In one scene, the passion of an upper-class woman remains torturously unfulfilled; it finds expression, if at all, in a "fiery" disorder of the "nerves." Her desires are assuaged, if at all, by a hyperconsumption of "synthetic perfumes" that "drowned the sense" (54). In a contrasting scene, the lower-class underworld is the scene of hypersexuality and overproduction. Lil's body, from her rotten teeth to her rotten womb – "(and her only thirty-one)" – offers a travesty of maternal creation (56).

Alongside this chaos, one is faced with the paradox of the city's reification. The urban masses are released to their most common desires; in their search for freedom, they find a base conformity. In an earlier draft, Eliot more explicitly defined the city as rent by these paradoxes:

> London, the swarming life you kill and breed,
> Huddled between the concrete and the sky,
> Responsive to the momentary need,
> Vibrates unconscious to its formal destiny.
>
> Neither knowing how to think, nor how to feel,
> But live in the awareness of the observing eye.
> London, your people is bound upon the wheel!
> (*Facsimile*, 43)

The city is the scene of a grand romantic experiment; its denizens seek unburdened life and noble savagery. What emerges in the absence of authority, however, can only appall. This is a social order of the lowest common denominator, community degree zero, which denies both unity or particularity. Indeed, the poem's one-line metonymic fragments – "Speak," "Tereu," "burning" – dramatize both the excesses and the reductions affected by an unchecked humanism. More ominously, Eliot argues that the anxious crowd, burdened by a lack of authority, willingly submits to the "observing eye" of efficient reason. Greed, sloth, the need to conquer and the need to submit, these conspire with an efficient technology to generate the vulgar order of the market. Eliot's circular imagery helps us to grasp the transformation that has been affected. The "wheel" of fortune has

been transformed into a wheel of torture; divine pattern concedes to the
inhuman face of technological domination. Elsewhere, the rings of Dante's
plotted universe gives way to the ritual patterns of the work day; "I see
crowds of people, walking round in a ring" (52). In this case, "fate" has
little to do with the whimsy of the gods. It has long since given way to
"formal pattern," the twin rails of reason and habit. To borrow from Marcuse, "'Fate' [has become] the law of an economy and society which are
largely independent of individuals, and violation of this law would mean
self-destruction . . . of a society in which the law of domination appears as
objective technological law."[30]

In this regard, the poem's most provocative claims concern fertility rites
and their modern desecration. Drawing upon Frazerian anthropology, Eliot
waxes nostalgically for a classical society founded upon ritual praxis. Specifically, he praises fertility rites in which participants mime the fall and return
of natural cycles. These rites are spiritual as well as practical; the performance of natural patterns organizes forces in relation to each other and
thus maximizes production. In the modern world, however, these rites
are everywhere travestied – transfigurative ecstasy appears only as brutal
rage, whereas ritual formality appears as blank automatism. The organizing power of ritual has been appropriated by a voracious market; the desire
for order and vitality has been manipulated by a technological apparatus
bent on profit. The logic of sacrifice has been freed from its spiritual context and now exists as a simple and transposable mechanism of efficient
production. Man continues to relinquish all pleasure, but, in this continual labor, he tends nothing other than the machinery of exploitation.
In one of the poem's more successful moments of irony, Eliot contrasts a
socially redemptive sacrifice with the all too bourgeois cultivation of private
property:

> "Stetson!
> You who were with me in the ships at Mylae!
> That corpse you planted last year in your garden,
> Has it begun to sprout? Will it bloom this year?"
> (53)

"The Fire Sermon," similarly, can be described as a parody of the Eleusinian
mysteries. Here, ritual participants prepare the scene and then meet as
representatives of an order that is neither creative nor communal. Their
passion is fully rationalized, subject to the patterns of the business day and
the brute formalism of the technological environment. The body is nothing
more than a "human engine / Like a taxi throbbing." At the end of the
work day, it automatically turns from its desk, eats without enjoyment,

and submits to the necessary act of reproduction. In this, desire feeds an impersonal machine; particulars of time and place are lost in a radical "indifference." The participants are apathetic to a technological fate they care neither to master nor understand; when the deed is done, the female victim "smoothes her hair with automatic hand, / And puts a record on the gramophone" (60).

It is fitting that Tiresius presides over this city and its painful rites. The prophet, in his androgynous decadence, mocks what Eliot sees as a more productive heterosexual union and neatly mirrors the horrific paradoxes of the modern world. Tiresius, in fact, sits beneath the wall of the marketplace; he emerges only after all values and distinctions have been dissolved by the economy (60). His dispassionate perspective, in fact, arises in direct response to the bland decay around him. He can be credited with "uniting all the rest" only because all has already been abstracted and neutralized (70). In fact, his prophetic power derives from the loss of particularity occasioned by the rational rule of equivalence. It is easy to predict the future of a world governed by routine and standardization, in which fate is determined not by the inscrutable whimsy of gods, but by the technological efficiency of modern production. In this, Tiresius's link with the tragedy of Oedipus is telling. In the classical drama, the prophet is witness to a guilty pride that, in its reversal, affects the restoration of social order. The tragic hero, in ritualistic fashion, has been singled out as a sacrifice for the health of the community as a whole. While the modern citizen may be guilty of a certain egotism, he can barely sustain anything so heroic as pride. Indeed, as Tiresius knows, if the citizen is to be sacrificed, it is as one of the many nameless tossed to the industrial machine.

Tiresius's appearance also coincides with one of Eliot's most weighted terms – "indifference" (60). Often in his work, Eliot interprets this word literally, as a complete loss of difference, the end of particular purpose and the loss of significance. In one early verse, the poet complains that his contemporaries are "Indifferent to what the wind does / Indifferent to sudden rains." In another, he sadly recounts how "Life departs with a feeble smile / Into the indifferent" (*Hare*, 16–17). In *The Waste Land*, "indifference" specifically coincides with the reductions affected by an efficient machinery. It appears at a moment when all has been rendered neutral by the industrial apparatus. Interestingly, the phrase "Like a taxi throbbing waiting" refers both to the secretary of the line before and Tiresius in the line after. Its muddling presence in the text mimics the ways in which mechanical processes in general neutralize identities. In this, it recalls Eliot's earlier prose description of an "engine":

The machine was hard, deliberate, and alert; having chosen with motives unknown to cut through the fog it pursued its course . . . The machine was certain and sufficient as a rose bush, indifferently justifying the aimless parasite.

As this passage suggests, the author of *The Waste Land* seeks "resolution," but not through a process of standardization. He yearns for an organic unity of heroic passions, while the machine can only organize and sustain "business men" whose souls "lay along . . . in one plane, broken only by the salient of a brown cigar" (*Hare*, 90).

In *The Waste Land*, though, Eliot's analysis of the modern condition only goes so far. One would think that his quasi-historical critique would point him back toward nature, toward material contingency and the mind's power to know and evaluate its place within the world. At its most humane, the poem seems to suggest a certain phenomenology of the sensual world, resituating the subject within the productive intentionalities of his environment. One finds hope in the image of the humble fisherman by the shore and in the graceful description that follows the command for self-control. In these instances, Eliot seems to yearn for a more balanced relation between the individual and his environment, one that is defined not by violence, but mutual accord. *The Waste Land*, however, ultimately obscures this materialist alternative. Eliot's disgust toward the material world denies the positive aspects of contingency. Nature is simply a place of chaos; history can only limit perspective and vex judgment:

> Son of man,
> You cannot say, or guess, for you know only
> A heap of broken images, where the sun beats,
> And the dead tree gives no shelter, the cricket no relief,
> And the dry stone no sound of water.   (51)

For Eliot, the material world remains unredeemed; it is a place of suffering only, the scene of spiritual trial. We must exist within the world, but that pain – "fear in a handful of dust" – readies us for purification; mortal experience – vexed by time and space – serves only to inspire desire for transcendence (51–2). Thus, as I hope to show here, Eliot ultimately fails to provide a suitable alternative and, in fact, poetically conflates the spiritual motive with an economic one. Ultimately, anti-naturalism, sexual manipulation, reductive rationalization – all he critiques is affirmed by the very structure of his poem.

These contradictions are submerged, somewhat slyly, within the poem's ambiguous water imagery. Eliot clearly warns of a potential "death by water" and his poem depicts multiple drowning victims, such as Ophelia, Alonso, and the Phoenician Sailor. His critique of romantic excess materializes as water's power to pollute and corrupt necessary boundaries; "A Game of Chess," for example, depicts a horrifically feminized environment in which "perfumes, / Unguent, powdered, or liquid – troubled, confused / And drowned the sense in odors" (54). Eliot, however, also refers to the cleansing, regenerative power of water; the poem opens with a gentle "spring rain" that stirs "dull roots" and concludes with a terrifying shower that prepares the way for a new order. Throughout, Eliot calls for baptismal renewal; he yearns, in fact, for a specifically feminized return, back beyond the "stages of age and youth" to a womb-like comfort (66, 63). In a similarly paradoxical manner, Eliot depicts the urban riverway as an anxious site of cultural exchange, a necessary point of contact with a frightening otherness. First and foremost, the river bears all the traces of urban pollution and carries the germs of cultural decay; London, Mylae, Smyrna – these once great trade cities have been corrupted by mixed blood and "demotic" traditions. Yet, elsewhere, the urban river affects a continual cleansing, washing away waste and importing new, invigorating traditions. In "The Fire Sermon," the "turning tide" washes away the sins of the city, flushing out debris from Greenwich reach to the Margate sands (61). Later, a dispossessed King sits at the river's edge, reeling in scraps from other cultures in hopes of restoring order (67).

Here and elsewhere in his work, Eliot's ambivalent depiction of water is always couched – not without wit – in the terms of commerce. It is not only that rivers and oceans bear the burdens of trade, but they actually mimic the destructive forces and flows of the market. The narrator of "Gerontion" is an "old man driven by the Trades / to a sleepy corner" (33). *Four Quartets* presents the mighty Mississippi as a divine "conveyor of commerce"; its cargo consists of "dead negros, cows and chicken coops" (*Quartets*, 35, 40). Most poetically, the fourth section of *The Waste Land* depicts an enigmatic sea-change as a form of economic transvaluation:

> Phlebas the Phoenician, a fortnight dead,
> Forgot the cry of gulls, and the deep sea swell
> And the profit and loss.
>
>   A current under sea
> Picked his bones in whispers. As he rose and fell
> He passed the stages of his age and youth
> Entering the whirlpool.   (63)

This passage is connected to the larger poem by a series of economic puns. "Current" is easily linked to the currency in Eugenides's pocket; the rise and fall of the tides mimic the "profit and loss" of the market; the tumult of the whirlpool mirrors the implacable "Wheel" of fortune. Here, as throughout the poem, "sea-change" is always implicitly economic, as the laboring body is transmuted into objects of exchange. As the Phoenician Sailor disappears on a trade expedition, his "death by water" seems linked to the loss of particularity occasioned by the economy (*Facsimile*, 119, 115).

It is, however, Eliot's depictions of seafarers and sea voyages that most clearly link the entrepreneurial plot with a Protestant one. In *The Waste Land*, we are introduced to a merchant who figures as the embodiment of all economic corruption, *contra naturam* and *contra culturam*.[31] Mr. Eugenides taints all he touches; he travels from port to port, mixing corrupt business with corrupt pleasure. His success in the marketplace depends upon the transgression of all values; his violation of natural order produces cheap goods of mixed origin and mixed quality. His association with the Smyrna fertility cults is clearly ironic, as his passion is directed toward the homosexual, and his pocket contains only dead fruit (59). Eugenides, despite his name, also figures as a force of national decay. As he himself is of questionable origin, his economic activity undermines national borders, whether they be ethnic, geographical, or linguistic. In the original draft, in fact, Eliot more extensively toyed with Shakespeare's "Full Fathom Five" in order to depict the ruinous effects of Eugenides's transactions:

> Full fathom five your Bleistein lies
> Under the flatfish and the squids.
> Graves' Disease in a dead jew's eyes!
>   When the crabs have eat the lids.
>   Lower than the wharf rats dive
>   Though he suffer a sea-change
>   Still expensive rich and strange
>
>   . . .
>   Flood tide and ebb tide
>   Roll him gently side to side
>   See the lips unfold unfold
>   From the teeth, gold in gold
> (*Facsimile*, 121)

The merchant's usurious activity, here signaled by a sickening repetition, at once exploits and destroys the natural order. His own body is perverted by greed; all that is human has been cut away, leaving only a hideous grin of gold. Like the subtle currents of the ocean floor, the market flows corrupt all particular values.[32]

Yet, in Eliot's work, the sea also beckons with the promise of redemption. Here, the poet's New England heritage proves decisive. His poetry returns again and again to the primal scene of the Puritan venture and finds structure and resonance in the narrative of the spiritual voyage. Throughout, the sea figures as a place of necessary trial, braved only by those whose wills are touched by true faith. The journey, at once physical and spiritual, serves to cleanse the body of its sins and prepare it for new life in the spiritual beyond.[33] In one early poem, for example, a narrator finds himself conflicted by "Some minor problems of the soul" and so sets out "along the wet paths of the sea" in order to be "renewed" (*Hare*, 29). Later, in *Four Quartets*, one of Eliot's Puritan ancestors turns away from the "Dung and death" of England and ventures forth to confront the "heat and silence" of the immense Atlantic (*Quartets*, 25–7). Importantly, this plot also shaped the original draft of *The Waste Land*. In a longer, pivotal version of the section called "Death by Water," Eugenides finds a positive counterpart in Phlebas, whose dangerous sea journey affects a change that is truly "rich and strange."

This version of "Death by Water" begins with a small paean to sailors and the sailing life. Here, the poet argues that the rough life of the sea scrubs the soul free of sin. The well-traveled sailor has been refined into a "concentrated will"; even at home, amidst the drunks and derelicts of the port town, he retains about him "something inhuman, clean and dignified" (*Facsimile*, 55). Eliot then recounts the kind of voyage from which this spiritual cleanliness may derive. His hapless crew must deal with dangers that threaten body and soul alike, from the insidious Dry Salvages to spoiled food, lack of wind, ruined supplies, and torrential storms. In each case, the men face ever-greater crises of the spirit: chance, pride, fear, and despair. They moan as the "sea with many voices / Moaned all bout us"; they scream before the "different darkness . . . dead ahead" (*Facsimile*, 61). Amidst the cries and the turmoil, however, Phlebas emerges in repose. He quietly performs his burdensome tasks, looking through worldly loss and gain with the same determined glare. He shuns all earthly temptations, whether pleasurable or frightening, and resigns himself to his mortal lot. Indeed, when the men find temporary relief from the storm and begin to dream of home and wealth, he stoically declares, "I laughed not" (*Facsimile*, 59). At the end of the journey, the crew approaches the white line of an arctic coast, a literally sublime moment. Phlebas, confident in his knowledge that his life's labor has been successfully performed, meekly consigns himself to a fate he could never comprehend: "And if <u>Another</u> knows, I know I know not, / Who only know that there is no more noise now" (*Facsimile*, 61).

The last few lines of this section, which alone appear in the final draft of *The Waste Land* as "Death by Water," can be interpreted in a number of ways. On their own, they appear alternately as a critique of romantic solipsism, an object lesson in existential nothingness, and, as mentioned, a description of the dehumanizing effects of the market. Generally, the isolated passage seems to suggest that the sailor is a victim of his own pride and now must suffer the assimilating vengeance of fate. Its final lines admonish any would-be hero who seeks to bypass the necessary suffering of mortal existence: "Gentile or Jew / O you who turn the wheel and look windward, / Consider Phlebas, who was once handsome and tall as you" (63). However, in light of the narrative which originally preceded it, the verse seems to suggest a more positive parable. The crew remains caught in a purely temporal dimension; their dreams of worldly success leave them victim to the brutal changes of fortune's wheel. Phlebas, however, with an eye always to the divine, finds a new innocence. His suffering body is transubstantiated into something purer, beyond the market and its violent fluctuations. With his sea-change, he forgets "the profit and loss" and moves back through "the stages of age and youth" to an earlier innocence. Indeed, it is Phlebas's humility before a larger order that grants him peace within it; his quiet toil and unquestioning submission grant him pride of place amongst God's elect. Ultimately, though, however forcefully one may be able to support either of these readings, it would be foolish to deny their accord. With its mercantile setting, economic punning, and poetic homologies, the scene ultimately conflates entrepreneurial suffering with religious suffering. The fallen world provides the raw materials for pecuniary gain as well as spiritual profit. Labor is the source of wealth as well as divine election; the entrepreneur and the Protestant both rework the world in accordance with an abstract plan that promises future reward. As Eliot coyly suggests in a note, "The one-eyed merchant, seller of currants, melts into the Phoenician Sailor" (70).

Importantly, this homology – this "melt"-ing – occurs through the logic of sacrifice. In fact, the entire poem – its content, its structure, its affirmative power – rests upon a forced submission of particularity to an abstract totality. Phlebas is celebrated for his humility; he sacrifices pleasure, spiritual and physical, for future reward. His fall is depicted as a loss of individual identity, a selfless act that renews the community as a whole. In the logic of the poem, he functions like one of Frazer's slain fertility gods: his "Death by Water" brings the nourishing rain of the next section. Phlebas, in fact, is homologous to the Grail Knight, who also braves the treacherous wastes in order to restore the kingdom. The Knight can only locate the ruined chapel if his search is free of pride; the kingdom is restored only through a selfless act toward the ailing king (66). In Eliot's poem, however, redemption figures as no return to natural innocence or even organic community. Whereas earlier fertility rites almost always entailed the hero's sacrifice to the earth and a reaffirmation of a natural order, Eliot's ritual is offered up to an abstraction. The loss of self is enforced by way of identification with a symbol; a neurotic particularity is dissolved in submission to patriarchal authority. When the thunder speaks, it does speak for communal values; greed, egotism, and lust – the sins of selfishness – these must be relinquished for the sake of social renewal. And, yet, Eliot's final sermon carefully avoids anything so egalitarian as a community; rather, it validates isolated acts of submission – "The awful daring of a moment's surrender" – before an all-powerful, mediating divinity. Its language remains, quite simply, hierarchical: "your heart would have responded / Gaily, when invited, beating obedient / To controlling hands" (67).

Eliot's need for a restrictive order takes many forms, some organic and natural. Here, though, this demand leads directly to an abstract hierarchy that is known only in death; suffering redeems, but in relation to a decisively nonhuman, unnatural presence. The individual finds meaning in his self-chosen submission to an unknown deity; community, if it exists at all, finds expression in a static, alienating order. A similar submission informs the poem's structural principles. The logic of abnegation underlies Eliot's effort to reconcile particulars into abstract formulae; here, fragments exist only to be superseded and resolved in universal mythic patterns. "Stetson," for example, is singled out not only as a representative of the great, exploitable masses, but as a cog in the poet's mythic method. Cleopatra, Dido, and Ophelia are called forth in order to coordinate a single sentiment of tragically spurned love, which is, in turn, reduced to an elemental "burning" (62). Throughout, particular experience appears as nothing more than crude material for symbolic order. In fact, in this poem, there is neither true individualism nor true community; all figures remain unbearably isolated as well as forgettably generic.[34] In this, Eliot most clearly adopts the economic mechanisms, the very mechanization, he sought to counter elsewhere. His poem provides not an end to pain, but a reaffirmation of the quasi-transcendent power of rationalization. The alienation of the individual, the suffering caused by exploitative labor, the radical imbalances of wealth, these are each "indifferently justified" by poetic form. Indeed, the "hand expert" that appears at the end of the poem bears, in its purposive anonymity, a striking resemblance to the "hidden hand" that supposedly balances the contradictions of capital (67).

This solution perhaps accounts for much of the confusion that surrounds the figure of Tiresius, specifically the debate over whether he serves as a positive or negative force of reconciliation. Within the context of the poem, he is a demon of rationalization, form without content; in his mechanical "blindness," he serves only to process and neutralize particulars. Yet, in terms of the poem's structure, he serves as a model for what Eliot himself seeks to accomplish. His efficient consciousness performs the necessary reductions and calculations by which the modern individual can be comfortable in his suffering. Like the poet himself, the impotent prophet only *expresses* reconciliation, but he does not actually *affect* one. In Eliot's words, it is "What Tiresius *sees*," and not what he does, that "is the substance of the poem" (70). As mentioned, the prophet is witness to communal sacrifice. Attuned to the workings of fate, he comes forth with knowledge of an apparently necessary submission. What Tiresius "*sees*," though, is the same romantic sublimation that Eliot depicts in "Tradition and the Individual Talent." He is witness to a suspect fate by which individual voices are subsumed into larger, nonhuman patterns and complex contingencies are organized by an efficient apparatus.

As mentioned earlier, this submission rests upon a conflation of the human and the transcendent. Through a subtle confusion of registers, human instincts and desires are imaginatively mediated and misdirected. The poem, in other words, diverts the possibility of real change by advocating the submission of potentially transgressive energy to an order that only seems to be divine. Emotions, individuals, and even political revolutions are sacrificed to what seems to be a necessary structure; in this, the temporal appears as the timeless, the irrational appears rational, pain appears holy. As Weber suggests, the Protestant submission to God only masks a submission to a much more treacherous, worldly power. When man in his labor resigns himself to a divine injunction, he submits to the enforced rationality of his labor, to the efficient logic that governs modern industry and its exploitative practices (123). Marcuse similarly argues that the modern individual misconceives the nature of his capitulation. Capitalism is "built on renunciation"; its organization of the masses depends upon an irrational submission to that which presents itself as divine ("Industrialization," 206–7). The decisive point is that this sacrifice seems "not only perfectly rational but also perfectly reasonable. All protest is senseless, and the individual who would insist on his freedom of action would become a crank."[35]

One could perhaps argue that the stylistic peculiarities of Eliot's poetry just as strongly resist rationalization. The ragged fragmentation, the accumulative imagery, the indulgent notes – surely this tendency toward excess bursts open the boundaries of an efficient totality. And, yet, as we have seen, it is precisely this poetic excess that is constantly consumed by the poetic structure. Voices *must* remain somewhat distinct, unrelated, and unredeemed, for only then does the power of rationalization become clear. Just as sin is necessary to redemption, waste is necessary to the activity of purgation; excess feeds the effort to reconcile the account. Indeed, any potentially divergent experience exists only to be objectified and synchronized in relation to the symbolic whole.[36] In this, the poem most clearly resembles Marcuse's description of bureaucracy as an apparatus that offers an imaginary reconciliation of particularity and domination. In a bureaucracy, Marcuse writes, "standardization proceeds along the lines of specialization. The latter by itself, provided that it is not arrested at the point where it interferes with the domain of vested control, is quite compatible with the democratization of functions. Fixated specialization tends to atomize the masses and to insulate subordinate from the executive function." In other words, *The Waste Land* is a bureaucracy insofar as its particulars are at once isolated and standardized, alienated and appropriated. That which appears unique is so only in relation to the larger apparatus that necessitates and thus denies its uniqueness. As Marcuse writes, the system fosters a "delusive harmony between the special and the common interest . . . The technical democratization of functions is counteracted by their atomization, and the bureaucracy appears as the agency which guarantees their rational course and order" ("Implications," 154). In Eliot's work, the potentially explosive tension between part and whole is always already tightly controlled; the tragic world of pride and sacrifice has been given up for the misery of specialization and compliance. The poet relinquishes material contingency for a highly efficient poiesis; the modern crisis – in all its vexed contradictions – finds a semblance of wholeness in a bureaucratic rationality.

5   WHAT THE CRITICS SAY

As the above comments suggest, Eliot's work is affirmative not simply in its content and structure, but also in its style, which allows individual interpretation to take place within the comforting embrace of a clearly defined order. Its particulars are always already semi-abstract, giving the illusion of difference as well as universality. The reader thrills back and forth between fragments that appear resistant and a well-oiled scheme that seems transcendent; throughout, otherness is confused with objectivity, manipulation is mistaken for reason. Here, Eliot's interest in tarot cards begins to make sense; he privileges a reading experience in which individual passions can be reinterpreted, and thus organized, in relation to generic symbols (52). Similarly, in the final section of *The Waste Land*, rigidly defined sects – gods, men, demons – apply their particular interpretations to the divine word. In this, as testified to by the actual content of their interpretation, the fantasy of individual expression meets with a competing desire for submission (66–7).

Moreover, in the very movement between these two levels, in the act of neutralizing particulars into abstract formulae, the poem ensures the dictates of rationalization. Eliot's work is consistently devoid of causal, contingent relations. His use of fragmentation ensures, on the one hand, complete isolation of the part, and, on the other, complete reification of the whole. Indeed, there is no middle ground of comprehension; the reader can either contemplate each image in its auratic power or mechanically arrange them into a lifeless whole.[37] If there was any tension between these two moments, any conscious friction in this transition, one would be tempted to say that the poem valiantly exposes the contradictions of capital. But Eliot consistently fails to provide any such foothold, any point of perspective from which the reader can understand the intensive unity of fragments and wholes. In this, the reading experience mimics the affective experience of industrial capital in general: the painfully contingent moment remains divorced from the abstract principles by which we try to understand the whole. Like Prufrock, we are unable to reconcile our alienation with the larger forces of domination; we can never critique, but only suffer and observe. Or, to borrow from Marcuse, we are no longer capable of "seizing the fateful moment which constitutes [our] freedom" ("Implications," 152).

This reading experience suggests that Eliot's work continues to please insofar as it redeems conditions that persist into the present. Its willful fragmentation confirms our distance from a horrific order, while its seemingly natural order assuages an increasing alienation. As suggested in my introduction, recent modernist scholarship seems to enforce a similarly affirmative logic of part and whole. In its efforts to avoid the excesses of its subject, it at once fetishizes and denies all particularity, both exaggerates and dissolves historical particularities. It should come as no surprise, then, that one of the most prominent lines of this scholarship takes Eliot's poetry as its institutional ideal. Beginning with Frank Kermode's work on the modern image, this particular tradition, even at its most critical, adopts Eliot's rationalized order as its aesthetic–political standard. Unable to reconcile part and whole in any historically contingent way, it turns to abstract relations that both obscure and extend that division. It should be made clear, though, that this criticism does not simply reproduce the logic of High Modernism in its content, for its very production can be seen as equally affirmative. The critical industry generated by texts such as *The Waste Land*, *The Cantos*, and *Ulysses* affirms at once the ideal order of the High Modernist tradition as well as its flexibility. Each individual interpretation attests to an expressive freedom, but each then also affirms the mythic order in which that freedom is possible. This apparently infinite ability to dissociate and recombine the elements of a modernist text is held up not only as a rational process, but as the fulfillment of history itself. A few examples:

Frank Kermode's *Romantic Image* (1961) offers a valuable discussion of the romantic tendency as it extends from the work of the Lake School poets to the New Critics of the early twentieth century.[38] This tradition, he argues, urges a dangerous rift between life and art, pure vision and worldly activity. It is defined by an uncritical celebration of the poet's abstraction from the world of contingency and by an irrational faith in a logos that shines like "a radiant truth out of space and time" (2). Kermode's study, though, typifies a critique of modernism that remains firmly imbedded in the logic of modernism. He seeks a poetics that resists the chaos as well as the totality of the modern world, the excesses of the imagination and the rigid control of the intellect (102). Much like Eliot before him, he argues for a synthesis of romantic "orthodoxy" and the rational elements of an "empirical-utilitarian tradition" (152). He hopes to counter the fragmentation of modern life with what he calls "mechanical and systematic modes of inquiry" (143). Indeed, with Eliot as his prime example, he argues that sensual experience must be given a common "symbolic value" (163). Tellingly, his analogy for efficient discourse derives from mathematics: the irreducible must be resolved "like the square root of two or like pi . . . like 1.414 . . . or 3.1416 . . ." (159).

Years later, in *A Genealogy of Modernism* (1984), Michael Levenson returns to the modern "disintegration of stable balanced relations between subject and object."[39] He detects "a persistent ambiguity in early modernism: the desire for autonomy of form and the claim that the root source and justification for art is individual expression" (135). Like Kermode, Levenson seeks to reconcile these competing tendencies, yet he rejects modern politics for a purely aesthetic unity. He turns to Eliot as the poet who most consistently resisted polemics and thus successfully negotiated between "the poem as a submerged unity and the poem as a chaos of fragments" (176). In particular, Levenson praises *The Waste Land* as it links particulars into provisional, yet always stable relations. By a continual process of objective comparison, experience is made meaningful (184). Levenson, too, hopes to dissolve the tensions of modernity into quasi-transcendent abstractions. Subjective chaos is redeemed by a "system" of ideal relations and static formulae; "No meaning without relations," he writes, "no truth, no reality, no value without order, without system" (185). Indeed, Levenson all but confesses to the affirmative power of these willful rationalizations: "Eliot's formula," he writes, "was the most successful formula and accordingly achieved cultural dominance" (186). Individualism and order, fragmentation and tyranny – thankfully, these potentially revolutionary tensions were absorbed with "the institutionalization of the movement, and the accession to cultural legitimacy" (213).

In *The Political Aesthetics of Yeats, Eliot, and Pound* (1991), Michael North provides a groundbreaking critique of the High Modernist right and its response to bourgeois culture. As he explains, "The anti-liberal reaction of such as Yeats, Eliot, and Pound can be characterized best by the inconsistencies it suffers in trying to oppose this contradictory system" (4). The High Modernist turn toward ideal communities and the past leads to an "authoritarian caricature of the liberal marketplace, where everyone can pick and choose because none of the choices really matter" (12). North then deftly analyzes the moderns' efforts to reunite the individual with the social whole. Not without cause, he refuses to accept anything other than dialectical negation; for him, reconciliation safely exists only in the mutual denial of fragment and totality. As North writes, when the modernists "phrased the claims of individualism and community in such an uncompromising way as to reveal their radical incompatibility . . . then and only then did their politics retain a promise of openness and freedom" (15). Their best work displays an intentional "conflict of part and whole in [its] architecture"; their masterpieces are "resolutely irresolute" (18). North, then, turns positively to *The Waste Land* because its structure suggests that "the particular can never transcend itself without falsification, and yet that very negativity would function as an inverted form of commonality" (103). In this, he refers us back to those imbalances and excesses discussed above and confirms the critical edge of High Modernism. *The Waste Land*'s revolutionary power derives from the ways in which its "stylistic discontinuity can become a 'standard' around which people may 'gather,' a disunity that paradoxically brings about unity. This quite different totality exists by implication in contradistinction to the repetitive, constrictive totality explicitly present in the poem" (105–6). Yet, as North recognizes, Eliot's *via negativa* is founded upon abstraction and thus serves as nothing more than an affirmative illusion. Through negation, ideals are always implied but never allowed material fulfillment; they exist as dreamy possibilities in a world that systematically denies their concrete realization. As we have also suggested, this logic tends to support a political quietism, an acceptance of the painful contradictions that haunt modern society. As North explains, "It is as if Eliot could only approach peace through conflict . . . as if he could imagine social solidarity only by extension of social chaos. Disorder thus becomes not a fault to be overcome, but a necessary moment in the process of arriving at order" (104). At its best, North's work, like High Modernism itself, seems unable to move beyond its own negations.

Ultimately, Eliot's work and its critical heritage recall Siegfried Kracauer's account of the affective power of "the mass ornament." *The Waste Land* is best defined as an indissoluble cluster of fragments that affirmatively displays the work of rationalization. Its parts are isolated, frictionless, sexless; they have been emptied of all substance in order to create an abstract design. Moreover, the figures that compose the ornament have no understanding of its totality; there is no point of perspective from which to link the particular to the abstract, "no line that extends from the smallest sections of the mass to the entire figure." These figures, who are also spectators, can only shuffle between immediate experience and a totality which, if at all, "must be understood *rationally*." In this, though, in its self-justifying perfectionism, the mass ornament mimics as it glorifies the double experience of capital, its sensual alienation and its abstract tyranny. Because its participants come from offices and factories, "the *aesthetic* pleasure gained from ornamental mass movements is *legitimate*." The suffering crowd turns to the ornament as "the aesthetic reflex of the rationality to which the prevailing economic system aspires."

As Kracauer explains, this is not a *reasonable* order, but a *rationalized* one. It perverts that reason whereby the individual may be able to lift himself out of subjugation, maintaining it only as the ability to dominate and to be dominated. It disallows critical thought about the "actual substance of life" and, instead, proffers as normative what is quite simply exploitative.[40] It is this tendency that makes Eliot's work typical of the period, and it is also what forces us to look elsewhere for a more critical alternative. Eliot seeks solace in an order that is all too human in its tendency to dominate and all too inhuman in its power to do so. His self-proclaimed classicism, in its emphasis on order and restraint, attains only a fatal semblance of beauty. In its confusion of the human and the divine, it everywhere excuses the domination of the material world as spiritually necessary. Indeed, all that might have grounded Eliot's critique within the material world is better developed elsewhere. Sensual phenomenology finds a more sustained expression in the work of Hulme; the valorization of labor is given a more humane expression in the sculpture of Gaudier-Brzeska; the commitment to a ritualized society becomes fluid and spontaneous in the poetry of H.D. Now we can turn to a classicism that deals *reasonably*, not *dogmatically*, with the pain of modernity.

PART II

Construction

CHAPTER 3

The modern temple: T. E. Hulme and the construction of classicism

> *Autumn*
> A touch of cold in the Autumn night –
> I walked abroad,
> And saw the ruddy moon lean over a hedge
> Like a red-faced farmer.
> I did not stop to speak, but nodded,
> And round about were the wistful stars
> With white faces like town children.[1]

T. E. Hulme's "Autumn" was the first of only six poems he published in his lifetime; it appeared in an early avant-garde plaquette called *For Christmas* MDCCCCVIII.[2] Importantly, Hulme's poem – and classical modernism in general – begins with a "touch," with an inevitable contact that suggests both limitation and fallibility. This poet is incapable of transcendence, of flying off into the ether, of all such romantic sloppiness. The harvest moon illuminates nothing but his imperfections and arrests the imagination. The natural landscape is a prison in which he must labor for only brief moments of respite. Moreover, there is no divine compensation for this kind of suffering – no rolling about in the earth, no lake isles, no Shantih, Shantih, Shantih. Symbolic reverie is here impossible; these mute forms refuse to cohere, to offer up an eternal wisdom. Perfection, if it exists at all, must be worked for on earth, against mortal restraints, by the sweat of one's brow. The ruddy-faced poet from North Staffordshire must work with his hands.

And there is no grousing about this mortal labor, either. Rather, one detects in the poem a conscious holding back, a willful reservation in the poet's voice. The speaker recoils from the imagination as if it were a curse, as if freedom would only release him into lunacy. He retreats from the heavens and seeks comfort in the earthly and the fallen. The farmer's worn visage serves to ground and diffuse the scene's potentially drunken energy. It offers the security of a dead weight amidst all this romantic flux. The poet, in fact, negates the very hierarchy of spirit and matter, intentionally confounds the terms of freedom and enslavement. Here, the "wistful stars" yearn for a completion that only the fallen earth can signify. Peace and sanity exist not in the heavens, but in the mute humility of the mortal world. The poem celebrates the peace and comfort of an earthly purposiveness, the inevitable tragedy of human endeavor.

Accordingly, this is a rough, muscular verse, akin to sculpture in its material toughness. We can see fingerprints in its clay, stubborn hollows and swellings in its line lengths. This quality is best exemplified by the poem's analogical structure. Here, farmer and moon never merge into a muzzy symbolic whole; rather, these figures remain separate as they touch and shape one another. The poet clearly distinguishes the two images with rigid breaks and by prominently displaying the term of comparison at the beginning of the fourth line. But look how the third line protrudes beyond the poem, like a farmer over his hedge. This line is not simply clarified, but fenced in by the image that starts the next. Moreover, the very shape of one term appears in the composition of the other. The moon already leans over, before we learn that it looks "like a red-faced farmer"; the "stars gather round" like town children before we are told that they seem "like town children." In both cases, the terms are neither indistinguishable nor autonomous. They exist in a vital, muscular dynamic; they leave their marks upon each other in an expressive tension.

The brief life of T. E. Hulme was defined by similar touches. He shaped all that he passed, leaving impressions that can perhaps never be hammered out. In hindsight, he appears as a central turbine for modernity's cultural swelter, addressing, adapting, and channeling the ideas and tendencies of the age. Socially, he was at the center of pre-war London's most advanced intellectual circles. He was a member of the foundational Poet's Club and then the Secession Club; he befriended and supported the newly expatriated Ezra Pound; he boxed with Wyndham Lewis in Soho Square; he debated with Rupert Brooke, Bertrand Russell, Jacob Epstein, Henri Bergson, Pierre Lasserre, Georges Sorel, and countless others. Professionally, he published on a variety of topics in the most progressive journals of the day. There was not a subject he did not address – modern sculpture, Byzantine design, parliamentary reform, pacifism; there was not a theory he did not revise – vitalism, impressionism, royalism, liberalism. A regular for *The New Age*, he also wrote for *Poetry and Drama*, *Commentator*, *Cambridge Magazine*, and *Westminster Gazette*. He translated popular versions of Bergson's *Introduction to Metaphysics* and Sorel's *Reflections on Violence*.

Not surprisingly, Hulme's versatility and his tendency toward overstatement have led to misinterpretations in all directions. He has been accused of being a romanticist as well as a classicist, not to mention a democrat, a fascist, a tory, a cubist, a futurist, a vorticist, a stagirite, a great lover, a warmonger, a farmer, and a racing cyclist. Despite these difficulties and the proliferation of Hulmes that has resulted, the original texts, when taken as a whole, convey a deep logical consistency. In fact, the repeated contradictions of the criticism, particularly as they circle around issues of romanticism and classicism, point toward the essential, if complex, unity of its subject.[3] In Hulme's hands, classicism was always an attempt to reform bourgeois culture and delimit its effects on art, philosophy, politics, and economics. His demand for "restraint" became a rallying cry for those who sought to block the aggressive energies of romantic individualism. His call for "tension" and "contingency" was appealing to many thinkers who wanted to halt the constant production and consumption of the modern. The unified value of his work, however, is that it does not oppose individualism with individualism, romanticism with a greater romanticism; rather, it challenges bourgeois culture by locating the tensions and contingencies within it. It examines romanticism's oppositional dynamic in order to disclose its inherent friction and thus the foundation of a more integrated, positive order. In other words, Hulme's classicism is deeply embedded in the vital world and only emerges from out of its dynamic contingency. Form, consciousness itself, is an historical effect that can at once be reintegrated, opened up to a new history. Ultimately, Hulme's seemingly contradictory adherence to romanticism *and* classicism functions within a rigorous dialectical materialism. His work neither fetishizes nor forecloses the possibility of freedom, but recognizes it only as it exists within a larger, flexible order.

Hulme's classicism can perhaps best be clarified by its difference from other, more institutionalized forms of classicism. Certainly, the cosmos described in the previous chapter, with its emphasis on labor, sacrifice, and myth, is also the cosmos in which Hulme lived and wrote. The violent experiences of modernity led many, Hulme included, to reject the promises of democracy and assert the social necessity of dogma. Yet, if scholarship seeks to open up this apparently closed history, it must look to differences of tendency. If romanticism and classicism exhibit a dialectical unity, and if each modern artist can at times be classified as one or the other, it is imperative to consider more subtle propensities, their historical causes, and their political implications. As argued in the last chapter, Eliot's classicism tends to emphasize the conservative aspects of the bourgeois order. His modernism affirms the structure of the market itself; the demand for "freedom" colludes with alienation, while the call for "order" finds an easy answer in reification. Hulme confronts the same crisis, but he remains suspicious of the endless activity of dissociation. He seeks not difference, but tension; he moves not away from, but through the mass. Moreover, Hulme refuses any romantic idealism that confuses the self with the divine. His phenomenology more radically takes the human outside of itself, not toward some abstract unity, but to a material other. The painful limitations of the material world disrupt self-complacency and thus provide the basis of a more conscious ethics. Perhaps, following Hulme, we can also define this difference in terms of historical precedent: one classicism, looking back to the rational conventions of Athenian society, is dissociated, static, relational; the other, founded upon an earlier, ritualized tradition, is integral, vital, and modal (272). Again, the first can only neutralize the passions of the living world, while the latter allows them to burst through and reshape a reified social sphere. For Hulme, labor is not rationalized and mimetic, but creative; humility is not exploitative, but communal; myths are not final, but provisional and empowering.[4]

Of course, certain personal experiences helped to shape this alternative. Early on, Hulme's exposure to agricultural labor informed a more attentive attitude toward the material world. Later, his miserable journey across Canada, his epiphany in Bergson's lecture hall, and the fall of the House of Lords helped to clarify a philosophy founded upon historical contingency and political ideology. Hulme's alternative, though, was not entirely personal; it arose only at the extreme end of a specifically modern tragedy. His work, and its increasing stridency, responds to a historical trajectory in which romanticism first isolates and then pushes the individual toward war. His essays first yearn for contact in a world that has become increasingly alienated and then demand restraint as that world turns explicitly violent. Throughout, personal experience combines with larger historical forces to occasion a materialist phenomenology that confounds all bourgeois ideology. Unlike Eliot and Babbitt, Hulme understands corporeal limit not as the boundary of an internal character defined in opposition to a corrupt world, but as the source of empowerment within a larger intentional community.

Hulme, unfortunately, could not fully clarify this alternative during his short lifetime, and, because of posthumous mishandling, his work's significance has remained somewhat confused since his death.[5] Taken together, though, the scattered shards and fragments of his essays can at least suggest something of an original unity. In their juxtaposition, certain angles and planes, faint outlines of arches and pillars will begin to appear; a structure will be revealed, concrete and tangible. What follows, then, is a study of a coherent metaphysic that, in keeping with Hulme's emphasis on the local, found expression in several different branches of thought:

(1906–7)   An early phenomenology of the body
(1907–8)   The theory of concrete language
(1909–12)   A materialist reading of Bergsonian metaphysics
(1911–14)   The politics of Romanticism and Classicism
(1914–17)   The religious attitude

As these homologous moments will suggest, Hulme's early materialism remained the foundation of his truly ethical order. This self-proclaimed "amateur" detected a snag in the otherwise smooth dialectics of bourgeois thought, a foothold of resistance within the flux of modernity, and there constructed his alternative order. His work thus exhibits a constant movement from the muddled and fluid realm of the subjective toward the vivid clarity of objective form; it transforms the "organic into something not organic," "the changing and limited, into something unlimited and necessary" (283). Ultimately, with the help of a few other modern philosophers similarly drawn to materialist dialectics – Bergson, Sorel, and Adorno – I will argue that Hulme's contradictions are always integral and progressive. His work, even at its apparently most dogmatic, transforms the romantic will into classical consciousness and opens up classical dogma into romantic desire. Throughout, force and form work together in a process that is at once critical and constructive.

(1906–7) "CINDERS," A SKETCH

Hulme's career began bleakly. In 1904, he was "sent down" from Cambridge in disgrace. Just two years later, in order to avoid working for the civil service, he was "shipped over" on a cargo boat to Canada.[6] There, wandering through the prairie lands from one isolated town to another, he sadly came to understand that "The cosmos is only *organised* in part; the rest is cinders" (9). "The flats of Canada," he recorded in his journal, "are incomprehensible on any single theory" (10–11). Hulme's earliest known work, "Cinders," finds both thematic and stylistic coherence in this melancholic relativism. In a seemingly random set of scribbled notes, the young philosopher begins to clarify the radical anti-humanism that informs all his later work. He deconstructs the pretensions of bourgeois individualism and bourgeois art by foregrounding the irreducible contingencies – the particular desires and material restraints – that confound all cultural production. As we will find, in this early critique lies the very hope of renewal; Hulme's emphasis on contingency becomes the point at which a more conscious social reconstruction is made possible.

In "Cinders," Hulme depicts reality as a formless ash-heap, a sterile wasteland in which "There is no inevitable order" (12). The romantic passion that once animated these cinders has been lost; the fantasy of total order has been snuffed out by modern relativism. In an argument cobbled together from Kant and Nietzsche, Hulme claims that "Pure seeing of the whole process is impossible. Little fancies help us along, but we never get pure disinterested intellect" (19). "Truth," if we may call it such, is merely the limited creation of appetite, a tentative order designed to serve immediate needs:

These little theories of the world, which satisfy and are then thrown away, one after the other, develop *not* as successive approximations to the truth, but like successive thirsts, to be satisfied at the moment, and not evolving to one great Universal Thirst. (14)

Religion, science, politics, and sexuality – each is a construction, a "manufactured chess-board" laid across the expansive waste so that we may exist with comfort and ease. These feeble systems only allow us to move from one position to another without having to acknowledge the truth, without dirtying our feet in the "primeval chaos" (13). In fact, language is utterly incapable of representing truth. Invented solely for the convenience of the mind, it expresses only vague passions and ideals. Symbols are believed to be realities, but they are intentionally mistaken for an order that could never exist: "These words are merely counters representing vague groups of things, to be moved about on a board for the convenience of the players" (8).

Tellingly, Hulme often described himself as a "philosophic amateur"; his theories were merely "personal impressions." He tended to exaggerate his North Staffordshire accent when speaking in public, and his arguments return again and again to his rural background and inexperience. In "Cinders," he affects a certain rustic simplicity, partly macho and partly naive. He presents himself as a low-minded dilettante, preoccupied with the most vulgar needs and desires. His metaphors are decisively sexual, his images graphically abject. Ideas are only "food" to be "devoured"; they should be judged "from the status of animals" (14). It is important to recognize that this scatology is not idiosyncratic. Hulme insists that it is not the mind, but the body that shapes the world's order. Subjectivity is substantiated in relation to the corpus and its all too material presence; reality is shaped by "the bodily frame which receives it." "All our analogies spiritual and intellectual are derived from purely physical acts"; indeed, even "poetry is an affair of the body" (20–1). For Hulme, in fact, the body is the site of order as well as variety; it mediates "flexibility and continuity into atomic structure." On the one hand, physical motives "are the only unalterable and fixed things in the world." "Disillusionment," he writes, "comes when it is recognized that all heroic actions can be reduced to the simple laws of egotism." But embodiment also implies an irreducible particularity and so a multiplicity of experience and desire. As he writes, "wonder can even then be found in the fact that there *are* such *different* and *clear-cut* laws and egoisms and that they have been created out of the chaos" (15–16).

One might argue that Hulme's turn to the material body works to objectify the ego and thus to revive the dissociative logic of bourgeois modernity. Kermode, in fact, argues that Hulme's classicism is nothing more than a quasi-scientific update of romantic ideology, using positivism to affirm the primacy of the subject (121, 128–9). But, even in this early essay, Hulme addresses this "Danger." He seeks to avoid any idealism of the self by foregrounding the ways in which physical contingency undermine purity. "Subtle associations," he writes, "which familiar images recall are insinuated into thought" (16). For Hulme, the boundaries of the physical body do not simply define spirit, but actively limit its movement. The imagination is inevitably restrained, thwarted in its search for infinite expansion by its location within the material world. While we seek perfection in a variety of forms, our constructions are always contingent, purposive, and thus limited. The individual stands arrested, struggling against his own constructions, self-defeated in his search for the infinite: "The absolute is invented to reconcile conflicting purposes. But these purposes are necessarily conflicting, even in the nature of Truth itself" (13). Even though the mind can perceive unity, it remains imprisoned in a decadent world of desire and necessity. The individual cannot attain perfection, yet he is not satisfied with the material world as given. He is always part-divine and part-animal, detached yet engaged. Spirit and matter are bound together, confounding desire as well as passivity.

This early essay similarly confounds the romantic impulse in art. As mentioned, Hulme describes a world in which symbols are "Separate from contact" and "quite divorced from nature" (12, 19). He laments a socially enforced gap "between a vague philosophic statement and the definite cinder, felt in a religious way" (21). In response, Hulme exposes the falsity of symbolic totality by describing the material terms of its creation. His fragments repeatedly refer to the "grit in the machine," the mud and dust out of which civilization has been developed and to which it will inevitably return:

> The eyes, the beauty of the world, have been organized out of the fæces. Man returns to dust. So does the face of the world to primeval cinders. (12)

Hulme continually strips the romantic image of its affirmative value. Aesthetic unity is depicted as a foolish dream, one that leaves us blind and impotent; aesthetic construction, though, regrounds our ideas within the world. Take, for example, the image of the dancer, which Kermode describes as an "uncomposite blessedness," the romantic image par excellence (53). For romantics from Wordsworth to Yeats, this image represents a perfect union of content and form, body and spirit; Hulme, however, fails to be charmed:

> Dancing to express the organisation of cinders, finally emancipated (cf. bird).
> I sat before a stage and saw a little girl with her head thrown back, and a smile. I knew her, for she was the daughter of John of Elton.
> But she smiled, and her feet were not like feet, but . . . . . [sic].
> Though I knew her body.
> All these sudden insights . . . all of these start a line, which seems about to unite the whole world logically. But the line stops. There is no unity. All logic and life are made up of tangled ends like that. (17)

Here, the possibility of romantic unity is ridiculed, its mortal limits laid bare. The dancer's feet are just feet, firmly planted upon the ground.

Hulme does not squelch the possibility of aesthetic pleasure, but he seeks to establish that power within the confines of the material world. Aesthetic value exists only in the recognition of limitation, in the acknowledgment of "that *fringe of cinders* which bounds any ecstasy" (17). Importantly, insofar as Hulme hopes to move beyond false symbols of comfort, to expose a necessary materialism, his aesthetic is based on the sensation of touch. Contact provides the comfort of material stability and sustains the hope of potential difference; it serves both to define and extend the self as it exists within the world. Interestingly, "Cinders" was originally conceived as a modern parable. The fictional Aphra served as its central figure and poet-hero:

> *Aphra's Finger*
> There are moments when the tip of one's finger seems raw. In the contact of it and the world there seems a strange difference. The spirit lives on that tip and is thrown on the rough cinders of the world. All philosophy depends on that – the state of the tip of the finger.

When Aphra had touched, even lightly, the rough wood, this wood seemed to cling to his finger, to draw itself backward and forward along it. The spirit returned again and again, as though fascinated, to the luxurious torture of the finger. (18)

Here, subject and object are inextricably linked at the point of contact. Spirit and matter coexist at the fingertip, in a state of "luxurious torture." Aphra returns to the point of contact because there he finds both unity and difference, power and pain. On the one hand, touch enforces a painful recognition of limit; the individual discovers a mortal world to which he must inevitably submit. It attests to an undeniable otherness, an impersonal order of stasis and discipline. On the other hand, touch affects a sensation of freedom and possibly divinity. It establishes the individual's formative power within and over the world. In this, as we will find in the work of Gaudier-Brzeska and H. D., Hulme begins to develop his defense of a rigid, classical formalism: the "hard and definite" object radically redefines the desires and possibilities of the modern subject.

Aphra's finger, in other words, points toward an alternative modernism, what Hulme would later call a new "weltanschauung." Throughout this essay, Hulme himself revels in "luxurious torture." He can barely contain his urge to debauch and corral. He tears across the ruined landscape with a proud intensity and stands over the ruins with smug contentment. He hunts down "mud" beneath "a girl's ball-dress" and stalks "chaos" behind the complacency of "Men laughing at a bar" (12–13). One detects a perverse glee in this thrashing of the civilized world, a joy in the fallen universe and its corrupt symbols. The finality of this ruin, the thoroughness of its chaos – these seem to offer both comfort and stability. This imperfection, though, hardly excludes the possibility of order: rather, the ash-heap suggests the possibility of reconstruction. "The definite cinder, felt in a religious way," implies not only critique, but the creation of a rational order (21). Hulme's essay concludes with a provisional hope:

A melancholy spirit, the mind like a great desert lifeless, and the sound of march music in the street, passes like a wave over the desert, unifies it, but then goes. (22)

Miriam Hansen offers the best description of this attitude and its affiliation with a larger tradition of materialist thought in the twentieth century. For her, Hulme's work is best characterized by its "dialectic of provocation and affirmation." It displays a typically avant-garde desire to "explode the organic unity of a poem from within." Yet its insistence on the "fragmentary" and the "non-organic" implies hope in a possible recreation of "absolute values." In this, Hulme's work recalls Benjamin's theory of allegory; its melancholic sense of the "empty world" implies, in its unflinching materialism, the possibility of a "'new sense of form,' a sense of 'construction.'"7 It is not surprising that Hulme next turned to aesthetic issues. His next two essays, "Notes on Language and Style" and "A Lecture on Modern Poetry," explore the act of artistic construction as it occurs within a dynamic field of desire. Looking closely at the lyric, Hulme redefines language as a difficult, yet malleable medium that unites the subject within a larger, integral community.

(1907–8) LANGUAGE, "HARD AND DEFINITE"

This next period has been the most rigorously discussed of Hulme's career, for it contains the development of his theory of the image and thus the foundations of modern poetry in general.8 But at precisely this ground-breaking moment, Hulme's work presents the critic with two serious problems. The most obvious has to do with gender: his writings on language engage a masculinist discourse of strength and clarity that will infect much of the classicist canon. His poetic theory seems to celebrate a specifically phallic beauty of Aphra, who "took the words, and they grew into a round smooth pillar" (28). The other difficulty lies in Hulme's discussion of the image itself, which clearly draws upon a traditional theory of romanticism. The following description, in its emphasis on subjective detachment, could have taken place during a walking tour of the Lake District:

> The beauty of London only seen in detached and careful moments, never continuously, always a conscious effort. On top of a bus, or the sweep of the avenue in Hyde Park. But to appreciate this must be in some manner detached, e.g. wearing workmen's clothes (when not shabby but different in kind) then opportunity for conscious reflection. It is the stranger that sees the romantic and the beautiful in the commonplace, cf. in New York, or in strange city, detached and therefore able to see beauty and romance. (44)

These two tendencies persist, in linked form, throughout Hulme's career and extend to those he influenced, particularly Eliot and Pound. In fact, his poetic theories, in their emphases on the masculine will and the pure sign, can be linked to fascist modernism in general. But, as even the above passage implies, Hulme's own work tempers these potential excesses with an aggressive materialism. His aesthetic theory counters its inherent romanticism, masculine or otherwise, with a sense of language's contingency and art's constructedness. Here, beauty is found only in workman's clothes, by a "careful . . . conscious effort." Aesthetic truth is neither immediately discovered nor spontaneously created; it exists only in a rigorous labor, in the tension that persists between a poet's physical experience and his language. With this logic, Hulme's poetic theory offers one of his strongest critiques of bourgeois modernity and thus provides the foundation for his later, more radical political theories.

In "Notes on Language and Style," Hulme reveals a budding interest in Bergson's vitalism as it provides an alternative to the hollow forms of the modern "intellectual machine." Rational thought, he argues, may be essential to practical activity, necessary for social order, but it is blind to the tensions and inconsistencies of the vital world; it deals only with "dead things." Rational discourse, too, only obscures the durational world it seeks to address; "We replace meaning (i.e. *vision*) by words," he writes, "These words fall into well-known patterns" (27). Hulme also follows Bergson when insisting that the poet "turn all his words into visions, in realities we can see" (24). The empty abstractions of conventional discourse, he writes, need to be replaced with "real solid vision or sound" (24).[9] For Hulme, in fact, the visual image is only the starting point for an even more concrete theory of language. He quickly shifts his emphasis from the thing seen to a tangible objectification of the sign:

the poet is forced . . . to construct a plaster model of a thing to express his emotion at the sight of the vision he sees, his wonder and ecstasy. If he employed the ordinary word, the reader would only see it as a segment, with no hair, used for getting along. And without this clay, spatial image, he does not feel that he has expressed at all what he sees. (24)

In this, the image is reconceived as a physical force, a "real solid." Recalling his account of Aphra, Hulme seeks a language that can be felt or touched. Poetry must approach the condition of sculpture, an aesthetic ideal we will discuss at length in chapter 4. Here, it suffices to say that literary achievement is something akin to a "statue in Paris"; "Each sentence should be a lump, a piece of clay . . . a wall touched with soft fingers" (25).[10]

Hulme may yearn for a total union of signifier and signified, a renewed logos, but the strength of this model is that it recognizes the incredible difficulty of all expression. Throughout his writings on language, the quasi-fascist fantasy of the organic sign is tempered by the inevitable tensions between language and the world and within language itself. For Hulme, language is no less resistant than stone or iron; the poet must shape a stubborn, everyday speech into the "solid image." In this, he claims that

"The idea is nothing"; significance is attained only in the "cindery thing done," in "the holding on to the idea" through its expression. Success rests upon the poet's strength, the result of his struggle with the "resistance of the material" (26). For Hulme, these tensions also inform aesthetic reception. The ideal work of art exerts a tangible pressure upon its surroundings; the hard forms of sculpture and poetry remain in the imagination (27). For the perceiver, this influence is palpable, predatory even. Certain forms can "arrest" the mind. In fact, they can "stand on end and hit you" (31). The entire creative process is indeed both involuntary and restrictive. The artist is "forced" to use a language that the perceiver, unavoidably, "feels." Nothing is created or perceived "out of vacuo" (26–7).

By foregrounding these tensions, Hulme suggests a theory of representation that undermines the romantic distinction between experience and expression, world and word. He hints at a more dynamic language and thus a more supple epistemology, one that is both perceptive and creative, conscious and willful. As Hulme explains, expression exists only in the tensions or "constraints" that exist between the various factors of its making; it exposes as it creates a field of conflicted energies (43). There is no one-to-one correspondence between word and thing, but neither do these two entities exist in isolation; rather, they form and shape each other, as they also impact upon other terms within reach. Considering a successful work, he writes,

It is seeing the real clay, that men in an agony worked with, that gives pleasure. To read a book which is *real clay* moulded by fingers that had to mould something, or they would clutch the throat of their maddened author. *No* flowing on of words, but tightly clutched tense fingers leaving marks in the clay. (26)

Here, in the willful activity of consciousness, tensions refine individual vision but only within the confines of a much greater order. The moment of contact tempers the "madness" of romanticism and the "agony" of positivism; the final object reveals a vital, yet stable order. Again, this theory suggests Hulme's growing interest in Bergson, who also describes the work of art as the point of impact between multiple forces: "The finished portrait is explained by the features of the model, by the nature of the artist, by the colors spread out on the palette." The final object conjoins the stable with the willful; "the *already-made*" becomes one with "the *being-made*" – "the fact of *seeing*" with "the act of *willing*."[11] Importantly, by defining expression in this way, these theorists strike at the heart of bourgeois subjectivity. Insofar as language is a dynamic field of tension, it firmly places the speaking subject within a larger, contingent order. Expression can never be simply escapist or reactionary; rather, it is always a medium in which human relations are clarified and potentially renewed.

Hulme similarly explores the creation and decline of common phrases and analogies. Every original and effective form of expression, he argues, eventually falls into decay and so must be replaced by a new one (39). This process, however, is not frictionless; the dead forms of the past inevitably limit the terms of creation. Formal staleness, in fact, inspires more precise modes of expression, but these latter arise only from within the confines of a larger expressive field. Each new form is created with immense difficulty, out of the inertia of the old, and thus exhibits its own solidity: "A transitory artificial impression is deliberately cultivated into an emotion and written about. Reason here creates and modifies an emotion, e.g. standing at street corners" (39). Here, force and form are not easily dissociated, for they exist through each other in a mutual give and take. The tangible impression must be worked through a conventional, reified order; in this, though, the former is made coherent and the latter is renewed. For Hulme, the activity of expression always figures as a negotiation of a significant order, what he calls "an infinite of limited *hard* expression" (34). Communication is a process of instigation and cooperation, moving in "ever-narrowing circles, to some third thing that seemed to lie behind both desires" (36). In other words, by materializing the tensions that always exist within sign systems, Hulme's thesis is carried into the social. In his formulation, language bears witness to the conflicting desires that define society as well as the possibility of their reconciliation.

The significance of this last point can be clarified by a close look at modernist theories of the image. Somewhat paradoxically, many modern poets understood the image as an analogy, as a "super-position" of two or more ideas or emotions. Oddly enough, from its inception, the poetic monad was founded upon an initial disunity or incommensurability of terms.[12] It is, however, not this paradox that concerns us, but the political agendas to which it was put. Poets such as Pound and Eliot tended to use analogy in a relational sense, as a way to unite the world's disparate forms and thus forge a higher, abstract order. Their smooth juxtapositions were engaged in the evocation of a greater, more universal term that stood tyrannically over all, whether it be "Tradition" or "The Great Bass."[13] Pound's "In a Station of the Metro," to take a quick example, uses three different phrases to conjure up the same ideal pattern. The mechanical branches of the metro system mirror the organic branching of the live bough which, in turn, mirrors the supposedly otherworldly power that unites the ghostly faces of the city. By establishing these relations, the poem attains a certain directive power and accumulative force (moving from modern mechanization to ancient spirit), but never does it once suggest contingency between its parts. Rather, its connective tissue remains unseen, immaterial. In his account of the poem, in fact, Pound somewhat embarrassingly admits that it "is meaningless unless one has drifted into a certain vein of thought." More specifically, he recognizes that he has transformed a "thing outward and objective" into something "inward and subjective." This imaginary reduction is, in fact, defended by an abstract babble concerning analytical geometry:

Thus, we learn that the equation $(x - a)2 + (y - b)2 - r2$ governs the circle. It is the circle. It is not a particular circle, it is any circle and all circles. It is nothing that is not a circle. It is the circle free of space and time limits. It is the universal existing in perfection, in freedom from space and time . . . It is in this way that art handles life. The difference between art and life is the difference of subject-matter only. (*Memoir*, 89–91)

In this turn to abstract form, Pound strips the analogical image of all that was critical in it, of its inherent duality and thus its resistance to totality. Not without a certain duplicity, the concrete image is decentered only so that wholeness can be reconstituted on a less questionable, imaginative level.

   Hulme, on the other hand, insists that analogy is a process of tension rather than relation. Analogies are not easily created or dissociated, for each incorporates linguistic material that governs and restricts its expressive potential. Indeed, with this emphasis on contingency, the Hulmean analogy tends to resist both abstraction and a crude materialism: the difficult process of representation does not give in to the tyranny of the idea or a simple positivism.[14] Like Pound, Hulme first considers analogy as a purely internal process: "the simultaneous presentation to the mind of two different images" (29). Poetry seems to be an act of maneuvering these images, positioning them within a relational whole that "suggest[s] an image which is different to both" (54). But the classicist quickly expresses "scorn" for this easy, idealist activity: "The things bring a kind of going straight, write them as analogy and call it literature, cf. marching in step, the great procession" (29–30). Hulme, therefore, provides another definition of analogy that limits this tendency toward formal abstraction. He argues that analogy exists not between abstract forms, but between two contingent objects. Its activity is both tangible and dynamic, a "continued close, compressed effort," a "deliberate choosing and working-up" (30). In this, representational entities exert a limiting, yet refining force upon each other. As Hulme explains,

If you only admit that form of manipulating images as good, if you deny all the other grasps, hands, for the cinders, all solid images, all patterns, then you can be clear, but not otherwise. (30)

Isolated, the terms of the analogy are equal, but insubstantial; they have little power to affect either true difference or a tangible unity. They become significant only when they exert pressure upon each other; in their mutual tension, they are made "conscious" and "whole" (37). As evidenced by his own poem "Autumn," Hulme thus moves beyond the romantic self as well as the finality of the dead word, toward some "third thing," something utterly "otherwise." His type of analogy, the "physical analogy," avoids all the modernist "tricks" in order to call forth a system that is at once vital and objective.

Again, Bergson comes to mind. Using music as his example, the vitalist describes the difference between a quantitative, intellectual order and a qualitative, intuitive one. The intellect, he explains, strips each note of its contingency in order to create a purely spatial arrangement: "[When] I intend explicitly to count [the notes] . . . then I shall have to separate them, and this separation must take place within some homogeneous medium in which the sounds, stripped of their qualities, and in a manner emptied, leave traces of their presence which are absolutely alike." An intuitive response, however, allows each note to jostle and shape its neighbors within a temporal duration: "I retain each of these successive sensations in order to combine it with the others and form a group . . . I limit myself to gathering, so to speak, the qualitative impression produced by the whole series" (*Time and Free Will*, 86–7). Elsewhere, in a text that Hulme himself translated, Bergson suggests that this latter, contingent order is necessarily imperfect, open, and resistant. Here, in the tangible juxtaposition of multiple images, the artist attains a certain liberation:

many diverse images, borrowed from very different orders of things, may, by the convergence of their action, direct consciousness to the precise point where there is a certain intuition to be seized. By choosing images as dissimilar as possible, we shall prevent any one of them from usurping the place of the intuition it is intended to call up, since it would then be driven away at once by its rivals.[15]

Several facets of this "intensive manifold" will be addressed in the next section. Here, though, as a theory of aesthetic order, it most clearly suggests a type of linguistic practice that, in its material dimensions, is at once unified and radically decentered.

Hulme, then, turns to the subjective flux of romantic poetry only to establish a flexible, yet conscious order within it. His account of linguistic contingency, in fact, presents us with a radically different kind of aesthetic politics. The analogical process he describes here extends well beyond the six-line poem. These linguistic tensions spread into the surrounding environment, polarizing and refining all they touch. Hulme again argues that aesthetic pleasure, like all pleasure, is generated by boundaries and restrictions. The self-contained art object has "no effect"; its "simple" perfection, its pleasurable illusion, exists only insofar as the work is detached from the material world (33). In contrast, the best art establishes a tangible order to which the subject is inextricably bound. This more radical art "depends for its effect not on a kind of half sleep produced, but on arresting the attention, so much so that the succession of visual images should exhaust one" (54). The poem "Autumn," for example, depends upon this play of arrest and exhaustion. Its analogical juxtapositions inspire a certain desire for unity, but the reader is carried along by the poem's force only to be restrained by its form. The reader is at once encouraged and halted, beckoned and denied by the poem's internal tensions. At the moment of restraint, though, desire is made conscious; the work thus inspires and clarifies a dynamic unity of willing and seeing. In this way, the intensive order within the work extends throughout the phenomenal world, shaping and forging its disparate elements; its structure spreads like crystal across water, strengthening and refining all that it touches. Thus, Hulme launches his most serious attack on the blindly reproductive activity of the bourgeois world and offers a new kind of aesthetic engagement. The difficult materiality of his art offers a foothold upon which the perceiver may stand amidst the flux and reconsider the possibilities of order.

As we will find, a similar kind of engagement informs both the abstract sculpture of Gaudier-Brzeska and the more directly political poetry of H. D. Here, though, it might be helpful to turn to a later thinker who also sought to move beyond bourgeois affirmations. Adorno's aesthetic theory foregrounds the same linguistic tensions, yet it more completely maintains art's power to challenge and restructure the productive logic of modernity. First, though, it is important to recognize that Adorno's earlier aesthetic theories are somewhat hindered by their absolute refusal to grant art a positive content. His early examinations of Beckett's plays and Schoenberg's compositions, for example, find resistance only by pushing negativity to its utter limits. He praises these works for their refusal to reconcile their constituent parts and thus for confounding the fetishization of popular art, the romantic unity of the cultural commodity. In these works, internal restrictions foreclose the possibility of immersion in either the sensual moment or an abstract unity; forces tug and pull at one another, denying the possibility of their realization and thus the possibility of affirmation:

If asceticism once struck down the claims of the esthetic in a reactionary way, it has today become a sign of advanced art: not, to be sure, by an archaicizing parsimony of means in which deficiency and poverty are manifested, but by the strict exclusion of all culinary delights which seek to be consumed immediately for their own sake . . . Art records negatively just that possibility of happiness which the only partially positive anticipation of happiness ruinously confronts today.[16]

Like Eliot at his most critical, Adorno here privileges a certain form of dissociation. The best modern art is self-denying, resistant to the false ideals of the past or the future, of politics or the market. It offers a fraught union of materials and structure, historical specifics and subjective ideals, and thus exposes the tensions that define contemporary existence. Of course, these works maintain the possibility of wholeness; their negativity inspires and thus exposes the spectator's desire for a positive fulfillment. This hope, however, exists only in a critical, negative form, as an impossibility and nothing more.

As Adorno eventually seems to realize, this theory might clarify the critical aspects of modern art, such as the ironic formalism of *The Waste Land* or the deconstructive punning of *Finnegans Wake*, but it obscures the constructive dimension of modernism in general and, alongside this, its preoccupation with materiality. Thus, Adorno begins to develop an aesthetic theory that more keenly focuses on the positive tensions that exist between the creative subject and the material world. In "Commitment," for example, he focuses on the fact that modern creative activity has become increasingly subjective. Art, he claims, has grown preoccupied with "the subject's decision and non-decision" and thus fails to acknowledge the "objective requirements regarding [the work's] construction" ("Commitment," 80). Elsewhere, he argues that realism and symbolism both partake in the romantic illusion that aesthetic expression is the ultimate reality. In these movements, subjectivity is celebrated "in the purity of the language, which, by spiritualizing language, removes it from the empirical realm to which it was committed" ("Narrator," 33). To counteract this tendency, Adorno advocates an aesthetic activity that foregrounds the artist's encounter with his materials. The best work reveals that moment when the attempt to organize reality meets with the inherent resistance of the real. First and foremost, Adorno validates this work as an expression of rationalization, as a conscious display of the subject's desire to master and organize an unruly environment. As he writes, "The organizing principle in every work of art, the principle that creates unity, is derived from the same rationality that its claim to totality would like to put a stop to" ("Commitment," 91). In other words, Adorno celebrates the aesthetic construct as it reproduces the contradictions of the world it rejects. Abstract art, precisely because it insists upon its autonomy, echoes the potential, and potential horror, of reified modernity at large. According to Adorno, the "uncompromising radicalism of [modern] works, the very moments denounced as formalist, endows them with a frightening power that impotent poems about the victims lack" ("Commitment," 88).

Yet if art's contradictions speak to the constructive activity of modern society, they also suggest the possibility of self-correction. Once again considering modern art, Adorno shows how a desperate subjective energy, in its attempt to establish coherence and authority, always inevitably exposes its historical or material origins. An "unleashed subjectivity turns into its opposite through its own momentum," exposing a "physical, non-aesthetic reality." In other words, art's desire for purity gives expression to that which it rejects, thus clarifying its strengths and limitations within a larger field of energy:

The literary subject who declares himself free of the conventions of concrete representation acknowledges his own impotence at the same time; he acknowledges the strength of the world that reappears in the midst of the monologue. Thus a second language is produced, distilled to a large extent from the residue of the first, a deteriorated associative language of things which permeates not only the novelist's monologue but also that of the innumerable people estranged from the first language who make up the masses.

As we saw in Hulme's work, this "deteriorated associative language" suggests an alternative sensibility, one consistently aware of the tensions between subject and object. It bespeaks both the horror of rationality as well as a necessary engagement with the material world, the possibility of critique and the power of organization. For both Adorno and Hulme, "There is no modern work of art worth anything that does not delight in dissonance and release." The best art continually proposes and confounds the possibility of unity; only thus does it "bear witness to what has befallen the individual in the age of liberalism" ("Narrator," 35–6).

Hulme liked to describe his poems as "gems," referring to the chthonic forces that give rise to their objective precision and clarity. Similarly, for Adorno, the lyric poem "crystallizes" human truth in its relation to society.[17] For both, the work of art exposes a modern excess of subjectivity, but also redefines that subjectivity as it exists within a larger, contingent order. Its language, then, is always "something double," existing at the boundary between the self and its others, at once individual and communal, spontaneous and ordered ("Lyric," 43). For these thinkers, then, art is a medium in which worldly relations are slowly shaped and clarified. The conflicted forces within the poem, between desire and language, mimic the hopes and failures of social organization in general. As Adorno writes,

Classical philosophy once formulated a truth now disdained by scientific logic: subject and object are not rigid and isolated poles but can be defined only in the process in which they distinguish themselves from one another and change. The lyric is the aesthetic test of that dialectical philosophical proposition. In the lyric poem the subject, through its identification with language, negates both its opposition to society as something merely monadological and its mere functioning within a wholly socialized society. ("Lyric," 44)

Adorno provides perhaps the best description of the classical aesthetic when he defines the work of art as "knowledge in the form of a nonconceptual object." For him, the work of art is always artifactual, and as such forces us to re-experience the worldly desires and tensions that went into its making:

The moment of intention is mediated solely through the form of the work, which crystallizes into a likeness of an Other that ought to exist. As pure artifacts, products, works of art, even literary ones, are instructions for the praxis they refrain from: the production of life as it ought to be. ("Commitment," 93)

Here, we return to the sensation of touch and the "strenuous effort." The aesthetic artifact reveals the traces of a mortal struggle. It bears witness to a material activity and thus engages the spectator in a conscious relationship with the vital world.

(1909–12) BERGSON BACKWARDS

Just about everything that Hulme admired in Bergson's thought was already present in his own: the emptiness of rational thought, the impossibility of pure vision, the intensive structuring of the material world. Hulme's theory of chessboards and cinders is based upon the same distinctions that Bergson drew between intellect and intuition; both thinkers condemned the ideological closure of the rational world and sought release in a more dynamic interplay of self and other. Hulme, however, first became interested in Bergson's work not for its specific content, but for its shaping influence on both his own thought and on modern thought in general. His writings on Bergson turn repeatedly to the manner in which the vitalist philosophy manages to shape and direct the otherwise chaotic energies of the phenomenal world. Paradoxically, then, Hulme was intrigued by "Bergsonisme" as it expressed the possibility of establishing concrete values in a changing world. In fact, the construction of British classicism would not have been possible without what has been seen as Bergson's largely romantic philosophy. In this, Bergson's influence extends beyond the "time" – children of leftist modernism, for it also courses through the spatial aesthetics of the British avant-garde.

In "Notes on Bergson," a collection of articles written for the progressive audience of *The New Age*, Hulme repeatedly delays the task of outlining Bergson's theories in order to describe its psychological effects on him and his generation. He begins with the "physical delight," the "giddiness" he felt when he first read Bergson's work. His experience was like that of a "relieving force," filling his mind with a "great excitement." His parched, cindery landscapes found life and fluidity in the "élan vital" (126). But, more importantly, Hulme praises Bergson for providing shape and definition to his own scattered musings. Clearly, he saw Bergson's work as a validation of his own; their confluence of thought suggests the possibility of objective order. But, more specifically, it was Bergson's language, in its clarity and precision, that provided a relieving security. In the following passage, Hulme describes the states he experienced both before and after his reading:

Certain elements present in one were present in the other. But these elements, which in the first state were tortured, vague, and confused, became in the second clear and definite . . . In the first place, there was a simple sentiment of relief. A solution was given to a problem which worried me . . . In the second place, the key with which this prison door was opened corresponded to the type of key which I had always imagined would open it. I had constructed for myself imperfect examples of keys of this type. I was shown the perfect and successful one which yet was on the lines I had vaguely imagined might be successful. (126–7)

Although the vitalist celebrates the soft flux of reality, his writing serves to clarify and harden that which is confused. His language exists as a practical form; it works to objectify and refine the muddled ideas of others. Ironically, in this, the vitalist is a source of "stability and fixity," of "final truth" (155).

The second installment of "Notes" continues to address the concrete influence of vitalism, but now as it affects the masses. Hulme begins rather sheepishly, discrediting his earlier enthusiasm for Bergson's theories. He claims that he has been incautious and bluntly declares the impossibility of philosophical change. Bergson's work does not offer anything new; the vitalist "solution" is as old as the "problem" it pretends to solve. Similarly, Bergson's fanatics are presented in static terms; they express an age-old need for order and conformity. His lecture audience is presented as an effete mob, a congregation of mindless supplicants, "with their heads lifted up in the kind of 'Eager Heart' attitude" (155).[18] Hulme, however, does find much that is positive in this spectacle. The vitalist philosopher, like the successful poet, has powerfully shaped language according to his needs. His ideas are not necessarily innovative, but they appear in an effectively innovative language, one that successfully competes against other "forces" and "factions" in a discursive battlefield:

These factions represent not only the various views it is possible to hold, but also the force with which these views press themselves on your mind. Beliefs are not only representations, they are also forces, and it is possible for one view to compel you to accept it in spite of your preference for another. (136)

According to Hulme, Bergson's theory has gained popular approval not because of any truth it might contain. Rather, like a good imagist poem, it impresses itself upon the modern mind, shaping its sluggish perspective. Its success is the direct result of its having attained a "definite and fixed shape" (132).[19] Here, too, Hulme's account of Bergson moves somewhat humorously away from all that Bergson represents. What begins as a liberating or relieving force turns into its exact opposite: a formative restraint upon modern consciousness. Vitalism's celebrated "newness" is reconceived as a coercive dogma. While Hulme might discredit the fanatical adoration of Bergson, he sees within it the possibility of a stable social order. The purely "accidental" fad suggests that "a certain kind of enthusiasm can crystallize" (129).

Not surprisingly, then, when Hulme finally turns to the content of Bergson's work, he inverts its central premises, emphasizing a static strain within it. In "Philosophy of Intensive Manifolds," for example, Hulme offers his first straightforward account of Bergson's metaphysics and the conflict between vitalism and materialism. He accepts Bergson's celebration of the former and explicitly offers his support in the battle against modernity's increasing stasis (136). But Hulme clearly distorts Bergson's definition of the élan vital as a "continuous" and "unorganized" creativity. Rather, he sees this energy as a "permanent part of reality," "a kind of eternal subject facing an eternal object." Paradoxically, the vital is defined as a "rock-like solidity" arranged in opposition to its environment (137–8). The most intriguing aspect of Hulme's discussion is that it allows Bergson's dualisms to take on the characteristics of each other. Just as instinct is often described as a "permanent, continuous and enduring entity," the abstract intellect exists within the radical contingency of the material world, as "the result of certain local physical conditions" (138). Throughout, Hulme emphasizes the eternal qualities of the former and the relative, self-satisfying activity of the latter. In fact, the specific composition of either entity is simply a matter of perspective: "Whereas at one time you felt sure that matter was the only permanent thing; you now find yourself in the position of taking the reality of individuality as such a base" (147).

If suspicions were not already aroused, Hulme later offers a substantial defense of the "mechanical conception of the world" (140). Hulme certainly laments the loss of freedom that mechanism entails. In a rational world, consciousness has no influence; "it makes no difference; everything would go on just the same without it" (142). He also bemoans the rational destruction of spiritual value, the displacement of religion with an easy faith in the "self-acting" motion of physics (144–5). However, Hulme also asserts that mechanization is historically inevitable and spiritually essential. Solid forms arise before us, blocking the easy path to perfection, but thus forging a much more rigorous standard of salvation. The materialism of modern life is a necessary "obstacle which stands in the way of any idealist or religious interpretation of the universe" (142). For Hulme, divinity is not a preternatural other, but the product of the struggle for its attainment. Salvation has little to do with the free expansion of desire, but exists in the painful acquisition of a "decent shape" (151). In an argument that conflates his theory of poetic creation with evolutionary creation in general, he writes,

> You may start writing a poem in an endeavour to express a certain idea which is present in your mind in a very hazy shape. The effort to express that idea in verse, the struggle with language, forces the idea as it were back on itself and brings out the original idea in a clearer shape. Before it was only confused. The idea has grown and developed because of the obstacles it had to meet. It may be, then, that the function of matter in regard to consciousness is this: It is destined to bring to precision, in the form of distinct personalities, tendencies or potentialities which at first were mingled. (189)

Here, Hulme celebrates not simply precision or intellect, but a restrictive process that lifts the self beyond itself and thus clarifies desire. As we saw in his theories of language, matter is valued for affecting a tension that is not "produced by the brain and is to great extent independent of it"; "At such moments of tension," in fact, "you reach a reality which passes outside your physical self" (189).

At first glance, Hulme's values are much more ordered, restrictive and permanent than those anyone could find in Bergson's work. His consideration of the élan vital serves only his much greater interest in a constructive materialism. As Michael Levenson correctly notes, "Bergson's philosophy was for Hulme a way not only of challenging the orthodoxies of science but of validating new anti-romantic literary impulses. For in Hulme's presentation of the position, its principle emphasis was sceptical . . . modest, tentative" (81). Sanford Schwartz confirms that Hulme "uses Bergson in a very un-Bergsonian manner. Bergson maintains that the artist cuts through a network of static abstractions to the transient stream of consciousness in real duration. Hulme, on the other hand, seems less interested in recovering real duration than in rendering the objects of perception as precisely as possible."[20] As we will see, though, Hulme's complex dialectic of spirit and matter already exists in Bergson's original theory. In fact, Hulme's work serves to correct two of the most common misinterpretations regarding the vitalist. First, we learn that despite Bergson's distinction between intuition and intellect, he develops a consistent monism in which intuitive forces give rise to intellectual forms. Secondly, despite the willful critiques of anti-liberals like Eliot and Lewis, Bergson's romanticism is everywhere tempered by an innate respect for phenomenological boundaries and tensions.

As in Hulme's work, Bergson's philosophy is founded upon the notion that life is intentional; reality is a field of indivisible tendencies that ceaselessly impinge upon one another. "Life," Bergson writes, "is, more than anything else, a tendency to act on inert matter," and a "tendency," he explains, "achieves all that it aims at only if it is not thwarted by another tendency" (*Evolution*, 96, 13). Indeed, for Bergson, anything that can be perceived is simply the final trace of a tendency that has been thwarted in its push through matter. Form is the last position of a desire that has been hindered in its effort to find fulfillment; buildings, bodies, oceans, and hills – these are merely the most recent effects of a continual striving. Bergson, for example, presents the image of a hand passing through a heap of metal filings, exhausting itself at a certain point, and then withdrawing. This once vital current, now arrested by matter, has left behind something utterly new: "We seize from within, we live at every instant, a creation of form, and it is in just those cases in which the form is pure [that] the creative current is momentarily interrupted . . ." (*Evolution*, 139). According to Bergson, some thinkers might try to explain this new arrangement by complex equations; others might imagine that a certain preordained plan had presided over the arrangement. But neither mechanism nor finality can define a process that is at once volitional and contingent. Force and form, acting and perceiving, these are indistinguishable in the vitalistic universe; "the road," he writes, has been created "with the act of travelling over it" (*Evolution*, 51).

Bergson's theory of evolutionary creation develops this monism and its most progressive implications. His discussion begins with the theoretical incompatibility of the laws of conservation and those of entropic decline. The apparent "constancy" of a system's energy seems directly opposed to its tendency toward "degradation"; while our solar system appears to have been born with a maximum of intensive vitality, it "has gone on diminishing" toward a cold extensivity (*Evolution*, 243). Bergson argues that some point of tension must exist at which these conflicting principles are united. Considering a theory of the big bang, he suggests that the élan vital pushes up through the lifeless forms of matter, which, conversely, push down and thus stubbornly restrict the power of the élan vital. What is perceived as life is only the boundary of these two oppositional forces:

So, from an immense reservoir of life, jets must be gushing out unceasingly, of which each, falling back, is a world. The evolution of living species within this world represents what subsists of the primitive direction of the original jet, and of an impulsion which continues itself in a direction the inverse of materiality. (*Evolution*, 247)

"All our analyses," he claims, "show us, in life, an effort to remount the incline that matter descends" (*Evolution*, 245). Importantly, though, Bergson explains that form here is simply the dynamic inverse of force. Matter is only spirit seen from the opposite side; in fact, the phenomenal world is composed of spirit in a state of tension against itself. The vital spirit tries to expend itself in infinite expansion, but is thwarted by an equal and opposite quantity of itself from the other direction. The specific characteristics of either of these "complementary tendencies" depends upon the position of the subject. As Bergson writes,

In reality, life is a movement, materiality is the inverse movement, and each of these two movements is simple, the matter which forms a world being an undivided flux, and undivided also the life that runs through it, cutting out in it living beings all along its track. Of these two currents the second runs counter to the first, but the first obtains, all the same, something from the second. (*Evolution*, 249–50)

Importantly, this monism incorporates the static and the changing. Certainly, movement within this field is finite and ordered; it inevitably erects its own rigid boundaries. But these boundaries, in turn, express as they generate the presence of multiple forces and their infinite creativity.

Bergson certainly exploits the deconstructive potential of this dynamic. For him, vitalism confounds both the romance of pure will (finalism) and the fantasy of an ideal order (mechanism). The apparent purity of his privileged terms – duration, intuition, the musical phrase – is always complicated

by the tensions and boundaries within each. Slowly, life is shaped into matter, while, just as slowly, matter melts into life. Reality is somewhat ordered,
but not fully determined; its objects are unique, but never isolated (*Evolution*, 42). Moreover, Bergson understands consciousness as a provisional
force that arises from within the material world and responds to its stubborn tensions. It is an intentional activity that continues as it revises the
dissociative tendency that is already present in life itself (*Evolution*, 186,
191). Consequently, Bergson maintains that consciousness is both active
and static; its power mimics the tendencies of reality itself both to dissolve
and congeal. Its willing is durational, its seeing is material; "The double
form of consciousness is then due to the double form of the real" (*Evolution*,
178). Importantly, if consciousness is always double, like life itself, it too
always exceeds its own boundaries, destabilizing the relations between inner
and outer worlds. Here, in the unity of seeing and willing, "the individuality of the body is re-absorbed in the universal interaction which, without
doubt, is reality itself" (*Evolution*, 11).

These last few points should help to explain Bergson's popularity amongst
modernist revolutionaries of both the left and right.[21] It is not simply that
the vitalist counters bourgeois rationalism with an organic unity, but that
his theory submits all ideological structures to a dialectical dissolution and
thus to a new history. The possibility of a reconciliation between willing
and seeing appealed to all sorts of visionaries and cranks. From Pound to
Stein, Gramsci to Mussolini, modernists across the spectrum were now free
to claim the immediacy of their perceptions. More importantly, though,
if intellect is a negation of a wider, dynamic reality, then "there has never
been a clean cut between the two; all around conceptual thought there
remains an indistinct fringe which recalls its origins." In this, history is also
at once open and ordered, conscious and collective; "the enterprise cannot be achieved in one stroke: it is necessarily collective and progressive"
(*Evolution*, 191–3). Ultimately, in regard to this dialectic, theorists of the
left and right differ only by what Bergson calls "point of view." While the
former may celebrate "unceasing life, action, freedom," the latter champions the potential of "a decent shape" (*Evolution*, 248, 251). Hulme's work,
of course, leans toward the latter, beyond the flux toward a provisional,
yet static order. For him, Bergson's theories prove that "There is nothing
infinite or ineffable about the fundamental self. It is a perfectly finite thing
and at the same time there is nothing miraculous about one's intuition of
it" (178). The élan vital inevitably falls into patterns, "stable crystallized out
states" (176). Indeed, this dialectic persists throughout Hulme's work, but,
as we will find, it is increasingly pushed toward the right. Hulme, as he

next turns to a dismal political situation at home and then to the war itself, loses patience with the slow work of crystallization and demands a more aggressive reconstruction.

(1911–1914) THE POLITICS OF ROMANTICISM AND CLASSICISM

At its most practical, Hulme's conservatism is exactly what one would expect it to be. In defense of a crumbling House of Lords, for example, he offers a standard right-wing rant for order and discipline:

The State or nation can only be in a healthy condition when it submits itself to a kind of discipline. There must be a hierarchy, a subordination of the parts, just as there must be in any other organisation. A pure democracy ends all this, for discipline can only be kept up when the centre of government is to a certain extent independent of the people governed. (220)

Here, Hulme drops his typically casual style in order to assert the necessity of a political order defined by "checks and restraints." He demands the construction of a stable institution that can keep the liberal "flux" at bay (220–1). But the logic that informs this argument, and Hulme's conservatism in general, is anything but traditional. First and foremost, Hulme consistently denies the objectivity of any political position, his own as well as that of the liberal. In explaining his taste for conservative politics, he explains, "Personally, I like and enjoy them; they state the truth as I see it" (214). Moreover, while Hulme consistently declares the need for restraint, he refuses to assign value to any one sector from which that power may derive. Unlike Eliot, Hulme resists political elitism by insisting upon the relativity of all positions and by upholding equal but opposing forces of discursive power. His sympathies do not necessarily lie only with the past, with race, or even with the House of Lords; in fact, he accepts the need for "all kinds of restraints" (221). This commitment to the subjective should now sound familiar. This fundamental bias, rather than any direct commitment to dogma, also underlines Hulme's political beliefs. Hulme everywhere stresses the dynamic processes by which political relations are constructed and thus maintains their openness. In this, he suggests the possibility of a social order that, like his metaphysical order, is at once conscious and flexible, necessary as well as negotiable.

Hulme's political essays revisit that relativism first considered in "Cinders." Political argumentation, he claims, has no formative value; its influence on the mind is inconsequential. Any particular position, he argues, "may look like an intellectual decision, but it isn't." Conviction and conversion are possible, but only through "emotional process." All belief is driven by "instinct," "appetite," and "desire" (207–8, 211). Clearly, in this, Hulme draws upon the popular work of the mass psychologists, particularly Sorel and Le Bon. But, as we know, he has always valued these subjective forces because of their inevitability, because of the objective forms toward which they move. Public opinion is familiarly described as a "fixed obsession," a perspective "too deep-seated to be moved by any argument" (211). The difference here, though, is that, now, in considering political ideology, Hulme moves beyond the hope of a mostly unconscious and accidental system. He begins to describe an ideological order that is not only knowable, but capable of being judged and manipulated.

For Hulme, the material construction of ideology suggests that it might be effectively understood as well as managed. Belief, as a response to need, falls within a limited range of possibilities; its permutations are predictable and thus subject to both analysis and control. All archeological research, he argues, implies "that civilisation is a recurrent phenomenon" (224). Human desire is "constant, and that the number and types of the possible forms of society are also constant" (222). For Hulme, this inevitability suggests the basic need for restraint as it reveals the particular restraints necessary for any given society. By a careful analysis, one can rationally enforce "the necessary relations which hold between things and the law of facts" (164). Importantly, Hulme's theory begins with radically subjective beliefs, yet it still confirms a certain social perfectionism. He argues first from a relativist position, claiming that all political opinions are the result of fear and desire. Even his own demands are purely subjective and have no special access to universal truth. But this very admission points toward its own sort of dogmatism. *As a conservative*, then, Hulme's call for order simply satisfies an emotional need. However, *as a political theorist*, he knows that order is both inevitable and knowable. Thus, his theory of political prejudice straddles the relative and the essential. It points toward an order that can be either revealed or denied by the individual will. Toward this truth, there are only "healthy" and "unhealthy" responses (224–5).

This position informs the paradoxical process that Hulme calls "conversion." Hulme does not foolishly hope to end ideology or even to replace one ideology with another. Rather, since prejudice is unavoidable, the political thinker can only ask for a clarification of its "first principles." The factors that determine belief cannot be destroyed, but it is possible to get at their "exact contours" (240). In other words, Hulme asks for a self-consciousness or doubling of ideology, one that removes the "veil which hides the man's own real position from himself" (233). He describes a certain "historical method" by which one can disclose the material tensions and inconsistencies that define any political position. He claims that "exhibiting the intimate connection between such conceptions – that of *progress* for example – and certain economical conditions at the time of their invention in the eighteenth century, does more than anything else to loosen their hold over the mind" (248–9). While this process entails the attainment of a certain objectivity, it is also, in turn, associated with a specifically conservative position. As Hulme understands it, conversion of this sort implies a movement above the political spectrum, but also a movement across the political spectrum, to the right. Liberalism, in fact, is defined by its inability "to perceive its own prejudices." Liberals and revolutionaries of all kinds foolishly believe that their purely relative values are "natural" and "automatic" (233). Conservatives, however, recognize ideological blindness and thus ideological necessity. The conservative acknowledges the fallen nature of the human and thus the need for absolute order. In other words, for Hulme, ideological blindness can be superseded by ideological freedom, but only for as long as it takes one to recognize the necessity of ideological blindness. The "historical method" entails not simply consciousness, but a conscious choice of illusions.

This argument clearly underlies Hulme's famous definitions of Romanticism and Classicism. According to Hulme, only a perverse romanticism could explain the current antagonism to tariff reform and the House of Lords. An irrational egoism governs the bourgeois intelligentsia, who "have everything to lose from the advent of unrestrained democracy, and who yet blindly believe in it as they would in a religion" (220). For Hulme, this romanticism is "a deeply seated and organised set of prejudices grouped round the word 'free' and 'natural'" (211). It is falsely founded upon the belief that "man is something rather wonderful" and so that "good will come even when things are left to themselves" (67, 222). We have seen this attitude attacked in the work of Babbitt and Eliot, but not with this same critical edge. Hulme argues that while every philosophy is relative, romanticism is distinguished by a failure to acknowledge its own limitations. The romantic is convinced that his attitude is neither historical nor ideological, but completely "natural" and "spontaneous." This presumption is based on a damning tautology: if the individual is essentially good, then so must be his beliefs. The impotent dreamer wrongly believes he can "deduce his opinions . . . from some fixed principle which can only be found by metaphysic" (67). For Hulme, this blindness is treacherously aligned with the voracious activity of the marketplace. The insatiable demand for freedom manifests itself in a horrific mechanism, a tyrannical succession of empty forms. Freedom turns into its exact opposite, the destructive order of the ceaselessly new, "a NEW art, a NEW religion, and even a NEW age" (237). Thus runs the standardized chaos of bourgeois modernism. The fallen worship that which damns them – they make a religion of themselves.

Conversely, the classicist acknowledges the binding patterns of subjectivity. His attitude, the only "honest" attitude, depends upon a recognition of the inevitable and thus the need for external restraint. Indeed, precisely because his attitude is an attitude, and because it acknowledges itself as such, it is the right one. In other words, the classicist accepts that the individual is inherently limited by his needs and desires. He sees the inner man as an "internal anarchy," a "sticky" ore of "fixed and unalterable composition" (241). Indeed, "Man is an extraordinarily fixed and limited animal whose nature is absolutely constant" (61). As we have seen, these subjective excesses fall into certain patterns that can be both analyzed and manipulated. The classicist does not defend limitation for its own sake. For him, humanity is necessarily limited, and his job is simply to find the best kinds of limitations. Certainly, then, at his most dogmatic, the classicist asserts that human nature, and thus its necessary laws, are unchanging. However, in his recognition of belief's constructedness, he maintains the possibility of an open order in which competing desires engage in a conscious negotiation of power. Hulme does not seek simply to deny or restrain subjectivity; rather, he wants it to partake in a "healthy" order, one that unites freedom with stability in a positive, constructive way. He seeks "regeneration" by way of an "irrational" dynamic, one that contests as it transforms order from the inside out (250–1). As Hulme will argue later, "Order is thus not merely negative, but creative and liberating. Institutions are necessary" (444).

This paradoxical position carries over into Hulme's admiring description of Georges Sorel as "a revolutionary who is anti-democratic . . . revolutionary in economics, but classical in ethics" (249, 252). Indeed, Hulme's many interests – pessimism, imagism, Bergsonian metaphysics, revolutionary conservatism – find a forceful coalescence in Sorel's work on social myth. In fact, Hulme's sometimes willful translation of Sorel's *Reflections on Violence* makes it difficult to ascertain where the work of each thinker begins and ends. This groundbreaking text opens with a definition of pessimism as a philosophy of conduct based on the necessity of restraint. The pessimist understands human weakness and acknowledges the obstacles before progress. He does not flinch before the fact that humanity falls into patterns, habits of conduct and belief; he regards "social conditions as forming a system bound together by an iron law which cannot be evaded, so that the system is given, as it were, in one block."²² Sorel, however, argues that while power and manipulation is inevitable, modern attitudes dangerously weaken or at least obscure these necessary restraints. Bourgeois humanitarianism, with its faith in reasonable progress and rational debate, tends toward the (albeit false) dissolution of social distinction. Any conflicting desire, socialist or otherwise, is mediated through the parliamentary machine, from whence it emerges in a socially acceptable, yet diluted form (54). Consequently, Sorel demands a return to violence as the true standard of ethical conduct. He privileges a proud hostility toward convention and a more aggressive program of social deliverance. Sorel's most vigorous passages counter middle-class middling with heroic immediacy; every great culture is characterized by a "war-like excitement," a vital force "displayed according to its own nature" (15, 122).

Sorel's discussion of myth depends upon a subtle social dynamic that pushes this position beyond its simple dualism. Following Bergson, he claims that certain types of language distinguish the bourgeoisie and the proletariat. The former, he argues, speaks through "the impersonal, the socialised, the *ready-made*" and thus obscures not only the truths of history, but their own machinations. The latter, however, in its self-imposed immediacy, puts forth "a mental effort which is continually endeavouring to break through the bonds of what has previously been constructed for common use" (3–4). Here, Sorel celebrates the working class for its living speech, a willing that is also a thinking. Their myths exist somewhere between passion and discourse; they enact as they express mass desire. As Sorel explains, these myths may appear to be eternal, essential, but they are composed of irreducible desires and specifically historical forces; they are "not descriptions of things, but expressions of a determination to act" (22). In their immediacy, myths tumble into physical presence; in their contingency, they strike the abstract into clarity. Desire becomes material, sentiments are made tangible; passion is voiced and, in turn, commanded. These methods of expression are not fanciful, but affective; they "throw a full light on things, which put them exactly in the place assigned to them by their nature, and which bring out the whole value of the forces into play" (130).

Certainly, Sorel's theory translates into a fantasy of the pure sign, and he can barely distinguish between the organic creation of order from below and its potential imposition from above. As we know, in fact, Sorel's myth of a general strike provided the blueprint for the fascist myth of national unity; his most widely abused definition, in its vagueness, allowed many leaders to sidestep the issue of origin altogether: "use must be made of a body of images which, *by intuition alone*, and before any considered analyses are made, is capable of evoking as an undivided whole the mass of sentiments" (130–1). Yet Sorel insists that these structures arise from within the mass and thus exhibit a great flexibility. He returns again and again to the primacy of the will, the desires that shape myth and thus ensure that it remains open, provisional. "When the masses are deeply moved," he explains, "it then becomes possible to trace the outlines of the kind of representation which constitutes a social myth . . . these myths have varied greatly in different epochs" (31). Indeed, myths can only honestly arise in relation to the present, and they may just as quickly fade away, "solely for our own time and for the preparation of the transition from one world to the other" (279). In contrast to Eliot or Pound, then, Sorel understands myth as it derives neither from some divine plan nor from a structural tendency within history itself; rather, it is forged between multiple desires and thus it is subject to multiple revisions. It is shaped, and reshaped, by local forces of production as they exist within "a complexity which is sometimes inextricable" (161). Certainly, for Sorel, as for Hulme, the law exists, or else there would be nothing to inspire this transgressive desire, but this law exists only in its enactment and thus remains negotiable. Here, as we will find in the aesthetic activism of Gaudier-Brzeska and H.D., political forms are constructed and tempered by personal forces; social order is always subject to "revolutionary tendencies" (165).

(1914–1917) HEROISM AND THE RELIGIOUS ATTITUDE

Undoubtedly, after the publication of "Romanticism and Classicism," Hulme's beliefs grew increasingly strident. In his later essays, he seems to abandon classicism altogether for an inhuman and anti-vital "religious attitude."[23] Here, the philosopher no longer maintains that subjective experience is productive of a stable order; he expresses great repugnance toward all that is "accidental" and "scattered." "Logic," he insists, "does not deal with the laws of human thought but with these quite objective sentences"; "ethics," too, is "an objective science, and is also purified from anthropomorphism" (443). In this, the trajectory of Hulme's career recalls that of many of his male contemporaries, such as Yeats, Eliot, Pound, and Lewis. The productive modes of modernity, particularly as they erupted in mechanical violence, pushed many members of the avant-garde toward more essentialized modes of resistance. It was in direct response to the threat of German invasion, and to what he saw as pacifist collusion, that Hulme abandoned "humanitarian ethics" for values that are "objective and absolute" (411). As we will find, though, Hulme never completely abandoned his earlier views. Despite his most dogmatic claims, he continued to define his faith as an "attitude." Amidst the flux of war, his rigid spiritual order is founded only upon a more skeptical relativism, a more radical, more rigid engagement with the fallen world (430, 444). What is troubling – and provocative – about this history is the way in which Hulme's dogmatism seems inevitably, and so easily, to arise out of his materialism. The late essays conflate classicism with religion and thus raise the question of whether any materialist order can be flexibly, or ethically, maintained in the modern world.

Hulme's "War Notes" were written in London while he was recuperating from a gunshot wound in the elbow. The writing is emotionally charged and decisively pro-war, but it maintains its openness to less jingoistic theories of war and seems genuinely interested in the ideological coordinates of any dissenting opinions. More radically, Hulme sets himself to the task of understanding "the mind of Germany" (333). He reveals a sincere respect for the country's history and even finds reason to praise Max Scheler as an "exceedingly intelligent German" (335–6). In general, Hulme's attitude is defined by a consistent lack of idealism, nationalistic or otherwise. His support for the cause is determined only by a careful consideration of "consequences":

> In this war, then, we are fighting for no great *liberation* of mankind, for no great jump upward, but are merely accomplishing a work, which, if the nature of things was ultimately "good," would be useless, but which in this actual "vale of tears" becomes from time to time necessary, merely in order that bad may not get worse. (397)

This pragmatism is governed by ideas that should now sound familiar. Hulme sees the war as a manifestation of his greater metaphysical scheme and perhaps all too easily translates the physical reality of the trenches into terms derived from his Bergsonian theory. In other words, he argues that the dynamic tensions of the war will eventually solidify into decisive lines of control. Europe, he claims, "is in a continual flux of which the present war is a highly critical intensification . . . as the war subsides, so will these boundaries be left where it places them, to determine the *form* of Europe during the coming peace" (332). It should be noted, however, that this conception of the war differs greatly from that of the bourgeois futurist. For Hulme, the battle is hardly a glorification of the market's continuous production and consumption. Rather, it figures as an intense state of pressures and resistances; it attests to the horrific stasis of all ideological positions and the potential solidification of violent attitudes.

Most importantly, as Hulme's analysis suggests, the greater battle is neither physical nor even economic, but ideological. The current conflict
masks a much larger war of attitudes and so will continue "long after
the conclusion of peace" (392, 250). He surmises that the Germans have
adopted the bourgeois language of "freedom" and "progress" in order to
defend motives that are strictly imperial. Their seemingly liberal position is
"neither Liberal nor even Liberalising," but conceals a desire to establish a
"European Empire, a Macedonian military empire." Conversely, the British
attitude is directed toward the "maintenance of the Balance of powers,"
the defense of a "European Commonwealth of Nations, a New Hellas"
(336). Hulme compares his country's effort to that of building and repair-
ing sea-walls against the flux; it serves only to resist the romantic extremes
of the modern age (397). Importantly, then, for Hulme, the trenches represent the decisive boundary not only between totality and democracy, but
between romanticism and classicism. The currently unstable situation will
inevitably favor a single ideological order that can either save or damn the
civilized world:

To-day it is a matter of force. What is being settled in the present war is the political,
intellectual, and ethical configuration of Europe for the coming century. All who
can see an inch in front of their nose must realise it. The future is being created
now. (336)

Of course, Hulme's response is to avoid the excesses of either attitude and
to maintain a healthy tension amongst nations. Not surprisingly, then, he
is convinced that England's call for balance is ethically sound.

In his efforts to define ideological alternatives, Hulme spends much of his
energy attacking not Germany, but the British liberal pacifists who refuse
to take his arguments seriously. In fact, he explicitly aligns Germans and
pacifists through his theory of romanticism, arguing that they have been
working together to advance values that undermine the stability of Europe.
Hulme's critique of the civic enemy should sound familiar. The pacifists'
refusal to "appreciate the issues of the war" is informed by historically conditioned prejudices. Their commitment to peace rests upon an "uncritical
acceptance of all the *Liberal* principles" (392). It depends upon a false belief
that all human progress, even that of the German, is "inevitable and of
necessity in one direction" (333). For Hulme, the pacifist values only that
which is relative to life and claims that anything which threatens spontaneous life is an evil. In fact, the pacifist believes that restraint is precisely what
corrupts man and leads him to war. Current hostilities have been fueled
solely by England's resistance to Germany's natural aims. Hulme, of course,
responds that this prejudice is nothing more than a "faded Rousseauism,"

"the remains of middle-class thought of the last century" (249, 395). It rests upon an "entirely false conception of the nature of man" and thus obscures the "true hierarchy of value" (395, 394, 333). More importantly, though, Hulme expresses great anxiety about the "the failure of logic to enact the [pacifist's] proper conversion." National danger lies precisely in this liberal blindness: "It is as if you pointed out to an old lady at a garden party, that there was an escaped lion about twenty yards off – and she were to reply, 'Oh, yes,' and then quietly take another cucumber sandwich" (398).

It is at this moment, when historical circumstances threaten the proposed balance of his metaphysics, that Hulme seems to abandon humanity entirely and adopt more rigid absolutes. This is nowhere more apparent than when the pacifists begin to put Hulme on the defensive. In "War Notes," Hulme initially praises himself for the clarity and patience with which he presents his support of the war. He claims that there is "no obscurity about the facts in this question; the *possibility* of hegemony is sufficiently clear" (403). But his confidence is quickly shaken by the pacifists' opposing claim that any support of the war, including Hulme's own, is fueled only by atavistic impulses and selfish needs. The war, they argue, favors those who would uncritically preserve traditional power structures, primitive brutes who are easily led by their instincts. Hulme is particularly disturbed by a series of lectures in which Bertrand Russell argues that the war effort is driven by "impulses of aggression" (393). As Hulme explains, Russell considers his own "ethical valuations to be objective" and those of the warmongers as only a "quasi-rational ground for the indulgence of impulse" (407). Hulme, of course, tries to dismiss this "largely insolent" dismissal as a sign of Russell's failure to understand the war (394). But he is obviously disturbed by this accusation insofar as it clearly mirrors his own. Both contend that the other argument is based on false, self-serving premises; both insist that these premises appear objective only because of the thoroughness with which they are engaged. Hearing Russell voice his own argument, Hulme is stymied. Relativistic tensions, which once seemed to suggest the possibility of beneficial order, now only affect a hopeless stalemate.

This theoretical impasse pushes Hulme toward an even greater ethical severity and a more rigid religious conclusion. He first argues that the underlying premises of pacifism fail to produce an effective value system. The "rationalist, humanitarian ethic" is not only blind, but dangerous; in its relativism, it affects an "unstable" conception of value. The values upheld by the pacifists are simply those of the "hedonist," and in that lies the all-too apparent destruction of civilization (408). For Hulme, this ridiculous attitude points to only one alternative. He argues that "Regeneration can only be brought about and only be maintained by actions springing from an ethic which from the narrow rationalist standpoint is irrational, being not *relative*, but absolute" (250). History, politics, economics, the great war itself – these all confirm a constant need to restrain and direct our fallen ways. Hulme loudly proclaims his faith: "I believe that the objective conception of ethics, properly realised, leads in the end to a way of looking at things, and to a scale of values differing fundamentally from that of rationalism" (408–9). Ultimately, then, Hulme's debate with the pacifists forces him to assert a complete discontinuity between relativism and the absolute, between the human and the divine. He argues that one can understand value to be either relative or absolute, and that this understanding is bound to the position in which one places "Life" on the hierarchy of values. A belief in the relative nature of value can only coexist with a hierarchy of values in which life is placed highest. This system is "rationalist, humanitarian: the fundamental values are *Life* and *Personality*, and everything has reference to that." Conversely, a belief in the absolute nature of value is bound to a hierarchy in which exist values that are higher than those relative to life. This is "The more heroic or tragic system of ethical values. – Values are not relative only to life, but are objective and absolute, and many of them are *above* life" (411).

Hulme, of course, recognizes that these absolute values have become nearly impossible to uphold. Any significant denial of the self goes against modernity's most fundamental prejudices. He maintains, though, that a serious recognition of life's imperfection forces us to reconsider its significance. The awareness of life's inevitable failure points the way toward a greater, abstract salvation. Thus, Hulme calls for a "CRITIQUE OF SATISFACTION" by which it is proven that the humanist truths are not only "demonstrably false," but "*unsatisfactory*" as well (436, 438). This critique exposes the "Vanity of Desire"; it shows that subjective visions are inherently purposive and thus eternally barred from the absolute. In this, moreover, the critique is the foundation of religious experience. It inspires a new "attitude of renunciation," a "feeling for certain absolutes, which are entirely independent of vital things" (433, 426). As these phrases suggest, however, Hulme's "religious attitude" is based on the same tensions and pressures that have been active throughout his career. The "Perfection" he describes here is dependent upon those materialist processes that also inform his stoic classicism, his radical conservatism, and, of course, his sculptural poetics. In fact, we find here terms that can be traced all the way back to "Cinders": the tragic stasis of the relative, the wishful blindness of nominalism, an all too material hunger. At this final moment, amidst the mud of the trenches and the hail of gunfire, Hulme is all too aware of the mortal condition, its radical sameness and inevitable failure. But now he revolts against that foundation and turns his ethical values against it. At the moment of his work's completion, Hulme reaches the top of his temple and kicks away the ladder.

In the end, one realizes that Hulme's "War Notes" were written primarily as a justification of wartime sacrifice. He insists not only that there are certain values that exist above and beyond those of life, but that the actual sacrifice of life is necessary to maintain them. In other words, the terms of this alternative ethical system are *literally* anti-vital, expressive of the ultimate material limit, death itself:

This ethic is not, therefore, bound to condemn all sacrifice of life. In a sense it may be called *irrational*, if we give the word *rational* the narrow meaning given it by the first ethic, i.e., those values are rational which can be reasonably based on *life*. It is generally associated with a more pessimistic conception of man, and has no belief in Progress. (411)

This ethic is "heroic," Hulme explains, because it upholds all that is "independent of the subjective feelings of particular men" (412). Its defenders are willing to abandon the self-satisfying constructions of liberal humanism for the impersonal perfection of "higher values" (415). This ethic is "tragic" because it entails a recognition of human limitation, of human mortality, as it is constituted by a greater order. The defenders of this ethic not only accept this limitation, but welcome it as the "bearer" of absolute values. Ultimately, though, it is important to recognize how this sacrifice opposes that of bourgeois society and its productive individualism. Like Marinetti and Eliot, Hulme suggests that the moment of death achieves a unity of the individual and its other, of the relative and the absolute. For Hulme, though, this moment is valuable not as a form of creative destruction, as an economic transmutation of human particularity, but as an expression of formal restraint. Death is the ultimate limitation, the final boundary between the mortal and the eternal. It attests to both temporal duration and absolute value. If we trace the arc of Hulme's career to this final moment, then, we find that humanity was valued insofar as it first shaped, then conformed to, and is now fully sacrificed to a greater order. Hulme, of course, was killed in September 1917 by an unexpected burst of enemy shell-fire.

Certainly, Hulme's late work offers a forceful defense of religious dogma. When pushed by the extremities of war, his thoughts on the phenomenal world are twisted into a rigid belief in the absolute corruption of humanity and the need for inhuman restraint. In this, his work most clearly resembles that of his conservative contemporaries. Like Eliot, Pound, and Lewis, he first posits contingency as the basis of knowledge and ethics, but, in the face of mass destruction, demands a more rigid restraint. Indeed, in his preface to Sorel's *Reflections on Violence*, Hulme retranslates classicism in its entirety in terms of this radical pessimism:

What is at the root of the contrasted system of ideas you find in Sorel, the classical, pessimistic, or, as its opponents would have it, the reactionary ideology? This system springs from . . . the conviction that man is by nature bad or limited, and can consequently only accomplish anything of value by disciplines, ethical, heroic, or political. In other words, it believes in Original Sin. (249–50)

This, also, is the impression of Hulme that was the most influential amongst his conservative contemporaries. Eliot, for example, was happy to see that "The classicist point of view has been defined as essentially a belief in Original Sin – the necessity for austere discipline."[24] Even in this final phase, however, Hulme's order remained tangible and thus continued to carry the self beyond itself and into the world. In contrast to Eliot or Pound, this classicist undermines his own potential absolutism by dramatizing the terms of its all too material construction, by disclosing those passions which ensure change. In this, his work preserves the possibility of a more flexible union of spirit and matter. Indeed, Hulme's insistence on provisionality forces us to wonder where he might have directed his interests if he had survived the war.

One would, in fact, like to think that this aspect of Hulme's work may help to establish a similar position from within today's flux. His sense of contingency offers a certain ballast for a world that has even further retreated into the discursive. His flexible ethics provides a more substantial way of negotiating a world that has been given over to its constant mediation. For sure, conversion to this way of thinking is a difficult process, and it seems nearly impossible to preserve its openness. Hulme, however, provides some guidance in one of his final fragments, a description of the subject's first recognition of ethical necessity:

Then having felt for the first time something binding, something objective, which he felt himself, to his own surprise and against his inclination, bound to follow, he may suddenly realise for the first time, that there is such a thing as Ethics. For the first time the real nature of an ethical value is revealed to him. (414)

Once again, Hulme insists upon the importance of touch, "something binding." For him, each touch enforces a recognition of worldly limit, a contiguity that is at once definitive and overpowering. But each touch also suggests an irreducible otherness; this continuous contact offers the relief of possible openness or renewal. In other words, this touch suggests engagement as well as access; it is the point at which community is constituted and potentially reconstructed. Drawing upon this hope, we can now consider two concrete attempts to establish this dynamic order: the next chapter turns to the trenches and one artist's efforts to rethink subjectivity as it is embedded in the communal; the last chapter considers several modern feminists and their efforts to rethink politics as a continuous negotiation of personal desire. We now turn to modernists who, in their unflinching commitment to phenomenological contingency, sought to establish and maintain an alternative social order that is at once knowable and negotiable.

CHAPTER 4

"A fairly horrible business": labor, World War I, and the production of modern art

INTRODUCTION

The story of the Great War begins (if not earlier) with the American Civil War and the invention of the mini-bullet, a rapacious mite that could tear its way through bold Blues and Grays from over 500 yards away. This story continues to 1900 on the shores of South Africa, with the introduction of the small-bore magazine rifle, a weapon that could draw blood from a distance of 2,000 yards. By August 1914, the ability of a prone rifleman to destroy his attacker had increased four-fold. As one enthusiast points out, "In terms of tactical bookkeeping, this meant that 1,000 defenders lying prone and firing at 2,000 attackers had an advantage of 7,500 bullets."[1] Given these statistics, twentieth-century warfare seems defined by progress, driven by advances in the greater effectiveness and faster production of destructive technology. Yet progress has its limits. With later developments, such as the machine-gun, the quick-firing artillery piece, and barbed wire, the world was ready for trench warfare, and nothing less than four years of it. These materials made it much easier to defend a post and thus forced attackers to dig into the ground and fight from a stationary position. Amidst the barrage of artillery, aggressors found themselves stuck in trenches and crouching in shell-holes. Once the bullets stopped and the smoke cleared, it became apparent to anyone still alive that no one had advanced an inch. Paradoxically, twentieth-century warfare, despite its novelty and intense productivity, is notable for its tendency toward stalemate, its incredible stasis and apparent endlessness. Its activity is infinitely varied, yet static.

This paradox was not immediately apparent to those involved in the war effort. Stubborn generals, for example, refused to relinquish the idea of an "offensive war" or the imaginative glory of the "break-through." They had only one solution, an old solution, to the new power of defense – more mass. They sought to counter artillery with greater artillery, to conquer numbers with greater numbers. This great barrage of artillery only destroyed the landscape, clogged roads and train lines – mass grew exponentially, yet positions remained the same.[2] Generals were further stymied by the lure of novelty. Strength was to be multiplied by invention, muscle by machine. New ideas, though, brought new needs, and the site of battle quickly became clogged with all sorts of gadgets and products, most of them unusable. The statistics are quite staggering:

The original BEF [British Expeditionary Force] of 120,000 men went to war with 334 lorries, 133 cars, 166 motorcycles, 300 guns and 63 aircraft. Such a force could easily be supplied without seriously disrupting regular industrial production. But by 1918 the BEF numbered nearly 2,500,000 men, who required 31,770 lorries, 7,694 cars, 3,532 ambulances, 14,464 motorcycles, 6,437 guns and 1,782 aircraft. Supplies were exhausted or destroyed at a prodigious rate, especially during gargantuan offensives. One mile of line required 900 miles of barbed wire, 6,000,000 sandbags, 1,000,000 cubic feet of timber and 360,000 square feet of corrugated iron. "A random selection of statistics," writes Dennis Winter, "shows 6,879 miles of railway specially built in France just for our army; 51,107 rubber stamps to have been issued; 137,224,141 pairs of socks to have been given out; 5,649,797 rabbit skins to have been cleaned and disposed of by the BEF; 30,009 miles of flannelette consumed in the cleaning of rifles."[3]

The war introduced the tank, the submarine, chemical warfare, novelties in communications, aircraft, railways, and automotive transport. The use of asphyxiating gas alone brought with it a whole new series of chemicals, pipes, fittings, screens, projectiles, respirators, rubberized fabrics, and non-splintering glass, not to mention new types of engineers, scientists, and soldiers. In the end, invention and mass combined only to stuff the field. Each attempt to achieve greater mobility added only to the stagnation.

This effect was felt on all levels, not only tactically, but physically, in the burden of weight and mass that each soldier carried. The weight of clothing and necessities issued to a soldier totaled over sixty pounds, enough to stop a man dead in his tracks. The official list includes the following:

Fork	Garters	Holdall
Table knife	Laces	Razor and case
Worsted socks	Soap	Spoon
Woollen vest	Body band	Woollen gloves
Pay book	Haversack	Mess tins
Cap	Great coat	Cotton drawers
Service dress jacket	Cord pantaloons	Puttees
Kilt and apron	Cardigan waistcoat	Cap badge
Braces	Shaving brush	Tooth brush
Hosetops	Comforter cap	Shirts, flannel
Hand towel	Field dressing	Ankle boots
Woollen drawers	Service dress trousers	Titles for shoulder straps
Hair comb	Identity disk (with cord)[4]	

As one soldier wrote, "The walk to the trenches with 'full pack' and a 'few' other things that we need, blanket included, the weight of it all nearly broke the back of 'yours truly' in two."[5] Quarters were also cramped and immobile, with much of the same clutter. One captain compared his tent to a decadent boudoir:

I have a wooden table; and two boxes, with the lids knocked off, placed one upon the other, make my chest of drawers. I sleep on a stretcher, placed upon two boxes. At night I can read or write by the light of a stump of candle; this ought really to be stuck in a bottle, of course, but unfortunately I haven't got a bottle! I even have a bath, which to be exact is a biscuit tin. There is even a bath mat, to wit, an old sack! . . . There is my revolver, my steel helmet, my gas helmet, my hold-all, a tunic, a clothes-brush, and a water bottle all lying just where I happened to drop them last. I shall add the finishing touch tonight: – there is an old steel helmet here, which doesn't belong to anyone in particular: I shall turn this up on the ground by the door of the tent, put some water in it, and chalk "Drink, Puppy, Drink" on it.[6]

Similarly, trains and other heavy machinery, laden with goods and materials, moved at a snail's pace. One soldier describes a two-hour train journey to the trenches that lasted over a day; the journey was "so slow that we literally got out and picked flowers from the bank."[7]

In light of this paradox, World War I seems to represent in exaggerated form the bourgeois economy in general. It offers a stark view of that process, outlined in the first two chapters of this book, whereby the demand for progress and freedom grows mechanical and repetitive. The front is the site of rampant production and consumption, and in its immobility exposes the ultimate reification of those processes. This effect is clarified by a careful look at the notion of "total war," which usually refers to a situation in which no sector of geography or society is immune to the hostility of enemy forces. In his famous treatise, Carl von Clausewitz explains that "war is an act of force, and there is no logical limit to the application of that force. Each side, therefore, compels its opponent to follow suit; a reciprocal action is started which must lead, in theory, to extremes."[8] It is important to recognize, though, that this apparently "limitless" phenomenon found expression only in the modern age, as a direct result of the international growth of the market. In other words, the Great War extended as far as the market did before it; nations could conflate civilian and soldier simply because economics had already done so.[9] England, in fact, could not support the war effort from its own coffers, but it had an effective system of industrial credit in place that was easily diverted toward the trenches. Also, England, "the workshop of the world," could barely produce enough surplus to sustain its troops, but it could call upon a vast overseas empire and a strong network of international relations that included, most obviously, the United States. Finally, the government could not conscript and train sufficient numbers to wage war, but, as the war was essentially fought by diggers and engineers, it easily supplied the labor in demand. It is no wonder that soon after the British declaration of war, Lloyd George expressed the government's commitment to "Business as Usual." He correctly predicted that war would ride the coattails of capitalism, quickly aligning itself with the already transformed sectors of society.

Insofar as this war rested upon the structure of the market, it was more dependent upon the worker than the cavalryman or the commander. In the trenches and at home, success rested upon workers' participation, their willingness to submit to hostile conditions and even more difficult labor. Indeed, given that 80 percent of the British population was working class at the time, it would be impossible not to speak of war morale as working-class morale. Importantly, this exploited majority exhibited an unquestioning loyalty to the war effort. Workers enlisted long before the government's formal propaganda efforts began; shortly after August 1914, the Trades Union Congress announced an industrial truce and thus formally relinquished the right to strike.[10] This commitment cannot be explained by economic hardship, government chicanery, or even widespread nationalist delusion. Rather, the lower classes saw the pain and suffering of war – the labor of war – as an affirmation of their own condition. The battlefield beckoned with a return to creation over labor, and community over commerce – it thus appropriated the promises of what had been originally conceived as a socialist revolution. In other words, the war was a glorified form of work and thus served to uphold economic relations and reinforce submission. In this, it forces us to reconsider the relation between ideology and material production as well as traditional theories of historical change, particularly those based on a romantic revolt of the proletariat.

This chapter, then, first addresses working-class participation in World War I and explores the trenches as a site of intensified labor, the literal production and consumption of human bodies. As I hope to show, a specifically bourgeois logic of pain and redemption was used to conflate the violence of labor with the violence of war. The rhetoric of sacrifice served not only to bind the potentially rebellious worker to the nation, but to ease the worker's calibration to new machines of destruction. Relatedly, art and literature of this time can be conceived as a special form of labor with a unique power to reflect and perhaps shape the paths by which desire finds expression in the material world. "War art" can be defined by its efforts to theorize, if not influence, the individual's productive relation toward other bodies and objects. Wilfred Owen's celebrated war poetry, as it is invested in *romantic* tropes and traditions, expresses a specifically bourgeois productivism torn between the demands of egotism and abnegation. As suggested by Freud's theories of narcissism and war trauma, this productivism could only find expression and affirmation in the violence of World War I: submission and hostility take on greater meaning in the field of battle, as part of a larger, spiritual effort. Henri Gaudier-Brzeska also fought in the trenches, but his art sought to ground subjectivity as it exists, actively and consciously, in relation to material objects. His work in stone, which largely adheres to Hulme's *classical* tenets, advances a theory of labor in which material resistance retards the expenditure of energy and the tendency toward sublimation. Sculpture, in its creation and reception, impedes the desires of the individual, thereby clarifying his power and position as part of a larger, worldly order. Ultimately, a look back at Marx's theory of "species being" suggests that these aesthetic alternatives denote larger alternatives of labor, one linked to the violent productivity of the modern age and the other with a radically different communal order. Most importantly, the former appears as a historical perversion of the latter and thus perhaps can be restored, by way of aesthetics, to its more humane form.

I

The connections between England's war effort and its voracious economy were felt in many ways. At both home and in the trenches, bullets and dollars tended to blur – government and the forces of production were aligned in one gigantic military-economic effort. England, for example, had maintained a naval stranglehold on German ports from the first days of August; many British "cargo" vessels were actually disguised and heavily armed "Q-Ships," and their officers defined all German vessels as necessary targets. The sinking of the Lusitania may have caused outrage and indignation across the world, but, as it was later revealed, the ship was secretly carrying munitions and had defied previous warnings in its area.[11] This relationship between money and munitions was also interestingly expressed in the images of propaganda. The aptly named "Feed the Guns Campaign" and London's "Tank Bank" poetically exposed the deeper pockets of the war effort. In the case of the latter, civilians purchased government bonds by literally depositing money into the side of a tank parked in Trafalgar Square.[12] For women, the connection between war and production was suggested in domestic terms; posters and placards depicted women sewing, gardening, and caring for machinery in the factory. One famous painting, in fact, depicted a rosy-cheeked and aproned munitionette cradling a shell as if it were a baby.[13]

For the lower classes, though, the war experience simply extended the labor of home. J. H. Leigh, a foot soldier, reports that his duties were "just the same as a tradesman in civic life, we worked nine hours a day, the Engineers do everything there, do all repairs to road, building barracks and married quarters, run the searchlight, run two ammonia plants for freezing meat, look after all the apparatus for pumping both fresh and sea water . . ."[14] Despite the need to train soldiers for the most basic use of artillery, the war demanded that laborers be laborers. The work of the infantryman was the work of the miner and the engineer. "Fighting" was a matter of pipes, ditches, walls, and machinery. Indeed, one of the war's greatest success stories is that of General Sir Herbert Plumer and his 2nd Army. Plumer had been assigned the near impossible task of overtaking the German-held Messines Ridge from the low ground. His troops, however, were perfectly suited to the job, as amongst them were several Welsh units composed of skilled miners. Plume abandoned traditional military tactics altogether and planned, brilliantly, to blow the ridge right off the ground. On 7 June 1917, at precisely 3:10 a.m., nineteen huge mines, containing nearly a million pounds of ammonal, were exploded beneath the Germans. The blast was clearly heard in England, seventy miles away, and the Germans went down in "tremendous columns of smoke, dirt, and flame."[15]

The work at the front, of course, was undeniably alienated work. Volunteers were tagged and positioned in terms of class. Those from the upper and middle sectors of society were quickly dressed and housed as officers, while those from the lower were hurried off to the trenches. According to Gerard J. DeGroot, "Class distinctions were essential to a smooth-functioning army. Army life was merely another form of the manager-worker relationship. This was particularly true in this war, in which the drudgery of trench life had much in common with the monotonous dehumanization of the factory."[16] J. M. Bourne, in fact, suggests that the BEF's command structure reproduced the logic of the factory's "line management," in which only the front infantry bore the burden of heavy labor.[17] Letters and diaries, in fact, rarely describe scenes of battle or even personal emotions. Page after page bemoan the back-breaking work and dull monotony of repetitive tasks. Take, for example, the following lament:

Tonight I think I shall be in charge of a party carrying such things as picks & shovels, sandbags, wine etc. up to the line. The men will be very heavily laden, and they will be carrying the stuff through a narrow trench, well over the ankles in mud. The job will probably take six or seven hours, and I shall not be sorry when we have got it over. The men are dead before the job is half done.[18]

Even the heat of battle was conjoined with the misery of work. Shooting and shoveling were often of a piece. Another soldier writes,

At last word to move – packs – left mine – packs again – then along trench and word to climb and over into fire trench – good to be moving – excitement now tremendous – the shrill and explosion of shells – the air seemed charged with noise and electrical. Fire trench – cleaned bolt of rifle – passed message – looking over parapet – half left wood – all in a haze of smoke across which passed shadowy figures – not much to see – wounded coming in – hopping . . .[19]

In such accounts, the word "duty" begins to take on another meaning altogether. Romantic sentiments be damned, one's duty was one's job. As George Fainstone clarified, in a letter to his wife, "We cannot leave our business. We have got to do our duty!"[20]

    The transition from factory to front was easy, if disheartening, for lower-class recruits. Workers, already conditioned to a lifetime of suffering and drudgery, quickly adapted to the alienating terms of the front. They brought to their service a sense of solidarity generated by common hardship and a self-deprecating sense of humor made it easier to respond to scenes of death and mutilation. Letters and memoirs, in fact, do not necessarily reveal an increasing sense of apathy; listless accounts of dismemberment and decay were sent home during all stages of the war. Unquestioning sacrifice and deference was the norm from the outset, and not despite the fact that trench life presented all of the dangers of the factory with the decent chance of a bullet through the skull.[21] The war, in fact, often appeared as nothing more than a hungry machine that drew few distinctions between the materials it processed. Soldiers understood the front as the site of industrial as well as human processing; their own bodies served as fuel, tool, and waste. Their greatest fears simply pushed wartime realities one step further; for example, widespread rumors of the processing of battlefield corpses was most likely based on the "Bone and Fat Bucket" campaign already underway back at home (Figure 2). According to Paul Fussell, one legend "held that fats were so scarce in Germany because of the naval blockade that battlefield corpses were customarily taken back by the Germans to be rendered at special installations." The British, it was rumored, had their own ways of dealing with fallen soldiers: fanciful images of a giant refuse plant – aptly named "Destructor" – poetically combined the threat of war with the threat of industry.[22]

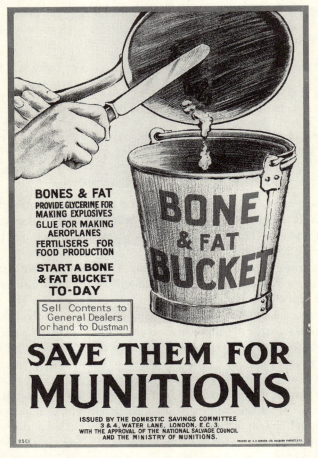

Figure 2 *Bone & Fat Bucket . . . Save them for Munitions*, 1914–1918.

Alongside labor, machinery was a decisive factor in shaping and sub-ordinating the troops. By mid-1916, General Haig and his commanding officers were chanting their one great mantra, "artillery conquers, infantry occupies."[23] With this strategy, they expressed a larger switch from a "human-centered" to a "weapons-centered" view of war. Soldiers were not excluded from frontline activity, but they were made to conform to the inhuman sizes, shapes, and power of heavy artillery. This point, of course, was not lost on the troops themselves. As Arthur Hugh Sidgwick explained, "The fact is, the war is become a fairly horrible business . . . It is really become a triumph of machines over men, & there's no kind of romance or beauty or decency in it any longer – not even any excitement, as the noise & the risk & the stink is there all the time." In another letter, Sidgwick writes that the mechanization of warfare had taken on a life of its own; he can scarcely imagine any other force impeding its growth. "At present," he claims, "I don't see any limit to the destructive capacities of artillery . . . The only question is, can we get an extrinsic limit? Will the civilized nations say they've had enough, & tell their gunners to stop? If not, we're in the Erewhon position: we've been beaten by our machines."[24]

The union of flesh and machinery most often took the form of senseless death. Soldiers were exposed to a constant barrage of metal that seemed not only hostile, but meaningless. Less obviously, but just as deadly, was the slow, painful process whereby the soldier-worker was forced to merge his vital qualities with the hard forms of the rifle, the shell, the tank, the aircraft. To survive his own machinery, he needed to adjust to masses, volumes, and speeds never before encountered in the civilian realm. For example, preparations for the Battle of the Somme demanded field-gun, howitzer and trench mortar for every seventeen yards of front. The movement of the heavy guns alone took weeks. Special pits and light railways were constructed to move the artillery forward. Over two-million shells were stockpiled and 1,508,652 of them fired during the first seven days alone. For communication purposes, 50,000 miles of cables were laid, 7,000 miles of which were buried well below ground level.[25] Then, during the battle itself, all of this material was set in motion over the rugged frontline terrain at speeds that were either too fast or too slow for human nerves and muscles. The precision that the machines demanded in their preparation was all the more impossible to meet during combat. This was made painfully apparent on the first day of the Somme, in a battle which one historian calls "the single worst day in the entire military history of the Somme."[26] General Haig and his subordinate, Rawlinson, left little up to their troops, the first group composed mostly of Kitchener's inexperienced and poorly trained volunteers. Their planned attack, perversely rational in its proposed execution, excluded all possibilities of human decision-making or spontaneity. After an initial artillery barrage that was meant to destroy German wire and trenches, the guns were to move from a general to a zoned attack, obliterating the enemy line at a given distance and then moving slowly forward at precisely timed intervals. Behind this creeping barrage of machine and metal, the infantry was supposed to advance, making hay of the few surviving Germans and taking over the territory piece by piece. Of course, the plan was far too complex and too rigid for any soldier, trained or untrained, to carry out successfully.

It was designed for machines, not men. Gun crews fired according to their strict time and distance tables, while the infantry either fell behind, thus left victim to the surviving Germans now returning from underground to their parapets, or ahead, left victim to their own artillery as it eventually caught up to them. By the end of the day, 57,000 British soldiers had been hit. Twenty thousand of them were dead.

These aspects of trench warfare suggest that the war's ultimate result was neither disillusionment, a lost generation, nor even the liberation of class, gender, or colony. Rather, the war seemed to affect, both at home and at the front, a greater conformity of man to machine, a more complete proletarianization of society as a whole. Training, of course, entailed depersonalization and regimentation as part of a larger, semi-mechanical unit.[27] As one lieutenant explained, "The first thing is to get them into a groove of doing things smartly and well, and without 'intelligent' thinking of orders before they obey them."[28] But it was the experience of battle itself that affected this process of mechanization, destroying all thoughts but the most pragmatic. After only days of battle, the average soldier ceased to interpret his actions in terms of high ideals; his mind was diverted toward the daily activity of survival, providing food, shelter, and protection for his body. By necessity, his gestures became rigid, abrupt, and unconscious; his face dull and blank. Arthur Hugh Sidgwick, for example, explains how working with the machines of war became a purely "automatic process." He claims that "there is no time for any process of thought, & that the only chance is to get the process automatic. The result is a little, outlying enclave of automatism in one's brain that has no relation to anything else." More ominously, he writes, "We simply sit at our machines, and mould our mind to them: the more we like them, the better."[29]

Eventually, soldiers resembled unconscious automatons, without thought or fear. As Colonel Sir Lionel Hall writes to his father,

It may comfort you to know that I have practically no fear out here. It is not bravery, it is simply an inexplicable fact. I have been half buried by shells bursting within a few yards but I am probably very busy at the time and so did not notice it . . . My only trouble of any importance is wet feet.[30]

Many, of course, embraced this transformation and willfully ignored the significances of their situation. Thinking itself grew painful; one needed to respond to mechanical horror with an even more rigid mechanization. The decent soldier was one who was able to lose track of himself, his past and its significance. Robert Peyton Hamilton, for example, neatly divides his frontline self from his home self. Expressing a common theme of self-alienation, he writes,

All this tends to make one lose one's personality and think always of the job; and, Governor dear, men dying so often and so near makes you think very small beans of human beings . . . There's no danger for the most conceited of infantrymen to think overmuch of 'emselves, provided they have a continuous dose of trench. Likely (and I hope soon) a rest from sandbags & blood will make me as swanky as ever; but at the moment, like the rest of 'em, I'm clinging to 2nd R. P. H. [his initials] by the skin of my teeth.[31]

A related theme was the change that occurred in one's hands; soldiers simply failed to recognize them as their own. According to Lieutenant S. A. Knight,

You have told me to write more about myself. I begin to think I am only what I see . . . I have been an absolute disfigurement to the landscape for days now – must spend some of my rest time digging myself out of my mud – it will be a long job getting to the original S. A. K. [his initials]. Have got a new pair of hands I don't recognize a bit. Will be permanently hard before long.[32]

In the end, labor and violence divorced man from himself. His own actions were no longer recognizable as his own.

Ultimately, the war experience served to affect a negative community of suffering and dehumanization. In the trenches, social equality was established through the complete subjugation of all. The bonds between soldiers were forged in a collective estrangement; together, they resembled a quivering, cowering mass. As one claims, "When you have ducked the same shell with a man over and over again, you develop a sense of comradeship, which you cannot get in any other way."[33] Another, lying wounded on the battlefield, recognized that the "splendid spirit of comradeship" was "born out of the horrors and hardships we had faced together."[34] Eric J. Leed defines the nature of this brotherhood as a horrific inversion of true equality:

The change of character experienced in war is synonymous with a social descent, "learning how to become a common man." The comradeship of war comes from a common sense of proletarianization, subjection to common burdens of never-ending labor. The men in this war are only anonymous fellow-sufferers of an "endless industrial process."[35]

The World War I belligerent partook in a solid community of fate, but one forged in fear, neurosis, and death. His hopeful volition gave way to the indiscriminate muck and blood of the trenches. The values of heroism and brotherhood made way for a common apathy.

In fact, for both soldier and civilian, the war was defined by an inability to distinguish between actions undertaken and actions undergone. In the end, the soldier-worker was both a complicit agent and a helpless victim; the effects of his activity appeared alien to his own volition. The end result was a broken passivity, an abject impotence and dejected privacy. A letter from Arthur Hugh Sidgwick helps to define this malaise:

It is not funk – or at least not like ordinary funk: the thing is too impersonal. If an actual foe was thrusting at you with a bayonet, it might be different: as it is, you know that the enemy is simply shelling a point or an area, and doesn't care twopence about you personally. Nor is it excitement. It is more a dull feeling of strain and depression, always (I fear) with the underlying suggestion that if he <u>should</u> happen to hit you, either it will all be over quickly & you will be out of trouble, or if you get wounded you will see England again.[36]

This "funk," at once devastating and impersonal, excruciating and mechanical, informs many letters from the front. Soldiers can barely describe, let alone analyze, the causes of their degradation, yet it shapes most of their thoughts. C. E. Montague offers another succinct description:

unaggressive, unoriginal, anti-extreme, contemptuous of all "hot-air" and windy ideas. instead of contracting a violent new sort of heat [he] . . . simply went cold . . . a Lucifer cold as a moon prompted him listlessly not to passionate efforts of crime, but to self-regarding and indolent apathy.[37]

This retreat to an essentially defensive character, in which the individual defines himself only as a survivor of implacable forces, suggests the victory of a power greater than that of any single nation. In fact, even the most casual look at the post-war world suggests a triumph of capital that continues to erode even the most rigid national borders. The returning soldier-worker, now afflicted with the impossibility of violence, no longer threatened the terms of his exploitation. The war had purged him of all revolutionary or anarchic feeling and thus purged the marketplace of any resistance.[38] As we will find, World War I began with the worst narcissism of the bourgeois subject, with the celebration of the individual life over and above the material world. But this romanticism, once embodied in physical form, returns with a vengeance to confront that subject. The history of the war entails a process in which the forces unleashed by the competitive capitalist ego take on an oppressive life and will of their own – as machines, as nations, as other soldiers – thus establishing their apparent permanence.

II

Despite the war's relation to the market, war morale – as it swept both upper and lower classes – had little to do with the possibility of financial gain. It was quite clear to most interested parties that conflict could only impede economic growth. English businessmen, for example, saw tensions with Germany as a hindrance to free trade and an obstacle to new markets. War would only endanger Britain's already precarious market position, which by 1914 consisted primarily of a financial go-between for potential belligerents. For the working class, volunteer pay was much less than that of all but the most impoverished workers. War offered all of the hardships that labor already entailed with the added possibility of getting oneself "scragged." But if the war did not directly support the economy, it served it ideologically, both as a direct confirmation of national might and a more subtle affirmation of modern productive relations and their effects. The scene of battle redeemed not only the physical pain and alienation of everyday life, but also the internal conflicts that define the modern subject. The image of man against man at once resolved and relieved tensions that can only be called sadomasochistic; it reconciled all-too bourgeois demands for both authority and liberation, restriction and release.

It has long been understood that England's troops entered World War I in a conscious attitude of revolt. For many soldiers, both middle and lower class, the war offered a potential triumph of spirit over matter, life over living death. It was to be fought in the name of vitality, revolution, and change, against a world governed by false relations and empty laws. For the young recruits, idealists to a man, the only life worth living was a life of one's own creation. The soul's vital activity, its pure willfulness, was the source of both truth and beauty. As one fresh recruit exclaims, "I can't describe all the things I've seen. We live by the hour and by Jove! It's breathless."[39] Another declares, "God knows what we might get up to, everything was so strange and entirely unconventional . . . we could have been in a different land."[40] Rupert Brooke's war sonnets, it appears, gave expression to a common joy:

> Now, God be thanked Who has matched us with His hour,
>   And caught our youth, and wakened us from sleeping,
> With hand made sure, clear eye, and sharpened power,
>   To turn, as swimmers into cleanness leaping,
> Glad from a world grown old and cold and weary,
>   Leave the sick hearts that honour could not move,
> And half-men, and their dirty songs and dreary,
>   And all the little emptiness of love!

Here, we find life purified and renewed by the spirit at war. A hygienic perfection of body and soul, a perpetual youth, is bestowed upon those in battle. A greater love, a more complete love, infuses a "world grown old and cold and weary."[41]

More specifically, the glories of war were sought in opposition to the empty transactions and dirty spoils of finance. The war was meant to provide relief from economic relationships and the conflicts they entailed, replacing instrumentality with immediacy, contracts with comradeship, accumulation with a glorious freedom. *For the individual*, battle was the site of pure expression, the antithesis of self-interest and self-consciousness. It represented the triumphs of emotion and activity for their own sake, apart from the restricted channels of commerce. The following account expresses a common dissatisfaction and an equally common solution:

When war was declared in September 1914, I was still seventeen, although I had started work. Everyone else in the very large office where I worked was considerably older; most of my colleagues were in the sixties or seventies. All the windows were kept shut in the large hall where a hundred men worked and the air was thick with dust and senile decay . . . I felt office life was hopeless. I longed for the open. No smoking was allowed so the rest of the office chewed tobacco and took snuff and spat upon the floors in a disgraceful fashion which made me sick. A cracked old voice from my department governor would request me to close the window if I dared to open it surreptitiously. "The wind is cutting my neck like a knife," he would say. What a pity it could not cut his head off, I thought. This had gone on for eighteen months, when war was declared.

Here was my golden opportunity for a healthy open air life . . . I promptly asked permission to go off and join the army . . . It was a great adventure – a change from the dull monotony of city office life where all was so safe and certain, where the chance of promotion was meagre and life could be mapped out for years ahead.[42]

Similarly, *for the group*, battle represented unmediated expression, communication and thus community between once-isolated subjects. Life during wartime was honest; comradeship was natural and spontaneous, free of the mechanized relations found in the factory or the office. Another early account:

It is a wonderful life out here, and a good life to have to live. There are many strange things about it. One is the extraordinary sympathy between men here. A man going up into the trenches meets a wounded man coming out. You say about four words to each other, and then part, feeling like brothers. Another thing is that you become quite childish again. I have a very good and loyal platoon sergeant, and as we marched the platoon back into the wood again, we both felt like children off for a holiday, and were laughing and chattering like anything.

In a later letter, this soldier laments the possibility of demobilization, "I don't like the thought of becoming a slave to Science again." He writes, "Thanks to the war I have broken free from it, and have been much happier since doing so."[43]

However, alongside the desire for renewal, for romantic transvaluation, war morale can be linked to another, seemingly antithetical, cause. New recruits just as often heeded the call for solid principles and traditional values. National borders as well as national traditions needed to be protected by an unquestioning sense of duty and committed sacrifice. In this, England presented itself as the last bastion of enlightenment values and bourgeois decency. King George, for example, initiated deployment in 1914 by telling troops, "I have implicit confidence in you, my soldiers. Duty is your watchword, and I know your duty will be nobly done."[44] Similarly, Lloyd George, in his famous Queen's Hall, speech, proclaims,

We have been living in a sheltered valley for generations. We have been too comfortable and too indulgent, many, perhaps, too selfish, and the stern hand of Fate has scourged us to an elevation where we can see the great everlasting things that matter for a nation – the great peaks we had forgotten, of Honour, Duty, Patriotism, and, clad in glittering white, the great pinnacle of Sacrifice pointing like a rugged finger.[45]

In this, Brooke's "cleanness" also symbolizes modest virtues, the "good form" of the public school. For many soldiers, battle suggested renewal, but just as often figured as a test of reason, compromise, and self-abnegation. In fact, many of the greatest disasters of the British war effort can be blamed on an all-too stubborn dependence on method and order. Officers worked strictly within a military tradition that had lost touch with the realities of modern warfare. In the name of "fairness," they refused to take risks, to encourage individual initiative, or even to surprise the enemy.[46]

   It would thus appear that war morale was informed by contradictory demands: a desire for release from the empty formalism of society and an apparent commitment to that very formalism, to reason and decorum. Tellingly, England presented its aims in terms of both progress and stability, freedom as well as order (incidentally, it accused its enemy, Germany, of both unrestrained chaos and a heartless, bureaucratic formalism). These contradictory attitudes, however, seem to derive from one and the same source. The desire for release and the desire for restraint are mutually dependent and decisively bourgeois. As we saw in chapter 1, the bourgeois of this period is a contradictory being, defined by an odd struggle against others of his kind. His pride exists in opposition to that of his neighbor; he asserts his individualism against a class composed of individuals. Self-love and self-loathing, then, commingle in relations that are at once senseless and compulsive. Moreover, while the bourgeois is celebrated for his initiative, his entrepreneurial spirit, he must abnegate, he must deny and repress. He must be proud as well as prostrate, revolutionary as well as humble. By August 1914, this largely internal struggle had apparently become too much to bear. Bourgeois ideology sought renewal on the battlefield, where its paradoxes were clarified and confirmed. Senseless competition, inexplicable pain and alienation, not to mention an unbearable inner torment – these found affirmation in the various configurations of international hostility. Modris Eksteins, in fact, defines the events of 1914–18 as "the civil war of the European middle class."[47] Similarly, Eric J. Leed calls the war an "expression of the bourgeois flight from itself, the projection of self-hatred, from within to without." As he explains, "the declaration of war could be greeted as the elevation of conflict from the sphere of economic life, where it was disruptive of community, to the level of a contest that at once demonstrated national solidarity."[48]

This phenomenon was strongly reinforced by a general protestant tradition which, as we saw in Eliot's work, defined personal sacrifice as the only path to glory. Amidst the dead and dying, soldiers found encouragement in the words and imagery of the Bible, the Book of Common Prayer, and, of course, *Pilgrim's Progress*. These texts helped to affirm the notion that perfection exists only in pain and violence; battle was valued as the scene of intense suffering and sacrifice. Well-versed soldiers found themselves "electrified" and "transformed" by frontline experience; first bloodshed was known as "baptism by fire."[49] As Canon J. H. Skrine explained,

War is not murder . . . war is sacrifice. The fighting and killing are not of the essence of it, but are the accidents, though the inseparable accidents; and even these, in the wide modern fields where a soldier rarely in his own sight sheds any blood but his own, where he lies on the battle sward not to inflict death but to endure it – even these are mainly purged of savagery and transfigured into devotion. War is not murder but sacrifice, which is the soul of Christianity.[50]

In this celebration of "endured" violence, we find a failing ideology seeking support for its own demands. This violence gives weight and significance to the abstract competition of business. Physical struggle materializes the financial hostilities of the bourgeoisie, confirms as it concretizes the absurdity of struggle against others of one's kind. Moreover, this struggle ameliorates an alienation and suffering that can no longer be justified at home. In war, in the effective chain of command, submission and hostility take on greater meaning; pain and labor are redeemed, their effects made tangible as part of a larger, divine effort. H. A. Vachell's *The Hill* offers the following bit of propaganda,

To die young, clean, ardent; to die swiftly, in perfect health; to die saving others from death, or worse – disgrace – to die scaling heights; to die and to carry with you into the fuller ampler life beyond, untainted hopes and aspirations, unembittered memories, all the freshness and gladness of May – is not that cause for joy rather than sorrow?[51]

As we can see here, material violence offers both precision and significance to an otherwise meaningless pain. The moment of physical struggle, removed from consciousness, from psychology, presents a "fuller ampler life." Death itself serves as testament to the competitive bourgeois ego, to the truth of romantic being.

Importantly, this violence affirms on two levels; as in the marketplace, personal pain is redeemed through the larger category of the nation. Each blow is a confirmation of the individual life and the allegiances to which it belongs. The flow of blood anoints the life now passing as it washes the community as a whole; the corpse represents the perfection of being, the final unity of self, as well as an ultimate sacrifice to a greater order. As Lloyd George explains in his famous speech,

> I see amongst all classes, high and low, shedding themselves of selfishness, a new recognition that the honour of the country does not depend merely on the main-tenance of its glory on the stricken field, but also in protecting its homes from stress . . . The great flood of luxury and sloth which had submerged the land is receding, and a new Britain is appearing.

Here, bourgeois self-discipline is equated with self-abnegation, which quickly leads to the "towering pinnacle of Sacrifice pointing like a rugged finger to heaven" (288–9). This turn toward abstract ideals, particularly the nod to heaven, was typical and quite devious. The end of "selfishness" is nothing less than the end of self, death for the nation. Personal pain is translated into a glorious martyrdom.

Importantly, the affirmative experience of war also involves a complex process of identification. The subject's unbearably conflicted desires find relief in a process by which he submits as well as identifies with various images of authority. For example, the rattled soldier often sought coherence in the potent images of the nation and the autonomous machine. These entities, precisely because they consisted of human power in an alienated form, easily met his complex demands. Man, split from himself, finds security in the hostile objects of his own making. With machinery, the very force that threatens to disrupt subjectivity offers a renewed sense of wholeness; the very cause of pain and alienation provides a false balm of wholeness and integrity. As Leed explains, even though soldiers feared machines, "identification of himself with autonomous technology became a source of personal power and authorization. Through this identification he could acquire the status of factotum and appendage of a suprapersonal power that lent those who derived their identities from it a renewed, if 'amoral' potency."[52]

As frequently, the activity of identification found its focus in another soldier, and, more often than not, that soldier was an enemy. Just as recruits within a single troop were stripped of their distinguishing features, so were men from opposing armies. On the field of battle, in the anonymous muck of the trenches, the forces of identification were given complete freedom. One's friend, one's enemy, the Bosche and the Brit, these grew indistinguishable as self-struggle was cast out into the world and made whole. In this, the torment of the split self was directed outward, where man truly struggled against himself. Self-love and self-hatred mingled in the moment of battle. Most obviously, these identifications were informed by common history and background; despite propaganda efforts, soldiers never completely abandoned pre-war sympathies and relations. In addition, the ability to identify was fueled by the dehumanizing and reductive effects of warfare; letters and poems frequently hint at the empathic bonds forged out of mutual fear and pain. Finally, it could be argued that identification was most intensely inspired by the need to preserve one's sense of self-worth. A self-preserving "narcissism" was often displaced onto images of a sympathetic or, more desperately, all-powerful enemy.[53] Freud's post-war work helps to clarify this phenomenon. His theories of narcissism and ego-idealism outline a process by which the torments of the bourgeois self, through the process of identification, find expression and affirmation in a violent world.

In many of his post-war writings, Freud grapples with narcissism's wider implications. The phenomenon confounds his previous distinction between ego instincts and libidinal instincts; it exposes complex processes by which desire is channeled back and forth between the self and others. Freud's work here begins with the issue of infant narcissism. Self-preserving ego-instincts, he claims, can be transformed into sexual instincts through the presence of a caregiver; an "anaclitic" process blurs the distinction between the selfish ego and, as is often the case, a maternal object. Object-love, he explains, is "derived from the child's original narcissism and thus corresponds to a transference of that narcissism to the sexual object."[54] Freud's work, however, also points to an opposing phenomenon, in which libido is directed back toward the ego. This secondary narcissism, a regression really, figures as an introjection of what the ego would like to be and thus typically derives from an image of paternal power. In response to castration anxiety, in the desire for stable ego-boundaries, the subject identifies with the father and establishes a stable ideal inside himself toward which he directs his libido. Of course, this ego-ideal is intimately related to the superego and thus figures as a powerful source of internal repression and socialization. Freud writes, "the formation of an ideal heightens the demands of the ego and is the most powerful factor favouring repression" ("Narcissism," 558).

Yet, as Freud argues, the desire to be the father is tainted by feelings of hostility. The subject at once envies and resents the paternal image; his narcissistic identification is always ambivalent, colored by feelings of anger and jealousy. It follows, then, that the ego's relationship to his ego-ideal, or super-ego, is also ambivalent and marked by a guilty resentment. The ego, in other words, has established its enemy within and thus reproduces, internally, its love–hate relationship with the outside world.[55] For our purposes, it is important to recognize that insofar as the ego can internalize this ambivalent relation, it can just as easily project it back out into the world. The inner turmoil of the ego, its confused pride and humility, in turn finds expression in created social relations. For Freud, these tensions universally reveal themselves in organized group formations. Ego-idealism gives way to the image of the leader, while masochism and guilt are satisfied by the strict chain of command.[56] It is apparent, though, that this internal ambivalence finds more direct expression in the experience of physical pain. Insofar as the individual seeks release as well as stability, insofar as if he likes to imagine himself as all powerful as well as utterly submissive, he finds immediate satisfaction in the experience of real bodily injury.

Freud points toward this conclusion in his various writings on war traumas and neuroses. When the body suffers, he claims, libido is diverted from its typical objects toward the site of bodily damage. There, it is at once released and restrained ("dammed-up"), causing a sensation both pleasurable and painful. "Two facts," he claims, "have been stressed by psycho-analytic research":

firstly, that mechanical agitation must be recognized as one of the sources of sexual excitation, and secondly, that painful and feverish illnesses exercise a powerful effect, so long as they last, on the distribution of the ego. Thus, on the one hand, the mechanical violence of the trauma would liberate a quantity of sexual excitation which, owing to the lack of preparation for anxiety, would have a traumatic effect; but, on the other hand, the simultaneous physical injury, by calling for a narcissistic hypercathexis of the injured organ, would bind the excess of excitation.[57]

We should probably dismiss Freud's shady biologism, as well as his desire to understand this phenomenon as representative of a larger metaphysical conflict between Eros and Thanatos. But we cannot deny the significance of his claim that violence serves both to release and bind the subject. The experience of the wound sets off a complex process of identification, one that gives shape and meaning to an already present inner torment. Freud, for example, notes how the subject tends to preserve his physically painful experiences, often by introjecting the inflicting object. This experience and re-experience of the original injury serves to ground an otherwise abstract anxiety. As he explains, physical injury "works as a rule against the development of a neurosis" (*Beyond*, 11). Here, as we will find in the poetry of Wilfred Owen, physical pain relieves the pain of the internally wounded. Love and loathing meet at the moment of bloodshed; the subject is both freed and restrained in the act of violence.

Ultimately, while Freud tends to universalize these processes, he recognizes how they are shaped by social contingencies and institutional frameworks. The ego's relation to its ideal expresses the subject's relation to a particular community. As this ego finds "significant analogies" for itself, it establishes the subject as both an individual and part of a particular social group (*Group*, 39). As we will find, this recognition sheds particular light on the issue of homosexuality and the seemingly homosexual experiences of the trenches. Several important studies, most notably Paul Fussell's *The Great War and Modern Memory* and Adrian Caesar's *Taking it Like A Man*, have tried to locate homosexuality at the center of the war's violence. In most cases, however, this work preserves essentialized notions of homosexual desire, whether it is given positive expression in the all-male relations of the front or whether it is described as transmuted, by way of repression, into violence itself.[58] Freud's discussions of narcissism and violence inevitably lead to the topic of homosexuality, but they consistently confound any essential notion of same-sex desire or its relation to violence. At times, he argues that narcissism allows identification with a powerful figure of the same sex and thus results in the formation of a common, social ideal.[59] Elsewhere, though, Freud traces the genesis of homosexuality to an original identification with the mother or, conversely, an initial hatred and rivalry between brothers that is transformed into a narcissistic identification.[60] In light of these varied instances, Freud seems to maintain that homosexual and homosocial relations cannot be reduced to a single psychological mechanism or primordial element. These tendencies, and the politics they entail, have their own history and respond to larger social changes. Similarly, we will find that while Wilfred Owen's narcissistic identifications are clearly linked to his homosexuality, the two cannot be equated. Many factors – political, economic, and social – inform his psychic relations and produce similarly violent results in many who do not readily identify with homosexuality. In other words, as I hope to show, his war experience is typical in that it expresses a specifically bourgeois, rather than homosexual, crisis.[61]

Consequently, we will need to recognize that the very act of narcissistic identification serves a specifically bourgeois subjectivity. Projection both extends and limits; it is an act of release and restraint, self-love and self-denial. In this, moreover, the act of identification confounds representative activity with material activity. The subject fixates upon that which affirms his inner conflicts, but in identifying with such, and only such, he transforms the external order of things. The situation is clearly circular and supports the unimpeded production (and reproduction) of the ego. We should perhaps recall Hulme's critique of an unchecked romanticism: the ego, profoundly convinced of his own perfection, transforms reality in order to reflect that perfection. Freud describes narcissists in a similar way; their relation to the world is marked by "an over-estimation of the power of their wishes and mental acts, the 'omnipotence of thoughts', a belief in the thaumaturgic force of words, and a technique for dealing with the external world – 'magic' – which appears to be a logical application of these grandiose premises" ("Narcissism," 547). In other words, insofar as the bourgeois ego is ruled by conflict, it can only "know" the material world in violence. In the process of identification, it wreaks havoc on the forms it encounters. Vitality exists only in the frenzy of slaughter; stability bears the grotesque features of death. With this in mind, we can now turn to one of the greatest martyrs of them all, Wilfred Owen, and more closely explore identification as an aesthetic activity. The violent externalization of bourgeois subjectivity is all too neatly mirrored in Owen's poetic transformation from suffering artist to suffering soldier-poet. His famous war poems, which have been praised for their compassion toward men and the world, seem to embody and affirm a larger crisis of modernity.

III

One detects a certain cruelty in the series of influences that led Owen to war. First, there was a domineering mother who preached the evils of the body. In the family Bible, several foreboding passages are underlined with Wilfred's name scrawled besides them. From the Book of Timothy, we find, "If we suffer, we shall also reign with him." In another, St. Paul exhorts us to "endure hardness as a good soldier of Jesus Christ."[62] The young Owen was taught to mortify the flesh and suffer his lusts. Anguish was equated with grace, endurance with salvation. According to Owen's brother,

Wilfred was beginning to be convinced that high attainment and the expected period of life were impossible to combine, and he was inclined when working well to fear it denoted early death; and when feeling robust and healthy to fear that this was a signal of lack of talent and a negation of all his hopes.[63]

But, for Owen, the rewards of Christian life proved too intangible. In retreat from this rather abstract system, he eventually turned to whom all suffering young artists turn: the sickly Keats. He read Rossetti's *Life of Keats* and "turned hot and cold and trembly over the first haemorrhage scene." A letter explains:

I never guessed till now the frightful travail of his soul towards Death; never came so near laying hold of the ghastly horror of his mind at this time. Rossetti guided my groping hand right into the wound, and I touched, for one moment the incandescent Heart of Keats.[64]

With Keats, Owen traded in his evangelicalism for a much more palpable, worldly beauty; he replaced the suffering Christ with the suffering romantic artist. In the moment of torment, the living self is both activated and proclaimed; personal pain is at once redemptive and expressive.

But even Keats represented only one stage in a much larger movement toward the material world. After all, the romantic attitude is as immaterial as the Christian. While its truths are much more personal, secular, they do not exist beyond the isolated flights of the imagination. Luckily, before Owen could test his poetic mettle, he was able to admire the beauty of real bodily pain. From October 1911 to February 1913, he worked as a lay assistant to a local vicar, and his duties included visits to the sick and poor. His letters outline a growing infatuation with these figures, an odd blend of pity and desire. In one, he describes a "scar-backed mining lad" who represents "Christianity in action." Another boy is pierced in pain, yet "his conduct, conversation, expression of countenance, during meeting, bids fair to speak louder to my soul than the thunderings of twenty latter day Prophets."[65] Importantly, Owen equally relishes the very act of describing this torment. After working through a depiction of a particularly miserable child, he defines his writing, not without glee, as "smooth and polished, formal, labeled, mechanical callousness!"[66] Here, as we will find in his war poetry, the very act of writing produces a sensation at once pleasurable and violent; the poet writes in order to master and mimic the subject in pain. Lyrical expression itself relieves a previously inner conflict; it reveals as it reconciles the tormented desires of the self. The lyrical voice at once asserts and denies the authority of the speaker, heals as it torments an already suffering subject.

Thus, even before his mobilization, before his first glorious battlefield corpse, Owen begins to fetishize the suffering body and attempts to reproduce its effects in the act of writing. "The Poet in Pain" offers the clearest account of this effort to define and resolve the unbearable conflict within:

> . . . If therefore my remorseless ache
> Be needful to proof-test upon my flesh
> The thoughts I think, and in words bleeding-fresh
> Teach me for speechless sufferers to plain,
> I would not quench it. Rather be my part
> To write of health with shaking hands, bone-pale,
> Of pleasure, having hell in every vein,
> Than chant of care from out a careless heart,
> To music of the world's eternal wail.[67]

Here, self-inflicted pain, like self-description, speaks to a prior inner division. The poet dismembers himself in order to know himself; his self-wounding proclaims the truth of an unbearably split being. The sight of blood, in fact, only "proof-tests" an already existent conflict. Paradoxically, it is at once released and revealed, freed and defined, and thus emblematic of that conflict. More generally, bleeding signifies both health and injury. It flows to the surface of the body, protecting life as it drains away. As we will find, for the war poet, these conditions cannot be dissociated. Only the body in pain can know of health, as, conversely, health demands a corrective pain. In this, the poem itself resembles a bleeding, its words "bleeding-fresh." Language is secreted from the tormented body, suggesting continuity and disruption. The act of speech is a moment of extension as well as definition, power and submission. Owen's voice is always doubled in this way, humble before its own authority. It is certain in its despair, tormented by its knowledge.

In this instance, though, the poet's suffering is a lonely affair. He can only damage himself, and so the conflict remains isolated, neurotic. As Owen eventually realizes, psychological torment is more completely affirmed in war, in a brutal engagement with others. His conflicted needs find greater expression in the landscape of the battlefield, in the images of dying bodies, the sensations of man-to-man combat, and even in his self-fashioned role as war poet. Owen's war poems, for example, turn again and again to those fleeting moments when life and death are intertwined. They focus on neither the triumphant soldier nor the dead corpse, but the slowly dying bodies that lay strewn across the battlefield. The following scrap typifies his interest in this liminal state:

> I saw his round mouth's crimson deepen as it fell,
>   Like a sun, in his last deep hour;
> Watched the magnificent recession of farewell,
>   Clouding, half gleam, half glower,
> And a last splendour burn the heavens of his cheek.

Here, as suggested above, life and death attain significance only in their contrast. While the poet cannot venture close enough to the physical point at which these two states meet, he is able to conjure the metaphysical space where they coincide. As a final index of vitality, blood rushes to the surface of the dying body. Life is glorified as it ends, its perfection exists in its passing – quite literally, as purpose and desire begin to recede and the body attains a certain self-evidence. The scenario suggests that the perfection of being is the end of being. The act of embodiment is an act of violence, of disembodiment. The subject is released, but into death, a "magnificent recession of farewell"; he finds order and stability in the same state, in "cold stars lighting" (123).

As in his account of the body in pain, Owen compares this experience to the poet's own activity. Poetry also affirms as it denies the life of its speaker, at once activates and alienates his desires. "Has Your Soul Sipped" also describes the beauty of a dying corpse, but focuses specifically on the mouth, a site of desire as well as speech:

> Though from his throat
> The life-tide leaps
> There was no threat
> On his lips.   (91)

The soul leaps from the soldier's mouth here as words leap from the poet's. The expression of life falters and dies as soon as it leaves the lips, without "threat." Its vitality, its pleasure, is immediately spent, on the battlefield or the page. A manuscript note sheds light:

> Consummation is Consumption
> We cannot consummate our bliss and not consume.
> All joys are cakes and vanish in the eating.
> All bliss is sugar's melting in the mouth.[68]

For Owen, the moment of pleasure, of consummation, is a moment of consumption; it cannot exist without punishment. Desire is exhausted in its painful experience; life dissipates in its living. Similarly, the poet expires in his expression. Poetry captures this perverse dynamic, granting it permanence and significance.

Owen's torment, however, found even greater release in the erotically charged configurations battle, particularly as they were informed by multiple reversals and identifications. In "Greater Love," he compares the clichéd romance of tradition and the home front with the "love pure" of the battlefield:

> Red lips are not so red
>   As the stained stones kissed by the English dead.
> Kindness of wooed and wooer
> Seems shame to their love pure . . .
>
> Your slender attitude
>   Trembles not exquisite like limbs knife-skewed,
> Rolling and rolling there
> Where God seems not to care;
> Till the fierce love they bear
>   Cramps them in death's extreme decrepitude.
>
> (166)

Throughout this poem, desire for another, desire to be that other, is fused with an intense hatred and hostility. This complex erotic charge finds fulfillment as the soldier, both literally and figuratively, merges with the object he destroys. In battle, though, the violent paramour reveals only that strange love he holds toward himself. He couples with himself in a deadly, merciless embrace. He makes love to his corpse, dies at his own hand. Tellingly, Owen claims to abandon the traditional forms of love. His "Greater Love" exists in a sustained physical violence, in "blinded" eyes and "knife-skewered" limbs. This transmutation of romantic love attests to the unbearable conflict of desire within. It confirms the unforgiving persistence of his desire for both authority and submission, the intensity of his self-love and self-hatred.

One of Owen's last poems, "Strange Meeting," further clarifies the power and necessity of this violent resolution. The speaker, thinking he has escaped the scene of battle down a "profound dull tunnel," finds himself in hell. There, he meets a wounded enemy soldier with whom he discusses their failed aspirations and false hopes. Both, we learn, sought the "wildest beauty in the world" and "the truth untold." Both, however, found nothing but "the undone years, / the hopelessness . . ." These men, of course, are one and the same; their exchange exposes a mutual crisis and torment. The setting and tone suggest a movement deep into the psyche; the soldier confronts only himself and begins to examine his confounded ego. In this, he seems to recognize the desires that led him to war. In the poem's oddly doubled speech, the so-called "enemy" explains,

> I am the enemy you killed, my friend.
> I knew you in this dark: for so you frowned
> Yesterday through me as you jabbed and killed.
> I parried; but my hands were loath and cold.
> Let us sleep now . . .   (149)

Here, the soldier exposes the battlefield as the site of perverse libidinal projection and a violent mimesis. The field of conflict is populated by narcissists and necrophiliacs, men in love with their own passionate deaths. Yet, his speech ends abruptly. The two men fall asleep; the violent identification remains intact and thus continues to work its powerful magic. Here, Owen signals the failure of his vision and seems to acknowledge the effects of his projections. But, in this abrupt ending, he also reveals the limits of his poetic ability, his failure to move beyond an essentially narcissistic mode. The world is either a configuration of his own violent impulses or nothing at all.

Ultimately, while Owen repeatedly grumbles about the political reasons for war, his work implicitly values the experience of battle. He seems to care little about the nation, but insists that the individual can find fulfillment only in the sustained physical pain guaranteed by national conflict. Throughout his work, the soldier's sacrifice grants him a greater wisdom and spiritual strength; he faces destruction only to rise from the ashes in exaltation. Owen understood his own role as war-poet in similar terms. There is a certain smugness about his poetry, a proud sense of initiation that no civilian could claim. In fact, many of Owen's poems are organized around a contrast between the soldier's glorious sufferings and the empty lives of those back home. Some of his most beloved pieces, "Insensibility," "Apologia Pro Poemate Meo," and "Greater Love," conclude with a rebuke to the civilian for his failure to appreciate the truth of war.[69] Apparently, only the frontline soldier finds the means to suffer and thus to write. There, he can submit to other men, but still emerge as their authoritative voice. In one letter, he explains, "I am much gladder to be going out again than afraid. I shall be better able to cry my outcry, playing my part." In another, he writes, "I came out in order to help these boys – directly by leading them as well as an officer can; indirectly, by watching their sufferings that I may speak of them as well as a pleader can."[70] This expressive conceit also seems to mark Owen's most famous poem, "Dulce Et Decorum Est":

> If in some smothering dreams you too could pace
> Behind the wagon that we flung him in,
> And watch the white eyes writhing in his face,
> His hanging face, like a devil's sick of sin;
> If you could hear, at every jolt, the blood

Come gargling from the froth-corrupted lungs,
Obscene as cancer, bitter as the cud
Of vile, incurable sores on innocent tongues, –
My friend, you would not tell with such high zest
To children ardent for some desperate glory,
The old Lie: Dulce et decorum est
Pro patria mori. (140)

Owen indulges in this description. He alone has experienced the world's extremes; he alone knows both the glory of man and his most lascivious desires. In this, Owen contrasts himself with the civilian, who has no access to the war's violent extremes. The fourth line from last ends as if it were a distinction rather than an admonition. Only Owen can speak of the war's sufferings with "such high zest." Only he can tell the "old Lie" with such conviction.

In the intended preface to his collected works, Owen betrays this mix of self-effacement and self-deification. He seeks not praise, peace or even understanding, but "pity": "The Poetry," he declares, "is in the pity." In this, Owen both humbles himself before his audience and radically distances his experience. He at once curses and cherishes his pain as his own – it belongs to him alone. Owen, in fact, dismisses his readers altogether. His experience, as both soldier and poet, seems to redeem itself. As he explains, "If I thought the letter of this book would last, I might have used proper names; but if the spirit of it survives – survives Prussia – my ambition and those names will have achieved themselves fresher fields than Flanders" (192). In this, in his emphasis on "the spirit" of battle, Owen continues to deny the terms of his involvement and its consequences. He can only understand his work as it negates the reality of Flanders or the Somme, as it conjures up images of "fresher fields." In the end, then, it seems absurd to speak of Owen the materialist or Owen the socialist. His poetry is thoughtless, acknowledging otherness only in violence. More absurd, perhaps, is to speak of Owen as a homosexual poet. His writing reduces all eroticism to a tortured narcissism and its willfully blind projections. Owen's work, the war's work, affects order and renewal, but only in their most perverse forms. This art destroys the mind and its world, giving both over to a violent productivity and senseless repetition.

IV

Henri Gaudier-Brzeska also served in the trenches. He, too, died *pour la patrie*. But what we know of Gaudier-Brzeska's frontline experience reveals a qualitatively different attitude toward the war, one that opposes the narcissism of the modern subject with a greater respect for the subject's relation to the object world. His "Vortex Gaudier-Brzeska," written at the scene of battle, contains the following anecdote:

I have made an experiment. Two days ago I pinched from an enemy a mauser rifle. Its heavy unwieldy shape swamped me with a powerful IMAGE of brutality.
   I was in doubt for a long time whether it pleased or displeased me.
   I found that I did not like it.
   I broke the butt off and with my knife I carved in it a design, through which I tried to express a gentler order of feeling, which I preferred.

For Gaudier-Brzeska, the rifle is primarily an "IMAGE," but one that actively shapes and determines the world at large. It is an image of bourgeois individualism, of "ARROGANCE, SELF-ESTEEM, PRIDE," and of corporate competition, of "ECONOMIC ACTIVITIES" that have now grown "NOXIOUS." Importantly, Gaudier-Brzeska recognizes that, despite its apparent autonomy, the rifle has been invested with a specifically human power and, in that, subject to change. He thus asserts his desire to transform the image, as well its consequences, into a "gentler order of feeling." In this, he claims to assert an alternative modernity, which he calls "THE VORTEX OF WILL, OF DECISION."[71] As this story suggests, Gaudier-Brzeska's work is informed by the notion that consciousness is conditioned and informed by its activity in the world. The self can only express and thus know itself in the process of its objectification. This relationship, however, does not reduce the possibilities of the will, for the manifold forms of the world continue to provide alternatives. When desire is arrested by the objects it encounters, the subject is made aware of its power within a specific environment. For Gaudier-Brzeska, sculpture serves to heighten this process, halting sublimation and thus exposing the subject's power as it exists within the world. In this, his work shifts our focus from the ego to its material relations; it replaces lyricism with sculpture, hero-worship with community, and destruction with the ability to discriminate.

In fact, all across pre-war Europe, sculptors were in revolt against the bourgeois humanist tradition as it had manifested itself in their craft during the nineteenth century. Influential figures such as Constantin Brancusi and Jacob Epstein railed against what they saw as a specifically bourgeois commitment to rational perspectivalism and visionary individualism; Rodinesque modeling was seen as a form of elitism if not escapism, a failure to engage the material world and its inherent limitations. Consequently, these sculptors defiantly privileged the primitive, totemic forms of pre-Hellenic cultures and the more aggressive activity of direct carving. They saw in these alternative traditions a specifically proletarian authenticity and a more honest engagement with the material world. As Charles Harrison explains, for many, direct carving was a form of socialist revolt, a way to resolve the division of labor between art and craft. Their primitive method was "an expression, however indirect and mediated, of class interests distinct from those of the English literary bourgeoisie."[72] Indeed, the vorticist group similarly privileged work. Pound argued that the modern vortex was most clearly expressed in three-dimensional work, "a much more energetic and creative action than the copying or imitating of light on a haystack." Hulme, too, thought that shape and mass were poorly expressed on canvas. The work of his favorite painters would be "even more interesting carried out as three dimensional shapes in wood or something of that kind."[73] Gaudier-Brzeska, who was a prominent member of this London circle, created sculpture that typifies these general trends and their political implications. His frontline experiences and avant-garde affiliation combined to produce work that is at once a challenge and an alternative to the correlation of modern production and modern violence.

From the start, Gaudier-Brzeska's life was defined by intense poverty and alienation. A true exile and a born sufferer, with dashing looks, Latin flair, and an early death in the trenches, he seemed condemned to romantic mythologizing. As Pound lamented in his *Memoir of Gaudier-Brzeska*, "A great spirit has been among us, and a great artist is gone" (17). Yet Gaudier-Brzeska's own writing reveals a cunning wit and a radically different perspective on his role as artist. His values are informed by a rather scathing critique of modern art and modern life; he laments the corrupt romanticism that has swept across Europe, pushing it toward the brink of war:

I believe that my country has never before been in so advanced a state of decadence. The Latin race is rotten to the core. Its flag has become violet, yellow, and green, the colours of the putrescence which fills the romantic paintings of Delacroix, presaging storms, wind, destruction, and carnage. The French disgust me more and more by their idleness, their heedlessness, and their excess of bad taste.[74]

Gaudier-Brzeska shares Hulme's belief that the excessive narcissism of his contemporaries is the direct cause of cultural decay. As the bourgeoisie project their greed outward, in material form, the world grows rotten. "Hysterical egoism" results in both aggression and impotence, violence and victimization. The bourgeois artist, too, can see "only himself"; he has "petrified his own semblance."[75] His art represents "only a repugnant sadism," triumphant in the "sufferings of a material body" (22).

Gaudier-Brzeska also shares Hulme's desire to oppose the decadence of bourgeois culture on its own terms. He wants to confront commerce and repetitive labor with an alternative productive activity, one informed by "will and consciousness."[76] As he explains, to define one's trade is an ethical task, for specific forms of labor imply specific relations to the material world:

> In trade, suffering, art, the town, the battle, I seek a collective happiness. I uphold the creative spirit in mankind, maintain it and make it triumph over the middle-class man who seems to deny its existence. If I abandon the workman, I take sides with the fat-bellied, flabby-faced plutocrat – a hideous idea . . . One thing I can absolutely decide, it is the only thing I can cut off at once, namely, to give up business for some craft. I am going to learn the technique of sculpture and wood for cabinet-making. I shall give next month to this, and it is with this I hope to earn my daily bread, and not by fleecing the masses. (25)

Gaudier-Brzeska very early abandons the romantic dream of pure creation. He recognizes that truth never exists on its own, but arises and must remain responsive to a larger environment. He rejects, in other words, the romantic idealism of self that turns man against man, that seems to "deny" the power and presence of the other. For Gaudier-Brzeska, expression has value only within the world, in a collective space. The value of any work exists in its materialism, its difficult construction and positioning in the world. Significantly, this quality is best represented by particular kinds of activity, namely, sculpture and carpentry. These arts unite not only mind and material, but individual expression and social order. The crafted object expresses as it shapes a positive relation to the community as a whole. Tellingly, he once rebuked a fellow artist for his stubborn isolation. Art, he argues, should serve the community: "You have ruined the best part of your life because of this pride which you place above the work which you could and should accomplish. This leads you inevitably to that narrowest kind of egoism which puts the self on the pedestal, labeled *Don't touch*, and makes hay with the primordial conception of the individual as part of a society, having relations with the other individuals who compose it" (159).

Certainly, Gaudier-Brzeska's alternative method also entails a certain kind of suffering. But for the sculptor, the creative struggle is always productive and responsive: sculptural work offers a more positive expression of freedom and stability. It discloses all that is original and new in the subject, but also that which is inevitable and necessary in the material world; it reveals human power as it exists and is limited by the conditional world. In one letter, he writes,

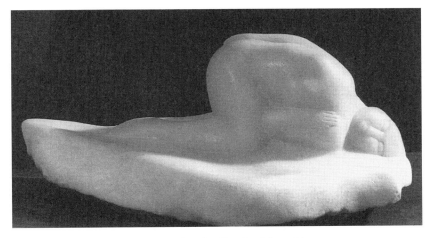

Figure 3   Henri Gaudier-Brzeska, *Mermaid*, 1913.

I have been reading about the Neo-impressionists. They are, like all artists, very idealistic: too idealistic, I think – mystical and not at all independent. . . . One's fingers should feel delight in touching the undulations of a statue, the eyes in beholding a painting. Philosophize after, to satisfy your humanity, but not before. In Art one must absolutely respect its limits and logic – otherwise one arrives at nothing worth doing. (58–9)

Here, sculptural activity is valued because it "respects" the limits of consciousness, the power of mind as it exists in the world. Whereas the romantic takes "immediate fright at the idea of limitation," the more honest artist engages limit as the source of truth as well as freedom. As the sculptor explains, "art does not lie in the dream, but in the marriage of the dream with the material." His advice is to "Work, always work" (58).

In these letters, Gaudier-Brzeska's work moves away from the one-dimensionality of the lyric toward the multiplicity of the worldly; it moves from line to mass, from myopia to parallax, from private to public perspective. His progress as an artist – and particularly the development of his use of relief – makes this transition explicit. His career begins with the relatively self-contained and flat space of the page, with lengthy experiments in line drawing and ideogrammatic symbols. Slowly, however, he ventures into low and high reliefs, and his previously flat forms begin to emerge from the page in depth. These reliefs suggest a tentative questioning of sculptural definition, a beginner's fear of commitment to sculpture in the round. His *Mermaid* (Figure 3), for example, seems to move toward full form, but the figure remains clinging to her plinth for security. The work's theme testifies to the liminal state in which the sculptor was now working, to a personal struggle between detached individualism and an animal fleshiness. A group of masks similarly points the way toward full modeling and a more mature feeling for mass. As in the work of many moderns, these masks provided the means to transform subjective emotions and lyrical feeling into solid, objective form. Like the lyrical personae of Pound, Eliot, and Yeats, they represent a possible reconciliation of ego and world, a process in which truth is seen to emerge somewhere between expression and material. Gaudier-Brzeska, however, can more fully exploit this process because he is working with material objects rather then linguistic fragments. When his sculpture finally emerges, it more completely avoids both the tyranny of the ego as well as the totality of the material. It consistently foregrounds the creative potential of all labor, the progressive coalescence of spirit and matter.

First and foremost, Gaudier-Brzeska argues that all sculptural activity is conditioned by the nature of its material, whether this be a found stone, a stolen gravemarker, or an enemy rifle. The unbearably physical dimension of this art distinguishes it from other, more technically developed modes of expression. Intentions and visions are always limited by the specific properties of the medium – the tangible qualities of weight, size, texture, and color. According to Gaudier-Brzeska, the good sculptor must try to avoid "arbitrary translations of a design in any material." He must remain "fully aware of the different qualities and possibilities of woods, stones, and metals."[77] For example, Gaudier-Brzeska's *Maternity* (Figure 4) depicts a female figure lying on her side, gently cradling a baby. The piece exhibits a lush compositional freedom that reveals the power of material creation as a slow process of shaping and nurturing. The creative union of spirit and matter – metaphorically presented in the figures' gentle embrace – is given expression in the fluid lines of the body, in the emergent swells and hollows of an otherwise dense block of stone. The piece is astonishing, however, in that it was carved from an irregularly pointed block no longer than a foot on any side. Its peculiar shape bears the traces of the stone's original oddities, yet perfectly conveys an organic fullness. The texture of the material, a lush *seravezza* marble, serves to establish serenity and warmth. Its soft glow coincides perfectly with the voluptuous mounds of the main figure. The final product exemplifies the mind's ability to work with, rather than against, materials in order to express a truth common to both.

Along with materials, Gaudier-Brzeska privileges the activity of direct carving. The worldliness of the sculptural process is confirmed in a difficult, physical activity. Pound's anecdote is by now famous:

Figure 4   Henri Gaudier-Brzeska, *Maternity*, 1913.

Gaudier, ætatis suae XVIII or thereabouts, met Epstein, who said, mustering the thunders of gods and the scowlings of Assyrian sculpture into his tone and eyebrows, "UMMHH! Do . . . you cut . . . direct . . . in stone?"

"Most certainly!" said Gaudier, who had never yet done anything of the sort.

"That's right," said Epstein, "I will come around to your place on Sunday."

So Gaudier at once went out, got three small stone blocks, and by working more or less night and day had something ready by Sunday. (*Memoir*, 76)

Pound defines Gaudier-Brzeska's sculpture as "energy cut into stone, making the stone expressive in its fit and particular manner." He claims that its power and particularity derive from the artist's struggle with the stone's "conventions and limits" (*Memoir*, 110). This difficult process exposes both dream and power, the artist's "will and consciousness" in relation to its specific object. Limitations clarify the tensions between mind and material; they make conscious the gap between vision and being. Of course, an intense system of mass and pressure inevitably results in deformities, but therein lies its power. What emerges might not be pretty, but it exhibits a radical sharpness and durability. Take, for example, the boulder-like *Standing Female Figure* (Figure 5). It was carved directly into a block of granite intended for machine-assisted, monumental masonry. The result is a hideous deformity, marked by scars and bruises. But, in accordance with its making, the work manages to convey an exquisite painfulness. The barely emergent head, flattened against its upper limit, suggests struggle as well as defeat. The chest and mid-sections, in their rough protruding, expose gravity itself, the palpable tensions of life itself.

Typically, Gaudier-Brzeska's work is slightly deconstructed, skewered, critical of its potential bravura. A work such as the *Hieratic Head of Ezra Pound* (Figure 6), for example, seems emblematic not because of its phallic intensity, but because it emerges from the ground with all the unexpected awkwardness that Pound himself exhibited in those years. It does not stand upright, but cocked to one side, its nose uneven and brow unclear. The wider block of hair does not protrude upward, in triumph, but seems to weigh down heavily, precariously, on the whole. Even the stone is defective, scarred and stained across its center. Pound, in fact, praised the sculptor for muting the work's original vigor and romantic masculinism (*Memoir*, 49).[78] Ultimately, the piece exemplifies a creative difficulty, a "palpable tension." Its beauty and intensity derive from its uneasy rhythms, its graceless imperfection. Its truth is that it bears witness to human endeavor as it occurs within the world. *The Hieratic Head* represents classical modernism (as well as Pound) at its best, in all its awkward, self-conscious commitment.

Finally, Gaudier-Brzeska privileges sculptural activity as an organizational process, for its ability to inform and clarify multiple relations within the material world. *In its production*, sculpture acknowledges as it arranges the objects that go into its making – inks, charcoals, papers, chisels, clay, granite, muscle, sweat, and bone. The activity between these objects results in a heightened consciousness of each, a recognition of their individual qualities as well as their place within the larger structure. *In its reception*,

Figure 5   Henri Gaudier-Brzeska, *Standing Female Figure*, 1913.

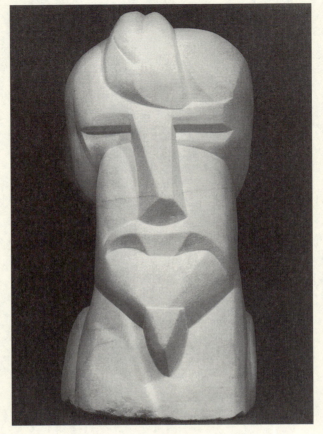

Figure 6   Henri Gaudier-Brzeska, *Hieratic Head of Ezra Pound*, 1914.

sculpture clarifies and creates its environment in a similar way. The final work takes up space, uniting and dividing the objects that surround it. Through its mass and form, it transfigures the physical relations and properties of its surroundings. Simultaneously, it organizes multiple lines of perception, whether they be visual, tactile, or intellectual. Richard Cork clarifies this effect in his description of one of Gaudier-Brzeska's larger works:

anatomical reality has been dispensed with in favour of an interlocking series of biomorphic shapes. Bellies, legs and antlers are all treated as the swollen parts of an ambiguous whole, and they burgeon mysteriously out of a decentralized composition which avoids any fixed focal point. The eye is forced to travel round the entire mass, searching for a clue with which to interpret the meaning of these huddled, vegetable forms. They appear willfully to defy analysis, and sprout from their base like natural outcrops of the alabaster itself.[79]

This effect defies final analysis because the interpretive process it demands is precise, yet open. Sculptural outcroppings are mimed by a continuous production of meaning; both burgeon out of a unified, vegetable whole. The shifts experienced as one circles around the sculpture clarify perspectives in relation to one another, making conscious the differences between them. Most importantly, this experience is common, if not communal. Through sculpture, the material world admits to both organization and freedom of view. The work combines spatial stability with individual position in a conscious, continuous whole.

This achievement can be clarified by a comparison of two works from different periods of Gaudier-Brzeska's career. The subject of both is the dancer, but one immediately realizes a striking contrast in the fundamental attitude behind each. The first, simply titled *Dancer* (Figure 7), embodies in both theme and style the romantic tradition we defined earlier. The figure exists only in her motion, what Kermode calls an "uncomposite blessedness" of form and force (53). Her slender body exhibits an ethereal grace, a symmetrical perfection that comes remarkably close to that of a simple line. She barely touches the plinth as one of her arms extends upward toward the heavens. However, there is something grotesque about this figure, something unhealthy. Her emaciated body seems tortured, stretched between a heaven she could never reach and a common world she despises. Her hip seems oddly deformed for an emblem of grace. She shields her face in shame, as one would before true beauty. The effect is one of increasing dissipation: one wants to clutch at the torso before it disappears for good, to stop the balancing act before its fall. But this slight wisp offers nothing for us to hold. Consciousness slips away, around the form, and into the ether. If the piece offers rhythmic dynamism, its movement is totalizing. The eye can only look up or down, in a straight line, with little power of choice. According to Stanley Casson, "There is no representation of motion here, only its full and direct expression."[80] This, of course, is the problem. Vision has lost touch with the material world and thus with the possibility of consciousness. Nothing is thought; nothing is expressed.

Redstone Dancer (Figure 8), completed several months later during the period when Gaudier-Brzeska grew closer to Pound and his circle, marks a radical departure for the sculptor. The sheer weight and muscular bulk

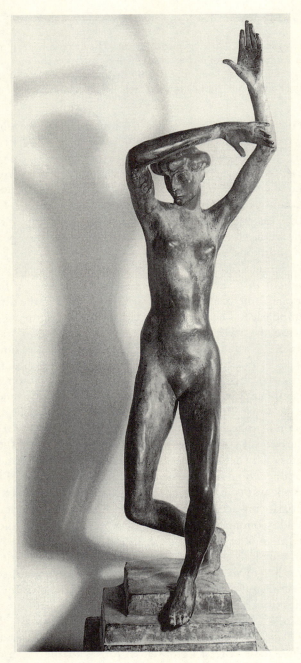

Figure 7   Henri Gaudier-Brzeska, *Dancer*, 1913.

Figure 8   Henri Gaudier-Brzeska, *Redstone Dancer*, 1913.

of this figure readily aligns it with the materialism we have been describing. Its thick torso and limbs, the earthy redness of the stone, proclaims its worldly presence. The figure's limbs and protrusions are subject to an intense centrifugal torsion. The vital outshoots of arm and leg are just as quickly drawn back into the figure, re-emerging with the earthly whole. And yet, in its grounding materialism, the figure also maintains a certain grace and vitality. The masses are perfectly balanced and delicately aligned; their slick, even surfaces and gentle curves evoke a beautiful, rhythmic flow. This beauty is perhaps signaled by the abstract shapes that mark the face and breasts. The geometrical forms seem to emerge out of the piece itself, as indices of an utterly material perfection. They represent the ultimate union of mind and matter, a truth both infinite and durable. According to Pound, "Into these so-called 'abstractions' life flows . . . The 'abstract' or mathematical bareness of the triangle and circle are fully incarnate, full of vitality and of energy" (*Memoir*, 137). Description, however, cannot account for an experience that is primarily sensual. The work is distinguished by the manner in which it physically evokes freedom and stability. The mind flows along its graceful curves, circles in and around its smooth limbs. But, quickly, instinct is defied, the will thwarted. Mass juts against mass and arrests all motion. The viewer is made intensely aware of his position and forced to contemplate the possibilities of change. In this, motion and mass are given over to freedom and thought; the material object establishes the possibility of conscious choice.[81]

The unique power of these forms forces us to question their existence in relation to the modern period as a whole. How does, for example, this sculptural activity differ from that of the average laborer? Or, rather, how does it avoid lapsing into the mechanical activity of that laborer? And how can the consciousness generated by this sculpture transform consciousness of production in general? Pound began to answer some of these questions in his *Memoir*. Primarily, he celebrated this sculpture for its ability to awaken his sense of form, to increase his awareness of the material world and its manifold properties. These works are valuable insofar as they direct attention to their surroundings and thus position the subject in conscious relation to his or her environment (*Memoir*, 126). Importantly, Pound also suggests that this sculpture is valuable in that it clarifies the human ability to invest the world with significance. The aesthetic artifact, in other words, exaggerates and clarifies the relationship between mind and matter, between creative power and its resistant objects:

And the "new form." What is it? It is what we have said. It is an arrangement of masses in relation. It is not an empty copy of empty Roman allegories that are themselves copies of copies. It is not a mimicry of external life. It is energy cut into stone, making the stone expressive in its fit and particular manner. It has regard to the stone. (*Memoir*, 110)

The artist with "form-understanding" does not simply accept the material world as given. The best work represents neither the desires of the sculptor nor the established forms of the natural world; rather, it exposes the power of the subject as it exists within that world, as it consciously negotiates the terms of existence. In this, though, Pound seems to imply that the activity of the artist heightens or exaggerates the necessary processes of life in general. As the artist drives energy through matter, he intensifies the activity of a world that is itself productive and objective. He creates as he clarifies the terms of his worldly existence, realizing himself and his world in the activity of production. In this, as we will see in Marx's work, aesthetic activity is valued as a specific form of labor, a more conscious and creative mode of existing within the world. It attests to the human capacity for transformation and stable order; it proclaims the possibilities of freedom and consciousness within an apparently closed order. In other words, for Marx and these moderns, it is through our sensual activity that we come to know ourselves and our community, and thus to negotiate its terms.

Gaudier-Brzeska opens his most radical "VORTEX" with the following three tenets:

Sculptural energy is the mountain.
Sculptural feeling is the appreciation of masses in relation.
Sculptural ability is the defining of these masses by planes.[82]

It is important to think of the masses referred to here as human as well as material. For the sculptor and his circle, human existence is conditioned existence, and human meaning exists only within a human community, in the individual's relation to others of his kind. Consequently, the world must be produced with love and compassion; labor should strive to establish a comfortable space for communal experience. In a telling letter written to his lover, Gaudier-Brzeska explains that community is our "one consolation." "We are part of the world creation," he claims, and so "When we are united we think neither of outer darkness nor of animal brutality" (186). All material activity, he writes, is born out of this desire for peace and freedom amongst others:

Dear, dear love, I press you to me with all my force, and only your help enables me to work. I thank you, dear Sun, lovely Star, for having created women and men that we may be united, mingle our personalities, melt together our hearts and, by the union of our passionate bodies, better liberate our souls, making of us a single creature – the absolute human which you have endowed with so many gifts. (187)

This loving attitude toward the material world, toward the living, social world, offers a poignant contrast to the work of the war poet. In fact, it was probably Gaudier-Brzeska's remarkable omnisexuality that informed his radical openness to the material world. His brief life was ruled by what seems to be a complete absence of narcissistic identification, by a true curiosity about other kinds of identity and other modes of self-production. Take, for example, the following passage, in which he describes himself as a playful "Pik":

I've been very lucky lately, for I've seen some lovely creatures – two superb women dressed so lightly that one could see their big bodies without corsets and their breasts small and well-placed on either side of their chests. One was a Hindoo and the other, I don't know, probably a Russian, but certainly not English; and for a man, again a beautiful Hindoo. He had a mouth so delicate and voluptuous that it looked like a ripe fig burst open in the sunshine: he had scarcely any clothes on either, and only the thinnest of vests covered a most marvelous chest. He walked like a tiger, proud and haughty, with eyes that flashed like steel. I think he was the most lovely man I have ever seen, the sight of him made me wild with pleasure; and, would you believe it, the English, with their hideous mugs, laughed like idiots as he went by. In this country it's a kind of crime to be beautiful. Pik would have loved to kiss that lovely mouth. (90)

One immediately notices how this kiss compares to Owen's. The difference in attitude – national, sexual, aesthetic, and otherwise – cannot be more starkly drawn. The war poet sought freedom in violence, unity in death. He worshipped a confounded self and its power to destroy. Gaudier-Brzeska, however, found unity within the world, life amidst others. Even amidst the violence of the trenches, he celebrates human existence as social existence. These opposed attitudes can also be judged by their effects. On the one hand, we find aggression and xenophobia, the implacable machinery of the class system, and a handful of decadent lyrics. Owen offers us the kiss of death, the kiss of betrayal. On the other, we see inspiring, enduring works, peace and calm, and the possibility of community. Gaudier-Brzeska offers the kiss of life, of renewal and hope.

v

I do not mean to suggest that Owen's poetry demands psychoanalytic treatment, while Gaudier-Brzeska's sculpture remains immune. Nor do I mean to intimate that lyricism will always impede our knowledge of the material world, whereas sculpture implies an ethical awareness to it. Rather, as I hope to establish here, a common, if complex impulse informs all productive activity and these two modes are only distinguished by tendency. In other words, the creative subject always seems both to activate and deny his being, to realize and limit his desire. The resultant work is both an expression of the self and an utter denial of that self, a manifestation of the ego and complete submission to something other. A certain violence always informs the subject's relation to the material world; more or less extreme forms of production are conditioned by larger social frameworks. Particular modes emphasize different aspects of this dynamic activity, the aggressive or the restrictive, the narcissistic or the social. Whereas a poet might realize himself and his desires in a comfortable range of worldly objects, a sculptor might be drawn to objects that directly confront and challenge his desires, that halt and thus reveal the possibilities for future action. The romantic projects his image everywhere, spatially and temporally, away from himself and into the world. He turns outward in search of an *individual* meaning he can no longer maintain on his own, in the isolated imagination. The classicist, however, recognizes objects as such, works through their unique properties, and contemplates the possibilities they contain. He too turns outward, but in search of a *social* meaning he could never establish on his own.

Wilhelm Worringer, whose work was well-known and respected by Hulme and his coterie, provides the theoretical link between the aesthetic values of the British avant-garde and Marx's more general theories of production.[83] In his 1905 treatise *Abstraction and Empathy*, Worringer argues that art's history has little do with skill, progress, or technology. Rather, aesthetic values are shaped by the hopes and desires of its creators; aesthetic qualities exist in response to the specific needs of the cultures that produce them. More specifically, Worringer argues that the work of art is typically the result of one of two culturally specific urges, the urge to empathy or the urge to abstraction. Some cultures, he explains, exist in a happy, pantheistic relationship with their surroundings and thus their art celebrates the vital energies of being. Others, however, experience a certain dread of space and thus seek to oppose that chaos with static forms. The genius of Worringer's study, however, lies in its suggestion that these two tendencies are actually part of a single aesthetic gesture:

In empathising this will to activity into another object, however, we are in the other object. We are delivered from our individual being as long as we are absorbed onto an external object, an external form, with our inner urge to experience. We feel, as it were, our individuality flow into fixed boundaries, in contrast to the boundless differentiation of the individual consciousness. In this self-objectification lies a self-alienation.[84]

For Worringer, the twin poles of aesthetic experience are "only gradations of a common need" (23). Every creative act is both vital and static, a moment of self-expression and self-alienation. With each stroke of the brush or chisel, the artist both activates and arrests his own being. He unleashes internal, vital energies as he submits to an external stability of form. Depending on his immediate needs and his cultural milieu, then, the artist might stress one or the other of these tendencies, but both are present in every creation.

Marx's early work defines a similar cultural dialectic, but relates it more generally to the historical transformations of labor itself. In *Economic and Philosophical Manuscripts of 1844*, Marx defines labor not as a singular activity or even an historical phenomenon, but as the very basis of existence and thought alike.[85] Labor is the "human essence" which drives "the entire movement of history . . . both its *actual* act of genesis (the birth act of its empirical existence) and also for its thinking consciousness the *comprehended* and *known* process of its *coming-to-be*" (84). As Marx explains, the human individual is inherently limited and thus eternally needy. He lives in a state of perpetual desire, bound to the material world for his existence. Consequently, his labor exists "as a *means* of satisfying a need – the need to maintain the physical existence"; it is thus his "*life-activity, productive life* itself" (76). In this, though, the individual is also a sensuous, or objective being; he depends upon worldly objects for his survival and thus only exists in those objects. "The worker," he writes, "can create nothing without *nature*, without the *sensuous external world*. It is on this which his labour is manifested, in which it is active, from which and by means of which it produces" (72).

And yet, for Marx, labor does not end in the satisfaction of desire or in the limitations of the object world. In his sensual activity, in his continual labor, the individual proves himself to be a species being. He does not produce only according to his most immediate needs, as the bird builds a nest, for he can also produce freely, according to the needs of every species. He treats himself and the objects of the world in their universality, and thus produces the possibilities that exist in all being (76). For Marx, then, the individual is driven to produce, but always produces beyond his needs. Caught within the material world, driven by need, he yet attains a certain universality. As Marx argues, "Man makes his life-activity itself the object of his will and of his consciousness. He has conscious life-activity. It is not a determination with which he directly merges . . . It is just because of this that he is a species being. Or it is only because of this that he is a Conscious being, i.e., that his own life is an object for him. Only because of that is his activity free activity" (76).

Importantly, production according to need provides the foundation for this other, universal mode. In fact, it is only because man produces in need, only because he must work through the differentiated objects of his environment, that he can attain universality. Out of suffering, out of that gap between desire and its realization, consciousness and thus choice arise. The object world provides not only the materials, but also the differentiating conditions by which man comes to know himself and makes his home. In fact, for Marx, the richness of need is synonymous with the richness of life; "The rich human being," he writes, "is simultaneously the human being in need of a totality of human life-activities – the man in whom his own realization exists as inner necessity, as need" (91). In painful, externalized labor, then, the subject discovers himself and his place in the world, as well as his essential powers to make that world his own. In fact, he not only proves that he is a species being, but raises the very standard of production, so that others too may "form things in accordance with the laws of beauty" (76). Herbert Marcuse provides an excellent account of this theory:

labour is "man's act of self-creation," i.e. the activity through and in which man really first becomes what he is by his nature as man. He does this in such a way that this becoming and being are there *for himself*, so that he can know and "regard" himself as what he is (man's "becoming-for-himself"). Labour is a knowing and conscious activity: in his labour man relates to himself and to the object of his labour; he is not directly one with his labour but can, as it were, confront it and oppose it.[86]

Labor does not serve to overcome difference; rather, in the creation of differentiated objects, it reveals man's sensual or objective relations. "Man," Marcuse writes, "can only realize his essence if he realizes it as something *objective*, by using his 'essential powers' to produce an 'external,' 'material,' objective world" (14).

Importantly, though, this positive mode of production, in its necessary objectivity and otherness, contains the terms of its inversion. If, for Marx, labor always entails a certain objectification, a certain estrangement or alienation, it entails the possibility of exploitation. If the individual must lose himself in the object in order to discover himself, his activity can be appropriated by others.[87] As Marx explains, the general product of labor is "labour which has been congealed in an object, which has become material: it is the *objectification* of labour. Labour's realization is its objectification." Under modern economic relations, of course, the worker loses control over this labor and thus its object: "the object which labour produces – labour's product – confronts [the worker] as *something alien*, as a *power independent* of the producer" (71). For Marx, then, modern economics exploits the original terms of labor, transforming self-activation into self-alienation. Private property is simply the "sensuous expression of the fact that man becomes objective for himself" (87). Simultaneously, the modern economy limits and distorts the worker's potential, the universal nature of his activity. The individual no longer produces freely, but according to the demands of the capitalist; he no longer creates in the fullness of his wants, but by the dictates of an assigned need. His universal powers are channeled into a single repetitive activity; his very being, in stunted form, becomes a simple means for being. Ultimately, this form of labor estranges the individual from himself and thus from humanity in general. As Marx explains, "In estranging from man (1) nature, and (2) himself, his own active functions, his life-activity, estranged labour estranges the species from man" (75).

Ultimately, if individuals understand themselves and each other through the objects of their labor, then the appropriation of that labor entails not simply the loss of self, but also the loss of community. As suggested, Marx understands labor as a social act; the worker, when he produces, produces an image of himself for himself and the other man. The object is "the direct embodiment of his individuality" and "simultaneously his own existence for the other man, and that existence for him" (85). But when the worker no longer experiences the potential of the species in his labor, he no longer feels that essential bond between himself and his community. Marx writes,

An immediate consequence of the fact that man is estranged from the product of his labour, from his life-activity, from his species being is the *estrangement of man from man*. If man is confronted by himself, he is confronted by the *other* man. What applies to a man's relation to his work, to the product of his labour and to himself, also holds of a man's relation to the other man, and to the other man's labour and object of labour. (77)

For Marx, the worker's relation to the material world has become impaired and impeded. He has lost touch with the fullness of his own powers and thus with the fullness of the species; consequently, he can confront others only as they have confronted him, "antagonistically" (74). Importantly, in this, Marx forecasts the rise of twentieth-century warfare. His theory points toward those same identifications and projections that inform Freud's work. For both thinkers, a violent internal division of the self is cast out into the world where it fractures society as a whole, turning man against man. For both, the split self finds relief in an activity that is itself divisive; the violent terms of modern life replicate themselves in ever larger forms. As Marx writes, "*just as* society itself produces *man as man*, so is society *produced* by him" (85).

One important distinction, however, persists. Whereas Freud fails to imagine an end to this state of affairs, and, in fact, argues that repression is socially necessary, Marx asks whether society can transform its hostile productive relations into a more humane order.[88] He bravely asks whether we can once again "produce things in accordance with the laws of beauty?" Of course, Marx's work suggests many answers to this question. In his *Manuscripts*, however, he seems less interested in a general revolution than in a gradual aesthetic re-education of the senses. Here, the positive transcendence of the modern situation is defined as "the *sensuous* appropriation for and by man of the human essence and of human life, of objective man, of human *achievements* . . ." (87). For Marx, as for Gaudier-Brzeska, this process entails a movement beyond immediate needs as they have been defined by the economy. The individual must practice a more inclusive sensuality in relation to the material world. His senses must once again "relate themselves to the *thing* for the sake of the thing" (87–8). This re-education, though, depends upon the perception and appreciation of specifically human creations. The senses cannot simply return to the object-world, for they must appreciate its human determinateness, the human ability to occupy and produce a stable world. Marx describes a now familiar process in which human artifacts obstruct easy identifications, thus at once halting and clarifying the desires that go into their making:

man is not lost in his object only when the object becomes for him a *human* object or objective man. This is possible only when the object becomes for him a *social* object, he himself for himself a social being, just as society becomes a being for him in this object.

On the one hand, therefore, it is only when the objective world becomes everywhere for man in society the world of man's essential powers – human reality, and for that reason the reality of his own essential powers – that all *objects* become for him the *objectification of himself*, become objects which confirm and realize his individuality, become *his* objects: that is, *man himself* becomes the object. The manner in which they become *his* depends on the *nature of the objects* and on the nature of the *essential powers* corresponding *to it*; for it is precisely the *determinateness* of this relationship which shapes the particular, *real* mode of affirmation. (88)

This is where art becomes important for Marx, where a carved stone or a lyric poem can transform the individual's relation to the material world. The aesthetic object exudes human determinateness; its excesses and exaggerations reveal those tensions that define the subject in relation to the world. In Marx's terms, this kind of object presents the "objectively unfolded richness of man's essential being" and thus "cultivates" the richness of human sensibility (88–9). In times of war as well as peace, art suggests history's openness, our ability to affect and transform human existence in more humane ways.

CHAPTER 5

Thesmophoria: suffragettes, sympathetic magic, and feminist classicism

"Deeds, not words!" – a fitting motto for the militant suffrage movement. From protests, pageants, and fisticuffs to sabotage, smuggling, and arson, deeds defined the movement from beginning to end. For women who had been effectively barred from public life, action was imperative and struggle a goal. Members argued that "revolt is a great and glorious thing in itself" and saw little distinction between "the joy of battle and the exultation of victory."[1] Yet one cannot deny the spectacular, performative aspects of the campaign. Firsthand accounts reveal that militant punches and kicks were often only suggested or mimed. In fact, one of the movement's very first "deeds" was nothing more than an imitation of spitting; as Christabel Pankhurst explained, "It was not a real spit but only, shall we call it, a pout, a perfectly dry purse of the mouth."[2] Often, suffragettes would tie stones to their wrists or wrap them in paper so that, when tossed, they would not cause any substantial material damage. Axes rarely fell, bricks dropped limply, and flags would poke through already open windows and doors.[3] Certainly, symbolic protest of this sort cannot be seen as a sign of cowardice or weakness. Militants proudly defined themselves as a "stage army" and self-consciously labored under the knowledge that "Who takes the eye takes all!"[4] Rather, the suffrage movement seems to confirm a powerful mutuality of deeds *and* words, and expresses the possibility of a society informed by their rational integration. In fact, as I hope to show, insofar as militants sought to exploit this mutuality, they defended it as the basis of an alternative, intersubjective community.

In the streets and on display, the militant body was at once active and expressive. Most often, it sought to obstruct civic flows, arouse the interests of the demobilized spectator, and then model and inspire alternative forms of behavior. In this, militants eschewed what they saw as the false promises of rational debate and the dangerous rhetoric of sympathy for a more active performance of their ideals. By miming and adapting various images of

199

power, they exposed the human passions behind them and thus their power
to be transformed. Their performative protest, in other words, exposed the
permeability of all political discourse. Militant spectacles, insofar as they
placed the desiring body at the center of the public sphere, challenged not
just the voting system, but the exclusionary logic that informs all modern
politics. These displays, like the ancient rituals upon which they were based,
occurred midway between the emotional and the discursive, the fluid and
the formal, the sensual and the sensible. They linked desire and image in a
dynamic, conscious whole, presenting clear alternatives and the ability to
enact them. This activity redefined politics as a ceaselessly creative medium,
one that conditions, and is conditioned by, multiple identities and relations.
According to Jane Ellen Harrison, suffragette and classicist, "Life is doomed
to make for itself moulds, break them, remake them."[5] For Harrison and
her feminist contemporaries, the relationship between the individual and
society was a continuum in which "the soul is like a bird caught in a cage,
caught and recaught ever in new births."[6]

These protests also offer a concrete example of classicism's power to challenge and transform the politics of the everyday. From its inception, the
suffragette movement was aligned with classical modernism in its opposition to the bourgeois culture of modernity. The militant's disgust with
the Liberal Party and the "sluggish respectability of the 'plain man'" clearly
echoes Lewis's attack on the "abysmal inexcusable middle-class."[7] Aptly,
Janet Lyon describes this "mutuality" as a "shared sense of deep disappoint-
ment that the promises for radical change, brokered by the language and
institutions of modernity's progressivist telos, had in fact been co-opted
by the modern instrumental status quo."[8] In other words, feminists saw
classicism as a viable alternative to the oppressive rationalism of modernity
at large. Classical ritual, particularly in its focus on the formalized body,
united action and symbol and thus became an important tool with which
to reconfigure the binary terms of culturally inscribed power. It was seen
as neither static nor reactionary, but as a continuous, effective argument,
a constant construction and reconstruction of those categories that govern the social. In other words, feminists adopted a classical armor not as
a form of escapism or in imitation of the male citizen, but to foreground
and thus maneuver from within a dynamic matrix of power and discourse.
Their emphasis on stasis, restraint, and clarity worked to expose and control
the construction of subject positions. Like Gaudier-Brzeska's sculpture or
Hulme's poetry, the stylized body was used to halt and inspire the desire
of others, to provoke and enflame the otherwise rigid relations between
modern subjects.[9]

The sections of this chapter, then, explore the political efficacy of classical modernism as well as the relations between feminist thinkers and a supposedly male modernism. In suffrage protest, Harrison's ritualism, and H.D.'s poetry, we find a charged matrix of worldly and aesthetic praxes. Each posits human desire as the basis of expression, and thus each finds a medium at once vital and static, affective and conscious. These sections, however, differ in their position along a single continuum; the first section offers protest at its most explicitly physical, the latter at its most textual. In this, I hope to dramatize not only the political connections between these phenomena, but the ways in which social praxis always entails a certain aesthetic activity and, conversely, the ways in which aesthetic activity cannot – even in its most rarefied forms – escape being political. According to Harrison, the stages of social praxis are "life with its motor reactions, the ritual copy of life with its faded reactions, the image of the god projected by the rite, and, last, the copy of that image, the work of art."[10] As we will find, this continuum served to counter the oppressive logic of modernity and its male-dominated avant-garde. Art begins and ends in a single dynamic matrix, and only thus offers the possibility of an alternative community. In fact, with this logic, modern feminists anticipate the more radical aspects of postmodern phenomenology, particularly M. Merleau-Ponty's theory of the expressive body. Their protests and poems align the condition of being-in-the-world with a specific mode of political engagement, the power of which has yet to be realized even in our own time.

LIFE

Insofar as militants defined their cause in opposition to their gendered subjugation, they also found themselves struggling against the attitudes and values of the larger bourgeois world. As they understood it, success depended upon their ability to move beyond the issue of the vote and to mount a much wider attack on a complex matrix of individualism, free trade, progress, and machinery.[11] The presumed consensus of the rational public sphere, the moral righteousness of individualism, the accessibility of the free market – these principles, they argued, only obscured and upheld specifically masculine interests. Essays and speeches typically denounced the sluggish machinery of liberal politics, the managed chaos of bourgeois economics. Emmeline Pethick-Lawrence, for example, criticized the Liberal government for conceiving freedom as an "ideal only of opposition, of vested interests, of inertia, and of prejudice."[12] Dora Montefiore argued that Herbert Asquith "is against the women because they are for peace and he is on the side of the capitalist."[13] As I hope to show here, militants sought to challenge their gendered status from within a specifically bourgeois world; their emphases on material restraint and the material dimensions of all political discourse worked to oppose the basic terms of a competitive modern economy and to erect an alternative, intersubjective model of social order.

The modern feminist movement, then, is first distinguished by its realization that the only effective campaign was one realized through direct physical action. Emmeline Pankhurst and her followers eschewed rational discourse and appeals to sentiment in order to focus upon the effective power of material force. Tellingly, in her famous address at Hartford, Pankhurst describes her work as an attempt "to bring enough pressure to bear upon the government to compel them to deal with the question of woman suffrage." She argues that "it is not by making people comfortable you get things in practical life, it is by making them uncomfortable."[14] As a whole, her movement measured effectiveness in terms of size, strength, and duration. Protests and pageants maximized pressure and discomfort upon their civic surroundings. A turn to arson and vandalism sought a wider and more lasting impact. The "argument of the broken pane" was perhaps the most successful realization of this strategy and as such attests to the power of the movement's anti-capitalism. In a seemingly random series of attacks on non-partisan shops and offices, suffragettes did their best to make the Londoner very "uncomfortable." The attacks exploited and exposed the interconnectedness of private and public spheres, particularly as that link was informed by economics. As Pankhurst claimed, "There is something the Governments care for far more than they care for human life, and that is the security of property . . . and so it is through property we will strike the enemy."[15] The attack, her daughter added, was developed for a world that was "very materially-minded; [opponents] do not care for argument, or anything of that kind – all that they want to know is, What are the resources of these women? Can we tire them out, or can they tire us out?"[16]

As these statements suggest, militant strategy was also informed by a decisively antiproductivist attitude, and it was most effective in its efforts to slow and retard social machinery. At first, opponents dismissed most tactics as mere nuisances – scraping golf greens, painting over house numbers, home and prison blockades.[17] But larger maneuvers – refusing the census, cutting down communication lines, and a rather peculiar week of self-denial – began to reveal a pattern. The most successful policies worked to create "a very paralyzing situation . . . an impossible situation."[18] Upon entering the streets, for example, militants first sought to block civic flows.

As one observer acknowledged, "More and more it became difficult to belittle the movement . . . which could hold up the traffic of London with processions two or three miles long, and decked from end to end with hundreds of banners, some of them of vast size . . ."[19] Similarly, in breaking shop windows and cutting down communication lines, militants halted the flows of the market. Their leader explained that "in this effort to rouse business men . . . we entirely prevented stock brokers in London from telegraphing stock brokers in Glasgow, and vice versa; for one whole day telegraphic and telecommunication was entirely stopped."[20] Most radically, in hunger-striking, militants interfered with the activity of the female body itself. This weapon, the "weapon of self-hurt," put perhaps the "greatest pressure" upon an otherwise smoothly functioning nation.[21] As Jane Marcus explains, "When woman, quintessential nurturer, refuses to eat, she cannot nurture the nation," particularly when that nation is defined in terms of a ceaseless production and consumption (1–2). As Lyon echoes, hunger-striking was directly opposed to the "'natural market' ideology of free trade economics" and thus served to expose and erode "the joints between economic coercion and sexual subjection" (116).[22]

The suffragettes' intransigent materialism, however, found its clearest expression in their valorization of restraint. According to the leaders, "our words have always been, 'be patient, exercise self-restraint, show our so-called superiors that the criticism of women being hysterical is not true.'"[23] At its most basic level, this emphasis served to counter misconceptions of the supposedly hysterical female body. As Lyon points out, "a discourse of anti-sentimentality and pure objectivity" provided access to "universalizing discourses that had been formative in the historical exclusion of women . . ." (115). But, as importantly, this emphasis, particularly when it took the form of hunger-striking, figured as a critique of an increasingly dissipated bourgeois community, one internally weakened by rampant production and the principles of exchange. For many suffragettes at the time, traditional forms of femininity were understood to be complicit with economic exploitation. Speeches and articles consistently condemned the social proscription of the domestic and the institutionalized pressure to reproduce. Many saw marriage as an "outrage on decency and freedom alike" that perpetuates "the view of women as vessels . . . for men's use and as automatic breeding machines."[24] Cicely Hamilton, in her popular study *Marriage as a Trade* (1909), found it impossible for a man to entertain any reverence and esteem "for a section of humanity which he believes to exist solely in order to perform certain animal functions connected with, and necessary to, the reproduction of the race."[25] Christabel Pankhurst similarly deplored "the doctrine that woman is sex" as the ideological product of a specifically bourgeois economy in which "the relation between man and woman has been that of an owner and his property."[26]

In *The Great Scourge and How to End It* (1913), Christabel Pankhurst pushes this critique to its most radical conclusions and presents sexual restraint as the basis of an alternative economy, a positive quality that increases human potential for thought and action. Her polemic begins by linking a recent rise in sexual disease with the subjugation of women. Widespread physical degeneration, as spread by prostitution, stems from the ignoble activity of men, the institutionalized discrimination toward woman, and the economic inequality of the sexes. Pankhurst inflects her critique of modern sexual practices with an attack on liberal society in general, claiming that the nation has been destroyed by sexual free trade and unchecked reproduction. "Men whose will-power fails them," she laments, "are constantly infecting and reinfecting the race with vile disease, and so bringing about the downfall of the nation!" (12, x–xi). It is within this context of national dissipation that Pankhurst voices her demand for restraint. She laments incontinence insofar as it "causes a waste of vital force which impoverishes [men's] moral nature and weakens their body" (60). Sexuality, she claims, "ought to lie dormant until legitimate occasion arises for its use, when it will be found to exist in full natural vigour" (61). In this, as in the most radical work of Hulme, Pound, and Lewis, Pankhurst presents an intriguing economy of energy and restraint, strength and clarity. What women admire in men, she explains, is "cleanliness and self-control – and even more than self-control, a mind which is too big and fine to harbour immoral ideas and intentions" (127). This dynamic system extends, as it does for the men just mentioned, well beyond the body. Pankhurst tackles the life of the mind when she praises the "active man who directs his energies more to his brain and muscles than to his sensual nature" (59). Uncannily, she even offers a quasi-Vorticist account of the work of art. After lamenting the foolish equation of art and voluptuousness, she claims that "Art is creative. Sexual excess is a waste of man's creative energy" (127).

This emphasis on restraint also points toward the militant reconception of discourse. Pankhurst's work offers a carefully crafted discourse of anti-sentimentality that expresses faith in women's ability to speak from within a supposedly rational public sphere. In this, perhaps, she could be seen to deny female sexuality altogether and thus capitulate to bourgeois notions of political identity. But her treatise reads as a conscious effort to manipulate ideological codes, and thus toys with essentialism, gendered or otherwise. The call for female restraint and the exposure of male sexuality

Figure 9   A poster advertising the suffragette newspaper, 1912.

is an intentional reversal of gendered roles, and, in this, it does not deny or erase the feminine body, but self-consciously girds it for participation in a discursive battle (Figure 9). As Pankhurst explains in her autobiography, "Much depended, in militancy . . . upon timing and placing, upon the dramatic arrangement and sequence of acts and events." The sites of suffragette struggle – streets, courts, and prisons – form, quite literally, a theatre of war, in which each spectator had "to reckon with us as representing womanhood."[27] For Pankhurst, restraint is not a form of emulation, but rather serves as a means of gaining mastery of the body and its representations. According to Lyon, "The control of the body – the code of this new order – everywhere patterns the discursive fabric of militancy." Pankhurst's work is "a reactive polemic that creates radical subject positions, first and foremost" (120).

Like Pankhurst, many suffragettes understood that identity, gendered or otherwise, was always negotiable and that the need for self-representation extended well beyond the issue of the vote. Olive Schreiner, for example, argued that "sex relations may assume almost any form on earth as the conditions of life vary . . . those differences which we, conventionally, are apt to suppose are inherent in the paternal or maternal sex form, are not inherent."[28] Cicely Hamilton equated her political turn with a growing suspicion of male-constructed ideals and symbols: "I became a feminist on the day I perceived that – according to the story – her 'honour' was not a moral but a physical quality. Once that was clear to me my youthful soul rebelled."[29] Emmeline Pethick-Lawrence, too, argues that "The world as we know it today is ruled by law, by custom, and by public opinion, and women are beginning to realize that it is a man-made world in the deepest sense of the word; it is a man-made and man-ruled world. Its laws are men's laws; its rules of commerce and every-day business are men's rules. Its moral standard, its public opinion, is formed by men." For Pethick-Lawrence, the suffrage movement is an effort to counteract the notion that "there is nothing that expresses the woman's point of view. There is nothing that tallies with the woman's soul . . . everything is arranged on a plan different from their own, and upon a system which has taken no account of their point of view."[30]

Informed by these experiences, the militants adopted an aggressive, material symbolism. They fully welcomed the spectacular, using pageants, deputations, and speeches to control and manipulate the processes of signification. Lisa Tickner, in fact, argues that the movement was most powerful as a form of symbolic militancy, in its turn to "object lessons, by signs and emblems and pictures, by processions, and many other visible and audible displays" (10). Its greatest success was probably not the vote, but "the legitimizing of new representations of women. Or, more precisely, the contesting, modifying and restructuring of representations of women already in circulation or in the process of emerging" (172). "Suffragette narratives and symbols, however, were perhaps most valuable in that they helped to shape new identities from within the female community. These representations, in other words, worked to inspire copies or duplicates, thereby influencing and informing other subjectivities. In fact, as Barbara Green argues, most suffrage writing self-consciously "takes up the performative nature of identity, revealing how feminist identities are produced through constant reiteration or performance" (7). In other words, feminist "experience" occurred within a certain performative loop, one in which origins and repetitions tended to blur, lost in the infinite variations of reiteration. By performing certain values or identities in public, militants inevitably called them into being. In the words of Emmeline Pethick-Lawrence, "While working for the idea of political liberty, we were individually achieving liberty of a far more real and vital nature."[31]

Lady Constance Lytton's masquerade as a poor spinster typifies this process. After repeatedly failing to become a victim of force-feeding, and in hopes of exposing hypocrisy within the legal system, the upper-class Lytton disguised herself as a lower-class militant. Not surprisingly, soon after her assumed economic reversal, she was arrested and subject to the most appalling torture. The political significance of the experience, however, depended upon its reiteration, in the fact that Lytton's narrative provided a script for others to follow as they too were forcibly fed. As Caroline J. Howlett explains, Lytton's experience needed to be voiced and thus complicates the notion of "authentic" feminine expression. For better or worse, the critic argues, suffragette activity provided "an image to be viewed rather than a 'real person,'" a "model for other accounts that followed, a model that working-class suffragettes then used to articulate their own experiences." Indeed, Lytton's own account of the affair and its aftermath suggests that even the most personal, incommunicable aspects of her experience contained performative, mimetic qualities. As she writes, "To think that I who have endured by far the least of all the 'forcibly fed' should be making people wake up more than all of them . . . It is the other more heroic and first ones who have really done what I *seem* to have done."[32]

With Lytton's example, it becomes clear how difficult it is to distinguish between the militants' active and representational strategies. Throughout the campaign, the female body functioned as the site of both work and signification. While its force was inevitably expressive, its expression released implacable forces. Deeds inevitably bespoke the need for change, and words were deployed for their ability to affect that change. Window-smashing, for example, was not only an exertion of power, but a very public display of "womanhood," solidarity, social change, and countless other fears and hopes. Similarly, the lengthy trial that followed the smashing not only provided a sanctioned forum in which to speak, but further served to disrupt the channels of power.[33] More complexly, physical activity gave voice to previously hidden spheres of opposition. Material protest gave rise – in the press and elsewhere – to voices of hostility and thus exposed an extensive matrix of power. Conversely, purely verbal acts unleashed hidden reservoirs of oppositional power. Militant words – shouted at government meetings, dinner parties, sporting events, and theater performances – inspired previously hidden hostility from the status quo. As Emmeline Pankhurst explained, one of the most effective militant acts consisted of nothing more than a question. For asking a question, just as men would have asked it, "girls were treated with violence and flung out of the meeting; and when they held a protest meeting in the street they were arrested, and were sent to prison, one for a week as a common criminal, and the other for three days."[34]

This conflation of deeds and words, power and knowledge, was most compellingly expressed in the slogan "You are an argument."[35] In fact, this conflation was used to characterize the vote itself. Emmeline Pankhurst defined suffrage as both "a symbol . . . a symbol of freedom, a symbol of citizenship, a symbol of liberty" and "an instrument, something with which you can get a great many more things."[36] Most importantly, though, this intense dualism informed the militant's understanding of the law. In a speech delivered in 1912, Emmeline Pethick-Lawrence draws upon a now-familiar dialectic of contingency and clarity; for her, reality is a complex matrix of force and form, need and expression. The desiring subject finds both restriction and definition in a single, negotiable continuum called the law. As she explains, "In common we have felt the compulsion of this Law that has brought us into association together and has made us part of a living pattern, woven by destiny in the loom of Time, to a rhythm and rune which is making the world's story." For Pethick-Lawrence, the law is simultaneously challenged and created, informed and revealed by a confluence of subjective positions. In fact, she argues that only because of "obstacles placed by enemies in its path, the idea for which we stand has dominated the human consciousness of the world . . . it is by the very enemy and the betrayer that the law is accomplished and destiny fulfilled." One cannot ignore the speaker's excesses, but Pethick-Lawrence consistently tempers her romanticism within the material world. The rhythms of force and form are the rhythms of history. The subject's power is made known only because it is contingent, immanent. It is both experienced and understood through the "material substance of things," "our own bodies."[37]

For militants, then, protest occurred at the border of the body and the law, between desire and its representation. Their strategies served to expose the infrangible union of power and discourse. As Emmeline Pankhurst argued, "Government rests upon force, you say. Not at all: it rests upon consent."[38] "In other words, if desire provided the terms of law, then the latter was always immanent and negotiable. In fact, while the suffragettes were always antagonistic to parliament, they were also quick to defend their respect for the law. In court, for example, they often argued that "We are not here because we are law-breakers; we are here in our efforts to become law-makers."[39] They repeatedly emphasized the distinction between criminal and reformer: "The criminal breaks the law to the injury of the State and for his own profit; the reformer breaks the law to his own injury, but for the salvation of the State."[40] Relatedly, suffrage protest worked to expose women's subjection to the law; a primary goal was to "be recognized as a person in the eyes of the law."[41] Efforts, in other words, were directed toward dismantling the bourgeois myths that pretended to remove women from the burden of social responsibility and thus from social power. Essays and speeches focused on the ways in which women – as mothers, wives, workers, civic agents, etc. – were affected by the law and thus needed to gain control of its construction. Sylvia Pankhurst, for example, attacked what she saw as women's enforced "outlawry," a state worse than that of the criminal, beneath the law, unrecognized and disempowered.[42]

By actively grappling with the law, militants challenged how it was understood and maintained. Their belief in the dynamic construction of the law moved them beyond democratic principle, beyond the rhetoric of individualism to a much more intensely integrated whole. Violent contingency, the traces of which often appear on the human body, evoked a radical intersubjectivity. According to Mary Jean Corbett, "Those who endure the physical force exercised against their bodies experience the material realization of suffragette ideology. Through these practices, they redefine the ethic of selflessness by bringing it into politics, where it serves as the basis for developing political community."[43] With this realization, militancy abandoned the myth of the universal subject and the empty abstractions of representational politics in order to explore the social as a modality of various interests and desires. The bourgeois public sphere and its seemingly rational laws, paradoxically constructed upon principles of exclusion and noninterference, were rejected in favor of what appeared to be more fluid processes of exchange and mediation. In fact, the importance of the movement seems to exist in its awareness that modern politics are essentially *negative* in character, founded upon the belief that the "individual" must *not* be encroached upon.[44] In response, militancy proposed a community that was radically *positive*, based upon a constructive or creative interaction between its constituents. Of course, community of this kind does not imply ideological freedom; the continuous negotiation of power denies the possibility of a stable, transcendent position from which that power can be clearly evaluated. Nevertheless, this community implies a point of access from which to grasp and perhaps reconfigure specific relations. As Corbett adds, the militant community "provided a ground for intersubjective connections rather

than a solution to or an escape from material and ideological differences"
(162).

Tellingly, militants often expressed, particularly at those moments of
intense suffering, a redemptive experience of larger forces and pressures.
Describing her own insurgency, Mary Richardson writes, "It was as if I were
compelled by something outside me . . . The idea that I could feel satisfied
with myself had not entered my mind. At such moments I was no longer
my small personal self. The cause had triumphed: that was what mattered."
Even in prison, she continues to feel a comforting "influence, almost of
a presence, beside me which gave me consolation and sympathy."[45] This
force was felt by many others. Constance Lytton, for example, describes an
intense process in which she was moved from "sympathy" with the cause to
a conviction based on "direct touch" and "first-hand experience."[46] Pethick-
Lawrence explains that "A life force has taken hold of us and has welded
us with all our different individualities into one . . . we individually and
collectively have been caught in the meshes of a Will that we may be used
in the accomplishment of its purpose."[47] These feminists – even at their
most romantic or mystical – yearn for undeniably material forces. Their
speeches express no wish for transcendence, or even freedom, but a real
respect and desire for a grounded, interconnected whole.

As I have tried to argue, militants understood themselves as both body
and sign. Their activity served as means and ends, a thing done and its
representation. As we turn to Harrison and H.D., this hybridity will help
us to distinguish between a collectivity that tends to subsume all difference
in a false equality and a collectivity that serves to understand and negotiate difference as a positive, constructive force. As we will also find, this
sensibility typifies modern classicism and particularly modernist thinking
about classical ritual. Militants bravely grasped those worldly tensions that
condition the subject and her relations, the definitive pressures between the
individual and the collective. Their work exposed a larger, intersubjective
matrix, one defined by the tensions of force and form, power and discourse.
The individual, her society, and the law itself, exist in a state of constant,
and conscious, negotiation. In the words of Pethick-Lawrence, each human
exists within a "living pattern" and achieves "human consciousness" only
within that pattern.[48]

RITUAL

In their protests and pageants, suffragettes often borrowed from the art and
literature of classical antiquity. Participants dressed in robes and wreathed
themselves with branches and fruits. They formalized practical, everyday

Figure 10   The "Car of Empire" on the Women's Coronation Procession, 17 June 1911.

activities and mimicked the gestures of the Greek heroines. Memoirs and narratives reveal "saints," "martyrs," and even "an overblown Adelphi heroine."[49] Importantly, this turn to antiquity was informed by an awareness that militant protest – in its imagery, organization, and publicity – recalled ancient transformative rites (Figure 10).[50] Spectacles were often structured around the patterns of sacrifice and rebirth. Service, particularly when it involved imprisonment and force-feeding, was interpreted as a process of suffering and redemption. According to Mary Gordon, "The Women's Social and Political Union leapt into being like a fire . . . It left behind a rebirth and a new situation." The member was "seized and used. She was both flame and burnt offering."[51] Jane Ellen Harrison, suffragette and anthropologist, offers a special perspective on this feminist turn to classical ritual. Her studies move away from the moderns' affirmative vision of a rational, enlightened antiquity to define a classical culture of the masses and material practices. The strength of her work is its account of the primal unity of mythic narrative and ritual enactment, representation and gesture. It redefines the bourgeois public sphere by emphasizing the difficult, intersubjective construction of power and the affective potential of the desiring body.

In *Prolegomena to the Study of Greek Religion* (1900), Harrison looks beyond the myths of fifth-century Greece in order to disclose the material conditions and motivations of their creators. According to Harrison, mythology "invents a reason for a fact" (*P*, 396). "Some of the loveliest stories the Greeks have left us will be seen to have taken their rise, not in poetic imagination, but in primitive, often savage, and I think, always practical ritual" (*P*, xvii). Harrison's assertion is grounded in the conviction that every religion is "conditioned by the circumstances of its worshippers" (*P*, 85). Myths, gods, divine names and attributes, these are but reflections of the mortal world, the material conditions that govern earthly life. In religion, Harrison explains, all depends on "primitive habit," the immanent relationships and lifestyles of the worshippers (*P*, 431). The myth of Demeter, for example, obscures an earlier ritual whose content "was 'physical,' the object the impulsion of nature." In the original rite, the worshipper "attempts direct compulsion, he admits no mediator between himself and nature, and he thanks no god for what no god has done" (*P*, 124). For Harrison, then, individual gods are but projections of human experiences and attributes. These ideal subjectivities owe their existence to mere mortals; divine power is simply alienated human power. As she writes, "the gods are as many as the moods of the worshipper, i.e. as his thoughts about his gods. If he is kind, they are Kindly Ones; when he feels vengeful, they are Vengeful Ones" (*P*, 214).

Importantly, Harrison's theory includes a rigorous ideological critique, one that aligns her with militants and classicists alike. As she explains, "A god can only exist so long as he is the mirror of the people who worship him" (*P*, 545). Insofar as "Man makes the gods in his image," his deities reflect larger social changes (*P*, 363). She turns this critical eye to the fifth-century and its unique deities, lonesome heroes, and popular poets. These various incarnations of the divine, she argues, affirm a social order driven by individualism and commerce. The Greek of this period – with his carefully departmentalized gods, with his rituals of "tendance" or exchange – is nothing more than an "archpatriarchal bourgeois" (*P*, 285). His life is neatly divided between work, rest, and recreation; his rituals are freely conducted "business transactions" (*P*, 3). Like his gods, his faculties have become "departmentalized" (*P*, 308). All is governed by an implacable "rationalism," by "ideas of law and order and reason and limit" (*P*, 352, 397). For Harrison, these attitudes must have been conditioned by "swifter changes": economically driven migrations, the shifting of populations, and a cosmopolitan cult of the new. As she explains, rationalism and commerce go hand in hand, serving to affect a superficial "sheen of passing and pathetic splendour."[52]

Harrison critiques this culture for its blindness, its violence, and its immaterialism. Its "Heroism is for individuals"; its people and gods "are cut clean from earth and from the local bits of earth out of which they grew" (*AAR*, 161). "As man advanced in knowledge and in control over nature," she argues, "the mystery and the godhead of things natural faded into science" (*P*, 314). Most importantly, she links the excesses of rationalism with the pragmatism of its language. "Eikonism," she explains, "takes the vague, unknown, fearful thing, and tries to picture it, picture it as known, as distinct, definite – something a man can think about and understand . . . The vague some*thing* becomes a particular some*one*; to use a modern philosophical jargon, eikonism *pragmatizes* the divine god."[53] Here, Harrison exposes a linguistic crisis that ensures the decadent solipsism of the Greek world. The language of pragmatism can only reproduce the human and thus obscures that which is other; these practices "comprised and confined the god within the limitations of the worshipper" (*P*, 258).[54]

Harrison, of course, laments the similar conditions of her own historical moment and asks readers to look beyond the affirmative myths of the Heroic age, beyond Homeric individualism and Platonic abstraction, and to consider an earlier period characterized by an intense materialism, immanent deities, and sensual rites. Earlier Greeks are celebrated for their "temperamental materialism," for being in "touch with the confusions of actuality" (*P*, 476, 215). Their fears and joys are never abstract, but earthly, tangible; they are haunted by the "actual ghost, not a mere abstract vengeance that haunts and pursues" (*P*, 217). Importantly, in this more primitive society, representative practices are conditioned by physical experience. Its more dynamic worldview is delicately balanced between form and force, abstraction and sensation. An evil Ker, for example, exists both as a real physical bacillus and as a representation of social fears. "In all these cases of early genii," Harrison argues, "it is important to bear in mind that the shared distinction between moral and physical influence, so natural to the modern mind, is not yet established" (*P*, 183). The elements of the social order are similarly hybrid. The ritual expulsion of the *pharmakos* is both a symbolic and a physical act. The scapegoat figures as abstract symbol and real physical threat; it serves a terror-stricken city in need of spiritual as well as physical hygiene (*P*, 103, 108–9).

With this turn toward ritual, Harrison also asks us to look beyond the omnipotent gods of fifth-century myth to an originally human force, beneath Olympian abstraction to a primal, chthonic practice. For her, early ritual provides an alternative model of social order and change, one based on the embodied subject and her situational needs. Typical of other modernists interested in ritual, Harrison locates desire at the center of this practice. She claims that most, if not all, rituals are initiated through passion, the "supreme mysteries of ecstasy and love." The Eleusinian rite of sacred marriage, for example, cultivates sensuality as the precondition for the revelation of the divine. "It is indeed," Harrison writes, "only in the orgiastic religions that these splendid moments of conviction could come" (*P*, 568). Importantly, Harrison links the desire for power with the performance or representation of power. "It is a natural primitive instinct," Harrison argues, "to try by all manner of disguise to identify yourself more and more with the god who thrilled you" (*P*, 474). As with suffrage protest, the ritual performance is hybrid, rooted in desire, yet utterly static. It allows the embodied subject to become divine, to "enter spiritually into the divine life . . . and so be made one with the god" (*P*, 487). The participant exists "half way on the ladder between earth and heaven"; "He is the God himself incarnate as one of his worshippers" (*P*, 475).

In *Ancient Art and Ritual* (1913), Harrison continues to define ritual as an empowering performance of the "thing desired" (*AAR*, 25). Here, she focuses specifically on sympathetic magic, which she defines as the "mimicking of nature's processes" (*AAR*, 129). In seasonal rites, she argues, the "savage utters his will to live, his intense desire for food . . . It is this, his will to live, that he *utters and represents*" (*AAR*, 65). Here, though, Harrison further argues that this unity of desire and representation is founded upon tension or restriction. To establish this theory, she asks that we look at human constitution not as a bundle of separate faculties, but as a continuous cycle of activities. She argues that perception, emotion, and action function concurrently, without hierarchy or telos. "When we talk," she claims, "of Reason, the Emotions, or the Passions and the Will leading to action, we think of the three stages or aspects of our behaviour as separable and even perhaps hostile . . . But in reality, though at a given moment one or the other element, knowing, feeling, or acting, may be dominant in our consciousness, the rest are always immanent" (*AAR*, 39–40). Importantly, though, for humans, "perception is not instantly transformed into action; there is an interval for choice between several possible actions." Suggesting the positive power of restraint, Harrison argues that "Perception is pent up and becomes, helped by emotion, conscious *representation*." It is out of this "momentary halt" in the cycle, this "unsatisfied desire," that "all our mental life, our images, our ideas, our consciousness, and assuredly our religion and our art, is built up" (*AAR*, 41). Like Christabel Pankhurst, like H.D., Harrison defines restraint as a creative force. The stymied participant at once utters and enacts desire, proclaims and thus repairs the terms of his or her existence. Sympathetic magic, then, occurs at the interface of desire and restriction, and only thus combines the active and the symbolic, the creative and the intelligible. In this, Harrison suggests that our experiences are always somewhat ritualized, seamlessly shifting between life and art. They incessantly combine dromenon, "things done," and drama, "performance" (*AAR*, 35).

It must be made clear, however, that this desire is primarily intersubjective, and its ritual performance often addresses the terms of human relations. In other words, public ritual extends beyond the expression of bodily need in order to address social inequality and disadvantage. In fact, for Harrison, social status exists only in its performance, in the part-practical, part-symbolic gestures of public protest. For the primitive as well as the modern, "the number of these 'dances' is the measure *pari passu* of his social importance" (*AAR*, 31). These performances do not simply express, but challenge social relations; their power is representational and transformative. According to Harrison, the ritual participant does "not simply 'embody' a previously conceived idea, he begets it. From his performance springs the personification" (*AAR*, 71). This change, though, extends well beyond the participant to affect the larger social field. The rite models activity and modes of behavior for the community as a whole:

the emotion is felt collectively, the rite is performed by a band or chorus who dance together *with a common leader*. Round that leader the emotion centres . . . This leader, this focus, is then remembered, thought of, imaged; from being *per*ceived year by year. He is finally *con*ceived; but his basis is always in actual fact of which he is but the reflection. (*AAR*, 72)

Ritual, much like suffrage spectacle, serves to conceive and thus enact new modes and relations. The performance of desire arouses the spectator's desire. Power is perceived in gestures that are then mimicked by the larger population. Moreover, that mimicry – because conscious – is open to choice and thus change. The process, at its best, is at once active and thoughtful, infinite and infinitely negotiable.

Harrison's discussion of the Thesmophoria offers the clearest example of this theory and its social significance. The Thesmophoria was an autumn festival in which women, purified for the occasion, lowered pigs into clefts or chasms in the ground. After some time, the women themselves descended into the clefts, brought up the rotten flesh and "placed it on certain altars, whence it was taken and mixed with seed to serve as a fertility charm" (*P*, 123). Harrison argues that the explanatory myth of Demeter and Persephone was only later appended to this seasonal rite, and thus obscures its original, sympathetic intention. Quite simply, "The content of the ritual was 'physical,' the object the impulsion of nature" (*P*, 124). Importantly, though, the mythological explanation testifies to the foundation of the primitive law. The myth, we learn, depends upon the personification of Demeter Thesmophoros as a law-carrier or law-giver. The second term, Thesmophoros, harks back to the carrying and laying down of sacred objects, or *thesmoi*. The goddess took her name from the ministrants, who were "called Thesmophoroi because they carried 'the things laid down'" (*P*, 137). The law, then, is based on ("laid down by") an earlier "thing done," and that "thing done" was performed in mimicry of the natural cycle. Harrison supports this argument by explaining that most ancient rituals entailed "things said" as well as "things done." The scholar argues that the words uttered during the sacred rites correspond to specific gestures and activities (*P*, 570). While today's creeds are simply dogmatic utterances, ancient speech functioned as an "avowal of things performed" (*P*, 156). Harrison's insight is that it was from this representative aspect of ritual that the formal law was derived. The binding curse or creed "on its religious side developed into the vow and the prayer" and "on its social side into the ordinance and ultimately into the regular law" (*P*, 142).

In Harrison's theory, ritual – in its intersubjective positioning and performative dynamic – functions as a continuous argument, a practical construction and reconstruction of those categories that govern the social. In fact, for Harrison, ritual activity everywhere overlaps with the habitual routines of the everyday. "Many," she writes, "perhaps most of us, breathe more freely in the *medium*, literally the *midway* space, of some collective ritual" (*AAR*, 206). The strength of this theory is its avoidance of the binary logic that governs modern politics. As a "universal transition space," ritual continually confounds those often gendered dichotomies that enforce contemporary configurations of power. It relocates desire within the public sphere and thus provides a point of access from which traditionally oppressed groups can negotiate their position. For Harrison, though, it is not that these groups are essentially identified with the body, but that all parties partake in a single matrix of desire and discourse. With this in mind, we can now examine the scholar's feminism and her account of modern feminism as the reactivation of community in its most elementary form.

We have seen how agriculture and agricultural rites served as the foundation of primitive society. Harrison argues that women, who presided over these activities, enacted and upheld the earliest forms of the law (*P*, 262, 272). Demeter embodies an originally feminine link between agriculture and law; as thesmophoros, she presides over the "things of this life, laws and civilized marriage" (*P*, 275). Partaking in an important modernist tradition, one exemplified in H.D.'s poetry, Harrison rewrites the ideological constructions of antiquity in order to counter current configurations of power. She looks beyond the judgment of Paris, which she calls a "beauty contest . . . vulgar in itself," in order to restore the image of three female, gift-bearing Charites (*P*, 298). Hera, we are told, had been worshipped long before the advent of Zeus; she may have been "forcefully married, but she is never really a wife" (*P*, 315–6). Harrison, however, claims that this early, earthly religion was inevitably superseded and obscured by the rational, abstract forms of patriarchal society. The "mystery of the godhead of things natural," she argues, was destroyed by "men advanced in knowledge and in control over nature" (*P*, 314). For Harrison, feminine power was systematically denied by masculine institutions. The dynamic materialism of the matriarchy was destroyed by the empty abstractions of patriarchy, by "Reason, Light and Liberty." Masterfully, Harrison examines the ancient myths in order to expose an ancient sex war that is surprisingly modern in its terms. She describes, for example, how the myths transformed an originally vibrant fertility goddess into the abstract, "sexless thing" called Athene (*P*, 301–2). She explores the ideological work at play when a male god such as Poseidon, angry with the civic worship of female deity, inflicted a triple punishment on her citizens in which "[women] were to lose their vote, *their children were no longer to be called by their mother's name* and they themselves were no longer to be called after their goddess, Athenians" (*P*, 261–2). For Harrison, mythic battles between gods such as Poseidon and Athene expose the historical basis of gender oppression. The tangible aspects of this struggle, still felt today, included the institutionalization of marriage and the political exclusion of women through the vote – in other words, the enforced logic of separate spheres.

Importantly, though, as Harrison traces the historical eclipse of female power, she also accounts for its inevitable return. Her theory, founded upon the negotiability of power, grants contemporary women a position from which to challenge institutional configurations of power. In "Homo Sum," in fact, we find that this challenge has already taken shape as the contemporary struggle for suffrage.[55] Harrison explains that her studies of the "psychology of primitive man" led her to a theory regarding the constructedness of gender. The sexes, she realized, are defined by an "artificial division of moral industry," and the "virtues supposed to be womanly are in the main the virtues generated by subordinate social position" (*HS*, 83–4). Harrison then defines the origins of the suffrage moment in terms of women's felt restriction, their increasing awareness and dissatisfaction with their public identities:

The beginnings of the movement are always dark and half unconscious, characterized rather by a blind unrest and sense of discomfort than by a clear vision of the means of relief. Woman had been told *ad nauseam* that she must be womanly; she was not unreasonably sick to death of it, stifled by unmitigated womanliness. (*HS*, 85)

Discomfort and desire, she argues, have produced new expressions of civic identity. Inequality has inspired various efforts to find the proper imagery and gestures that best serve to empower women. Eschewing essentialism, Harrison sees the suffrage movement not as an expression of genuine womanhood, but as a ritualized effort to rewrite the terms of cultural power. She argues that the "superficial" activity of the movement, which is sometimes ugly, sometimes coarse, needs to be understood in terms of the "essential soundness" of the campaign (*HS*, 86). Militant activity is defined as women's "awakening of the *intention to act*, to act more efficiently and to shape the world more completely to our will" (*HS*, 113–14).

Harrison ultimately argues that contemporary feminism restores desire to the political arena. In "Scientiæ Sacra Fames," she boldly claims that the feminine ego is "extensive" and that the feminine mind is "resonant," subject to "induction from the social current." While man often conducts his life according to his own pleasures, woman is tied "somewhat closer to the race. She has more social, racial tact."[56] Harrison thus consciously reverses the logic of separate spheres, deploying a specific argument used against women's political involvement in order to assert the necessity of that involvement. The very qualities which supposedly make women unfit for participation in the rational public sphere provide the basis of a radically different, more humane social order. Since women "may be more racial, less individual," they "may be of use for the whole body politic" (*SSF*, 134). As they are "in intimate contact, close touch with the bigger will, the larger life," they can help society to grow "conscious of its unity, its interrelations" (*SSF*, 135–6). Importantly, though, Harrison backs away from any essentialism that these claims may imply. She is not sure whether this attribute is "wholly induced by social conditions, or a factor inherent in sex." She is only concerned with the way in which it can influence "popular prejudice" (*SSF*, 126–7). Her point is that contemporary feminism restores a general principle of sexuality in its relation to intellect and thus counters "the old obsolete dualism between body and soul" (*SSF*, 140). As she explains,

Intellect is never wholly and separately intellectual. It is a thing charged with, dependent on, arising out of, emotional desire . . . We can watch the physical and emotional sides of knowledge in our own minds. Anyone who makes even a very small mental discovery can note how, at the moment of the making, there is a sudden sense of warmth, an uprush of emotion, often a hot blush, and sometimes tears in the eyes. Who can say that a process so sensuous and emotional, or at least attendant by concomitants so sensuous, is insulated from a thing as impersonating as sex? (*SSF*, 140–1)

With this, Harrison concludes that feminism demands a "binocular vision of the two sexes," an intellectual hybridity that makes "co-operation desirable, because fruitful" (*SSF*, 142, 140). Anticipating one of H.D.'s most celebrated images, she concludes with a small paean to a deity that is "neither male nor female, but a thing bisexed, immaculate, winged" (*SSF*, 142).

ART

For Susan Stanford Friedman, H.D.'s early work, and indeed early modernism in general, is complicated by its association with patriarchal attitudes and conservative politics, with the "totalizing mythos of the reactionary center." Imagism, in particular, comes under attack as the "critical cage" of a rigid, phallic modernism, from which the female poet needs "liberation."[57] Consequently, Friedman praises H.D.'s turn away from these suspect aesthetics toward the nonrationalist, nonmaterialist perspectives and mystical hermeticism of the later epics. H.D.'s work is read as it "mediated the influence of patriarchal traditions and led to a poetry centered on woman as both authentic symbol and questor."[58] It is valuable as "a case in point for the gendered history of modernism, for the situation of a woman who writes out of the position of the Other," and as an expression of woman's "'difference': her recognition of, desire for, and pride in multiple forms of 'difference.'"[59] Difference is, of course, the key term here, and at times Friedman repeats it with a revealing compulsiveness:

Penelope's Web sets out to explore the *difference* of H.D.'s prose oeuvre: its difference from her poetry, its difference from male modernism as the Penelopean Other enacting its own agency, and the difference it makes to a literary history of modernity. The production, publication, and reception of her prose enact that difference . . . Gendered more directly than her lyric poetry, linguistically more experimental in its excesses, her prose is a difference that necessarily makes a difference in our reading practices.[60]

This valorization of an absolute and mystical "difference," which is paradoxically presented here as a measurable quantity, informs H.D.'s scholarship as a whole. Those concerned with modern feminism and alternative modernist traditions, seem unable to interpret H.D.'s strength as anything but negative or oppositional. Cassandra Laity, for example, also argues that "H.D.'s decadent revisions helped her, therefore, to create a myth of womanhood counter to the myth of manhood represented by male modernist anti-Romantic programs for poetry."[61] Similarly, Rachel Blau DuPlessis claims that the excesses, repetitions, and radical instability of H.D.'s most experimental writing suggest "an overlayered centre of authority in female and mystical otherness."[62]

Friedman's work helped to initiate a late-twentieth-century triumph of a particular kind of modernism committed to "difference" or "otherness." In "Modernism of the 'Scattered Remnant,'" "Exile in the American Grain: H.D.'s Diaspora," and *Penelope's Web* (each repeats her argument nearly verbatim), she celebrates an alternative "modernism of the margins, a modernism based on an identification with those left out of the cultural mainstream."[63] Of course, biographical and historical evidence leaves us suspicious of the class and racial dynamics that inform the moderns' attraction to otherness. More importantly, though, insofar as Friedman defends a modernist tradition based on individualism and otherness, she rewrites the totalizing ethos of the period. Quite simply, this celebration of "perpetual marginality" tends to subsume that very difference it hopes to establish.[64] If H.D.'s "epic art places her squarely in the center of this modernist mainstream," then it does so precisely through that fetishization of otherness that regulates modern society as a whole. The poet's presumed "difference" tends to replicate and reinforce a romantic, not to mention bourgeois and masculinist, dialectic. Ultimately, in Friedman's work, one finds a revival of those binaries that tyrannize the earlier period. H.D. comes out the clear victor in a "prototypical confrontation between the polarities that permeate the modern world: man against woman, science versus religion, fact versus faith, objective versus subjective reality, reason versus intuition, the rational versus the irrational."[65] To define history in these terms cannot be redeemed, even when it serves to revive a forgotten, yet valuable poet. "Otherness," whether violently critiqued or blindly romanticized, can never "oppose and transcend" the tyranny of the modern, for it can only reinforce the very logic upon which modernity's sexual, racial, and economic oppression is founded.[66]

Although I do not deny H.D.'s tendency toward romanticism or even her powerful deconstruction of typically offensive tropes and styles, I hope to establish here that her most powerful work focuses on the intense intersubjectivity of experience and only thus entails a certain social, if not explicitly political, engagement. In other words, if H.D.'s poetry results from, and gives expression to, a certain marginal experience, it consistently emphasizes the creative tensions and pressures that exist between texts, subjects, and societies. It typically eschews polarities, dialectics, and even sympathetic identifications in order to focus on a single political matrix of expression and desire. Thus, I now turn to a third point on the continuum of deeds and words, to the most formal mode of engagement, the work of art. As we will find, H.D.'s ritualized verses reveal the dynamic unity of often gendered binaries, such as subject and object, public and private, work and world. Her work, at once ecstatic and effective, does not avoid political responsibility, or even define that responsibility through the individual; rather, it raises the possibility of an integrated community that always already incorporates the marginal, the feminine, and the poetic. As H.D. explained, "My work is creative and reconstructive, war or no war, if I can get across the Greek spirit at its highest I am helping the world, and the future."[67]

Much like Harrison, H.D. consistently depicts spirit as an immanent, affective presence. Her earliest collection, *Sea Garden* (1916), celebrates powerful, irrational forces as they both inform and clarify the objects of this world. Her poems are charged with a dynamic, fluid energy, yet their images remain vibrant, crisp, and intensely static. H.D.'s sea flowers, for example, are caught amidst violent drifts and tides, but it is precisely their openness to these conditions that lend them their beauty. Subject to elemental forces, their features turn "hard," "bright," and "fresh." The "marred" rose and "slashed" reed are "doubly rich" for their torment. Conversely, these precise forms, in their graceful motions and swift mutations, suggest the presence of elemental forces. The reed that is "lifted" gives shape to the wind; "pebbles drift and flung" reveal the motion of the sea.[68] In "Sheltered Garden," the poet tries to define the personal significance of this charged, contingent landscape. She first condemns the imaginative excesses of romanticism, its solipsism and glutted self-satiety. The isolation of the mind is at once claustrophobic and suffocating. "I have had enough," the speaker claims, "I gasp for breath . . . beauty without strength, / chokes out life." Repulsed, the poet demands a crisp, spare beauty marked by irregular pressures and tensions. A true classicist, she seeks the pleasure of a "terrible / wind-tortured place." She yearns for the sensation of "some sharp swish of a branch" and urges violent forces that "break," "snap," and "scatter," and forms that lie "torn" and "twisted" (19–21).

With this poem, it becomes clear that while H.D.'s work suggests a unity of form and force, it resists a romantic conflation of the two. Her world is defined by tension and contingency, and it is always at once tangible and expressive, vital and objective. As Eileen Gregory explains, the most remarkable quality of H.D.'s poetic landscape is its "liminality," a constant negotiation of "boundaries between inner and outer, between self and other." Its central qualities are at once "deeply subjective and radically impersonal . . . they represent deep interiority infusing in outward shape or motion, making it vibrant and golden."[69] These aesthetics are based on processes akin to those that inform militant protest and classical ritual. H.D.'s clear, crystalline images do not exist in isolation, but are embedded, and indeed result from multiple tensions within a dynamic field. Their existence is neither spontaneous, isolated, nor permanent, but conditional, resulting from their subjection to larger forces. As the poet observed,

I grew tired of hearing the poems referred to, as crystalline . . . For what is crystal or any gem but the concentrated essence of the rough matrix, or the energy, either of over-intense heat or over-intense cold that projects it? The poems as a whole . . . contain that essence or that symbol, symbol of concentration and of stubborn energy.[70]

This "energy," insofar as it informs and shapes the phenomenal world, is also decisively human. The winds and tides of H.D.'s poetry suggest the shaping power of desire itself. Throughout her work, we find an intense passion that cuts and marks all in its path, leaving its traces on both body and world. Subjects exist in a constant liminal state, between a palpable intimacy and a formal clarity. For H.D., the human body remains caught and purified by the elemental drift; subject to contingent forces from within and without, it grows intense and knowing. Take, for example, the fascinating "Pursuit." Here, H.D. depicts a lover's hot chase through a classical landscape of wild hyacinth and dwarf cornel. The speaker, in her lust, tracks the sensual traces of her quarry:

> . . . the stream is trampled,
> the sand on the stream-bank
> still holds the print of your foot:
> the heel is cut deep.
> I see another mark
> on the grass ridge of the bank –
> it points toward the wood-path.
>
> (11)

The desiring body shapes the landscape; its wild arc transforms all in its path. These traces bespeak of a passion perhaps greater than that of the natural world, a specifically human power to transfigure that world. Yet, in turn, the desiring body does not remain stable. As the speaker traces the path of her beloved, she clutches, falls, and stammers. Slowly, in this mimetic chase, she begins to merge with the object of her desire. H.D.'s ambiguous use of speech suggests a dynamic conflation of hunter and hunted:

> Did you clutch,
> stammer with short breath and gasp:
> *wood-daemons grant life –*
> *give life – I am almost lost.*   (12)

The speech comes at a moment when the speaker herself is "almost lost"; what she imagines to be her beloved's plea also seems to be her own. She cries out for "life," for renewal, but also for stability. She fears that she has become another, not simply the other she pursues, but other to herself. It is telling that this transformation climaxes in the act of speech, a speech which is part gasp and part denotation. Desire creates a self that is "doubly rich," caught between desire and expression, power and consciousness.

In another poem from this collection, H.D. echoes Harrison in that she associates this torturous desire with the process of becoming divine. In "The Cliff Temple," we find a similarly treacherous landscape of sharp rocks and jagged cliffs. Once again, we are presented with a chase and a pursuer who is "splintered and torn." This hunt, however, proceeds upward, toward an ever-receding height. It leads the speaker from the booming winds of worldly passion to the crisp clean edges of jagged rock, from the obscure chaos of desire to the clarity of the divine. Ultimately, the struggle itself enacts divinity. The ruggedness of the landscape and the suffering of the body brings forth the divine. As this final speech suggests, the god exists in its absence, in the desire it inspires:

> I have stood on your portal
> and I know –
> you are further than this,
> still further on another cliff.
> (28)

The inability to reach the divine, the lack of fulfillment, is itself divine. The desiring subject always already exists at the portal of the temple, conjuring both the power and knowledge of the other.

As we can see, H.D.'s work, much like that of Pankhurst or Harrison, consistently privileges tension and restraint. For the poet, creation depends upon the constancy of desire, and desire is fueled by the experience of restriction. In fact, throughout her work, H.D. warns against sexual fulfillment and consummation. She often pleads for chastity, claiming that the artist can "retard" his powers by "neglect of his body." The "love-region" must remain in a state of constant excitation, "its energy not dissipated in physical relation."[71] It was in the twenties, however, when H.D. revisited her early classicism, that she developed a clear theory of the desiring subject. In "Notes on Thought and Vision," the poet argues that the subject reaches her full potential only through "definite physical relations." Her image of the "over-mind" suggests that all identity exists in the play of desire and material resistance:

> I should say – to continue this jelly-fish metaphor – that long feelers reached down and through the body, that these stood in the same relation to the nervous system as the over-mind to the brain or intellect.
>
> There is, then, a set of super-feelings. These feelings extend out and about us; as the long, floating tentacles of the jelly-fish reach out and about him. They are not different material, extraneous, as the physical arms and legs are extraneous to the gray matter of the directing brain. The super-feelers are part of the super-mind, as the jelly-fish feelers are the jelly-fish itself, elongated in fine threads. (*NTV*, 19)

Albeit bizarre, H.D.'s image of the over-mind provides a consistent inter-subjective model. The over-mind, subjectivity itself, exists only in mutuality, in a kinetic coupling that is at once sensuous and conscious.

Importantly, this model also suggests the possibility of the subject's empowerment. Like many other modernists working with visionary traditions, H.D. recognizes that perception, as rooted in the body, in desire, is also creative. "The centre of consciousness," she explains, "is either the brain or the love-region of the body" (*NTV*, 20). To illustrate her theory, she turns to the sacred rites of Eleusis, in which "One must understand a lower wisdom before one understands a higher" (*NTV*, 31). The rites entail a three-step process that moves from "Crude animal enjoyment" to pure "over-mind consciousness." Physical lovers figure as prototypes for "spiritual lovers," the latter having the power of "concentrating and directing pictures from the world of vision" (*NTV*, 50). As in Harrison's work, body and vision, "seed" and "word," coexist in a single, dynamic process. Subjection becomes subjectivization, and a position from which to negotiate power. As H.D. argues later, "Two or three people, with healthy bodies and the right sort of receiving brains, could turn the whole tide of human thought, could direct lightning flashes of electric power to slash across and destroy the world of dead, murky thought . . . could bring the whole force of power into the world" (*NTV*, 27).

Tellingly, it was by exploring her psychic experiences in Greece that H.D. found the most compelling links between desire, restraint, and vision. In *Tribute to Freud*, the poet recalls how her trip to Greece was supposed to culminate with a visit to the seat of the visionary priestess at Delphi. At Itea, however, she and Bryher were told that the trip was too dangerous: "But no, now that we were so near, we could not go to Delphi. We were going in another direction, Brindisi, Rome, Paris, London . . . we obviously *were* leaving."[72] For H.D., though, these intense feelings of restriction and longing were the direct cause of her *own* visionary experience. Unable to visit the oracular seat, detached from the excitement of the temple, the poet finds her passion transmuted into ecstatic symbols. Well-versed in psychoanalytic theory, H.D. places these projections squarely between the wish-inspired dreams of Freud's work and the mystical, otherworldly speech of the mystics. Each one can be translated, she argues, "as a suppressed desire for forbidden 'signs and wonders'" or "an extension of the artist's mind, a *picture* or an illustrated poem, taken out of the actual dream or day-dream content and projected from within" (*TF*, 76). For H.D., the visionary event is significant precisely because it is both personal and impersonal; the seer is caught between her intense passion and abstract form. One image, she claims, is "so impersonal it might have been anyone, of almost any country. And yet there was a distinctly familiar line about that head . . . dead brother? Lost friend?" (*TF*, 66). Time itself seems to straddle the mythic and the ordinary, as H.D. conflates the "formal handling of a subject which has no racial and no time-barriers" with the specific instances in which it has been retold and "translated" (*TF*, 69–70). Not surprisingly, the deity that presides over this hybrid experience is none other than the winged Nike. The goddess appears upon a ladder, between two realms, the worldly and the divine. For H.D., the image, like those found in her early poetry, is "doubly rich" (*TF*, 83).

H.D.'s poetry repeatedly explores this relay of desire, restraint, and creativity. Her verses are populated by "broken" lovers and distraught visionaries whose powers exist only in a passion deferred. "Fragment Thirty Six," for example, presents the following, frustrated lament:

> I know not what to do,
> my mind is reft:
> is song's gift best?
> is love's gift loveliest?
> (165)

The speaker cannot decide whether to seek fulfillment in the arms of a lover or attenuate and thus transmute her passion into the clear words of song. Masterfully, H.D. presents the lips as the source of both desire and language. Kissing, of course, would "slake / the rage that burns." With this act, all tension would subside as subject and object dissolve into one. The speaker, however, wonders whether she should turn away and "press lips to lips / that answer not . . .?" The verse aptly conveys the nervous transmutation of passion into speech. In the absence of fulfillment or response, in its willed deferral, kissing becomes song. The lips offer a precise image of the painful doubling or enfolding that defines all experience. Difference and unity, engagement and detachment – it is this "brokenness" that produces song:

> so my mind hesitates
> above the passion
> quivering yet to break,
> so my mind hesitates
> above my mind,
> listening to song's delight.
>   (167)

It becomes apparent here that the song is already being sung. The poem itself is an expression not of a decision made, but of an attenuated state. Both sensual and sentient, aroused and detached, the speaker writes herself within the dynamics of desire. Restraint produces language, as language heightens and prolongs passion. "Strain upon strain, / sound surging upon sound," such runs the relay of passion and expression (167).

"Eurydice" explores this sensual coupling as the basis of a more exhaustive phenomenology, as it both confirms and denies subjective wholeness. The poem begins with an eerie elemental layering; the infernal landscape is lit by "flame upon flame" and the upper earth reveals "Fringe upon fringe of blue crocuses" (51, 53). This metaphysical doubling is quickly translated into a drama of intersubjective dynamism. For Eurydice, the Orphic gaze is not simply that which returns her to hell, but a sort of perpetual torment:

> So for your arrogance
> and your ruthlessness
> I am swept back
> where dead lichens drip
> dead cinders upon moss of ash;
>
> so for your arrogance
> I am broken at last.
> I who had lived unconscious,
> who was almost forgot . . .
>   (51)

The presence of the other, here figured as both tangible and visual, disturbs the romantic isolation and comfortable solipsism of the buried woman. The aggressive male ego demands dependence and subjection, leaving the speaker "broken," defeated. Yet this presence also serves to distinguish the woman, to render her whole, distinct, and conscious. The subject exists only in this mutual recognition, in the mirroring "reflex of the earth" (52). For H.D., it is precisely this double state, at once a dependence and a detachment, that empowers the speaker. If Eurydice is "broken," she now exists midway between desire and knowledge, between body and thought. As she proudly announces:

> At least I have the flowers of myself,
> and my thoughts, no god
> can take that;
> I have the fervour of myself for a presence
> and my own spirit for light . . .   (55)

This relation, and the power it generates, is infinite. As we saw the cliff temple continually recede into the heavens, here the fall into hell is endless. Eurydice's phenomenal pain is eternal, and thus eternally creative. She continues to gather presence and strength from her surroundings, and wields them in her speech:

> Against the black
> I have more fervour
> than you in all the splendour of that place,
> against the blackness
> and the stark grey
> I have more light;
> . . .
> and I would sink into a place
> even more terrible than this.   (54–5)

Here, the speaker aligns her own presence with the enfolded space that surrounds her. In manipulating the contours of that space, in controlling relations within the primal matrix, she locates a "terrible," earthly strength.[73]

"Eurydice," in its elemental layering and intersubjective positioning, comes closest to defining the incarnate *matter* of H.D.'s poetry. It explains what we find often in the verses: "flame upon flame," wavebreak upon wavebreak," "strain upon strain," and "white on white." Throughout, basic elemental forces continually collide and overlap, resulting in clear, objective forms. H.D.'s poetry offers a world continuously doubled over onto itself, ceaselessly bifurcated or enfolded. It suggests a single dynamic matrix that, in its constant redoubling, produces subjects, objects, and the possibility of consciousness. There has been much effort to claim this enfolded, bifurcated space for a specifically feminist, lesbocentric polemic. But while H.D.'s work occasionally links the intersubjective with a more specific state of invagination – see "Cassandra," for example, in which a divine "shaft" leaves the maiden a "bitter, broken thing" (169–70) – it more often points toward an open sexual dynamism and the universal terms of all intersubjective relations (170).[74]

In fact, H.D. suggests that the poet's activity merely intensifies a universal activity of being. The poet's desire – like desire in general – mimics the creative activity of the world at large. Her voice speaks not *against*, but *with* the world, actively engages its tangible forces and vivid forms, its passions and their representations. To borrow from Peter Nicholls, we can call H.D.'s work a "mimesis . . . which somehow supplements its model" (30). It inflects everyday objects and events with a certain "otherness," and thus "opens a gap or breach within the rhythmic flow of social life . . ." (31–2). This notion is confirmed in H.D.'s short essay "Responsibilities." Here, the poet privileges art that seems "conjured to life from some region inhabited by half-spirits, half-humans." While the best verse is often "innocent" and "remote," it is defined by a "greater, sterner intensity" of life. For H.D., this intense doubleness, this middling between work and world, between image and desire, serves to "redefine and reconstruct boundaries and barriers, and reinvoke some golden city, sterner than the dream-cities, and wrought more firm to endure than those riveted of steel and bleak with iron girders."[75]

This supplementary process, which may also be described as a form of sympathetic magic, can be seen in H.D.'s celebration of gift-giving. In H.D.'s poetry, gifts are always natural, and their exchange mimics natural processes. However, in gift-giving, both object and activity have been singled out and abstracted from their common surroundings. In this manner, accepted relations of dependency and power are critically examined and challenged. In "Hermonax," for example, the speaker presents the sea with the gift of its own creative activity:

> Broken by great waves,
> the wavelets flung it here,
> this sea-gliding creature,
> this strange creature like a weed,
> covered with salt foam,
> torn from the hillocks of rock.

> I, Hermonax,
> caster of nets,
> risking chance,
> plying the sea craft,
> came on it.
> Thus to sea god,
> gift of sea-wrack . . .
>
> (58)

Masterfully, the elements of the scene – the tides, the gliding creature, the feeble nets – suggest a dynamic matrix within which various forms of life negotiate for power and position. The speaker's gesture simply redoubles this activity, taking and giving that which has already been given and taken. The act serves only to define and clarify his particularly humble position within the tumultuous landscape, to counter "chance" with "craft." In other words, through mimicry, the speaker attempts to know and thus manipulate his position within that matrix. Tellingly, his speech is marked by a reiteration and amplification of identity, "I, Hermonax," and it concludes with a recognition of his position within a large economy of exchange.

In "Holy Satyr," H.D. once again turns to this supplementary process, but now cunningly confuses notions of originality and imitation. Here, the passion of the speaker manifests itself in a much more complex creative process:

> Most holy satyr,
> like a goat,
> with horn and hooves
> to match thy coat
> of russet brown,
> I make leaf-circlets
> and a crown of honey-flowers
> for thy throat;
> where the amber petals
> drip to ivory,
> I cut and slip
> each stiffened petal
> in the rift
> of carven petal . . .   (148)

At first, the speaker seems to adorn the holy satyr with variously crafted objects. Her work serves to supplement and augment a beauty that is half-animal and half-divine. Yet, after the eighth line, we find a curious slippage and conflation of materials. The satyr seems to disappear entirely, and we are left with nothing more than the collected bits of flower, ivory, and horn. There appears to be no original object here; the speaker herself creates what she desires. In fact, the second line tells us that the original model is already a representation; it is already "like" something else. Ultimately, human desire, the passionate nature of the goat, is answered only by itself. The final product "return[s] our hymn, / like echo fling, / a sweet song, / note for note" (149). The speaker realizes herself to be the satyr she both creates and mimics; her activity is itself half-animal and half-divine.

What needs to be clarified is how this poetic ritualism can, in turn, transform relations based on desire, how the seeming escapism and frigidity of the classical work of art can be realigned with political activity. A return to Harrison is helpful here, as her work explicitly traces the continuum of aesthetic and political praxis:

The god arises from the rite, he is gradually detached from the rite, and as soon as he gets a life and being of his own, apart from the rite, he is a first stage in art, a work of art existing in the mind, gradually detached from even the faded action of ritual, and later to be the model of the actual work of art, the copy in stone.

The stages, it would seem, are: actual life with its motor reactions, the ritual copy of life with its faded reactions, the image of the god projected by the rite, and, last, the copy of that image, the work of art. (*AAR*, 191–2)

The work of art, born of emotion and want, is but "a later and more sublimated, more detached form of ritual," that yet retains its social potential (*AAR*, 225). As an expression of desire, it offers the audience a life transformed, "a different kind of life, it is the life of the image-world, of the *imag*ination" (*AAR*, 210). It can feed and nurture the mind with possible "alternatives," and thus "enhance and invigorate the whole of human life" (*AAR*, 211). For Harrison, even the most abstract aesthetic creations are inevitably earthbound, arising from, working against, yet ultimately returning back to life itself. "Earth pulls hard," she argues, and thus conditions, as it is conditioned by, the work (*AAR*, 229).

Harrison's theory carefully avoids art's potential for sublimation. The work may serve to "discredit the actual practical world," but it never insists "on its actuality and objectivity" (*AAR*, 227). While the good work of art generates desire, it absolutely refuses identification. Thus, the energy that would be lost in its framework is blocked and diverted back toward the world at large. In other words, for Harrison, classical art, in its very stasis and cool detachment, offers perhaps the most powerful form of political activism. As she explains, "Art . . . sustains and invigorates life, but only does it by withdrawal from these very same elementary forms of life, by inhibiting certain sensuous reactions" (*AAR*, 236). More precisely, "the life of imagination, cut off from practical reaction as it is, becomes in turn a motor-force causing new emotions, and so pervading general life, and thus ultimately becoming 'practical'" (*AAR*, 210). With this formulation, Harrison offers a valuable counter to the oppositional logic of the avant-garde. By locating material tensions and restrictions at the very center of representational practice, she confounds distinctions between worldly and aesthetic praxes. Ritual art does not exclude the possibility of contemplation, but denies the possibility of an autonomous, purposeless space from which the world may be addressed. Art, as routed through intersubjective desire, is always already material, purposive, and social. Its beauty is collectively determined, conditioned by "a keen emotion felt toward things and people living today" (*AAR*, 237).

H.D. similarly conceives art's relation to society. In "Notes on Thought and Vision," aesthetic appreciation is defined as a more intensive, more refined experience of desire. Aesthetic beauty is similar to that of the "loved one," but its detachment denies fulfillment and thus "enflames" mind (*NTV*, 22). Similarly, in "Helios and Athene," the work of art is described as a medium or "go-between." It exists midway between human desire and divinity, between bodily lust and abstract form. Ultimately, its coldness disallows "self-complacent admiration." Good art does not supply a "final resting place," but forces the viewer to return to the practical world (327–8). H.D.'s formulation also denies the binary logic of modernity. It suggests neither an objective world nor its symbolic transcendence; rather, it offers a clear expression of desire that finds both origin and return in social praxis. Her art, then, serves to heighten, foreground, and thus suggest possibilities as they already exist in life's praxis. It impedes and opposes the romantic flight of the modern world, a flight into the subjective, into the future, into war, and thus offers a momentary pause or rest, out of which a more responsible action may arise. For Gary Burnett, "What [H.D.] calls the 'sacred' . . . is precisely the ability of the 'torchbearer' . . . to carry on with the responsibility of art in the face of this destructive spirit, to forge an art which is new without being violently severed from the past." Burnett nicely captures the supplementary quality of H.D.'s poetry, for he recognizes that her classical abstractions are "also always a presence," a "responsible inhabitation of the present."[76] Adalaide Morris, in a stunning article on H.D.'s *Trilogy*, more explicitly links this supplementary quality to ritual practice. She argues that H.D.'s poetry "not only *means* but *does*"; "it labors," she argues, "to create a formal break with everyday life, a ritual space that invites the reader to return to, reexamine, and rearrange the *ethos* of a community in crisis."[77]

Ultimately, though, we need to recognize that this classicism serves to occasion a critical experience of pain. Its beauty is teasingly offered and denied; its passions remain torturously unfulfilled. We have seen this tension in Lewis's cold, externalist method, Worringer's theory of abstraction, Hulme's aesthetics of touch, and Gaudier-Brzeska's work in stone. It is perhaps most keenly felt in the militants' strategic use of restraint and self-abnegation, in their painful contortioning of the body and in their celebration of the slain martyr. In these rituals, desire always encounters its rigid, static double, if not death itself. Harrison comes closest to defining the power of this experience. For her, the ritual work of art offers "reality caught – held somehow, at a distance . . . a spectacle of reality fettered." As she explains, "Art to me is very like a dead face or a sudden halt in a dance, but the noise of life and its flutter must be there if you are to feel the silence and the binding spell."[78] H.D.'s poetry, of course, similarly plays with stasis and pain, but thus casts its "spell." For her, though, this stasis provides not only tension, but also stability, a common presence or space around which community can consider itself. In other words, the dead space of the poem is also a space of collective life, a space transversed *into* collective life. In the words of Gregory, it signifies as it inspires "threshold states celebrated collectively," in which "the tribe as a whole renews itself" (123–5).

H.D.'s various statements on the Eleusinian rites offer the most striking account of this painful beauty and its affective power. In "Notes on Thought and Vision," the poet argues that while the "Eleusinian mysteries had to do with sex," sensuality was countered by "a certain amount of detachment . . . a certain amount of artistic appreciation" (*NTV*, 29–31). Similarly, in "Helios and Athene," she claims that the participant neither surrendered to desire nor achieved detachment, but experienced a love that is "the merging and welding of both, the conquering in herself of each element, so that the two merge in the softness and tenderness of the mother and the creative power and passion of the male."[79] In the poem "At Eleusis," however, H.D. does not simply describe, but enacts this rite and its divine pain:

> *What they did,*
> *they did for Dionysos,*
> *for ecstasy's sake*:
>
> now take the basket,
> think;
> think of the moment you count

most foul in your life;
conjure it,
supplicate,
pray to it;
your face is bleak, you retract,
you dare not remember it:

stop;
it is too late.
The next stands by the altar step,
a child's face yet not innocent,
it will prove adequate, but you,
I could have spelt your peril at the gate,
yet for your mind's sake,
though you could not enter,
wait.

What they did,
they did for Dionysos,
for ecstasy's sake . . .   (179–80)

With the poem's contrasting registers, H.D. presents a rich doubling of deed and word, power and thought. Her verses alternate between the abject and the divine, between passionate engagement and formal gesture. The italicized refrains, in fact, confirm the worldly enactment of the divine. An anonymous, ecstatic "they" have performed the power of the god. Through their activity, they did not merely conjure, but became that which they desire. The poet, however, is not content with description or even suggestion, for she demands the reader's complicity and her poem enacts the intersubjective dynamic of this rite. The speaker engages us directly in the second person, calls forth an erotic potential thus far obscured. The contrasted registers inspire and impede our own desires, encourage and deny the possibility of fulfillment. This restraint is most dramatically felt in the transition between the second and third verse, when the speaker shouts "Stop." With this "sudden halt," the moment of unity is forestalled, and thus power and power relations are made conscious. The priestess bars entry, and commands us to "wait," presumably in order to achieve understanding, for "mind's sake." Ultimately, we turn away, but now enflamed by a conscious desire, by a renewed potential that still seeks outlet. Passion is heightened, but now mediated and made thoughtful. Consummation is yet possible, but informed by consciousness. The painful feeling of restriction transforms dream into knowledge. As mortals, we wield the power of the divine.[80]

CONCLUSION

For H.D. and her feminist contemporaries, the notion of an expressive body shook the very foundations of modern thought and practice. If desire informs discourse, there is no longer any support for the dualistic, regulatory logic of the public sphere. Moreover, the absolute unity of mind and matter suggests a dynamic field of engagement, an endless and creative negotiation of all power. With this logic, the modern feminist movement anticipates postmodern phenomenology and its most radical implications. In *Phenomenology of Perception*, M. Merleau-Ponty similarly argues that the intentional body shapes the world that it knows.[81] First and foremost, the body's situational specificity implies an integral unity of feeling, knowing, and acting. "All my knowledge of the world," he writes, "even my scientific knowledge, is gained from my own particular point of view, or from some experience of the world without which the symbols of science would be meaningless" (viii). Importantly, it is precisely this situatedness that implies the possibility of change. As Merleau-Ponty explains, "The subject is no longer the universal thinker of a system of objects rigorously interrelated"; rather, "The world is not what I think, but what I live through. I am open to the world, I have no doubt that I am in communication with it, but I do not possess it; it is inexhaustible" (xvi–xvii). As I hope to show here, this phenomenology, with its emphasis on intentionality and resistance, on desire and its social patterning, suggests the continued significance of modern feminism, and, more generally, modern classicism. Merleau-Ponty's work links the classical landscape with an alternative, postmodern order and thus with a radically different, anti-dualist concept of truth and its political consequences.

Merleau-Ponty begins his most important work with an account of the body in action. In contrast to most Western theory, he argues that bodily motion is hardly rational or mechanical. Physical movement, whether sensory or muscular, involves a certain ideational grace. It occurs somewhere between the psychic and the physiological, between unified idea and material causality. For Merleau-Ponty, in fact, the body has its own "consciousness" of the surrounding world. It exists somewhat like a medium or relay, a flexible surface that learns to negotiate internal desires and external pressures (75, 80). In this, the body defines the subject as "being-in-the-world," as a certain modality of intentions and responses in relation to a specific environment. This condition is most often habitual and nearly unconscious, but it always implies the unity of nature and culture, of instinct and pattern. The body is continually reshaped in its negotiative function; internal desires are transformed and diverted by external relations and experiences. According to Merleau-Ponty, "Everything is both manufactured and natural in man, in the sense that there is not a word, not a form of behavior which does not owe something to purely biological being – and which at the same time does not elude the simplicity of animal life" (189).

For Merleau-Ponty, the condition of embodiment, of being-in-the-world, entails the possibility of both consciousness and freedom. In its most basic activity, embodiment provides the material *foundation* for consciousness; the union of body and mind is not "an amalgamation between two mutually external terms, subject and object, brought about by arbitrary decree. It is enacted at every instant on the movement of existence" (88–9). For Merleau-Ponty, the self seems to exist in two modes that tend to overlap and coincide, one "impersonal" and "biological," the other "personal" and "human." The former is almost always unconscious and habitual, yet it provides the materials by which consciousness and, ultimately, culture, arises. It provides the groundwork for a learned "ability to mark out boundaries and directions in the given world, to establish lines of force, to keep perspectives in view, in a word, to organize the given world in accordance with the projects present of the moment" (112). As importantly, embodiment also provides the *conditions* by which consciousness is renewed. The organic and the conscious self "never quite coincide" (87). Intentions and thought processes shift in relation to one another; the system is marked by an uneven dynamism, an inassimilable "principle of indeterminacy" (169). In other words, the habitual stability of consciousness inevitably meets with changes in the world, with inconsistencies and dissonances that renew consciousness. Ultimately, that which "enables us to centre our existence is also what prevents us from centring it completely, and the anonymity of our body is inseparably both freedom and servitude" (85).

Importantly, this condition has a social dimension; in fact, identity is most powerfully shaped by intersubjective relations and reactions. For Merleau-Ponty, the acquisition of habit is defined as "the rearrangement and renewal of the corporeal schema," the "motor grasping of a motor significance" (143–4). The skillful use of an everyday object – such as a cane, a hat, or a car – is neither conscious nor rational; rather, it expresses the body's ability to transform its intentional schema. In these instances, "Habit expresses our power of dilating our being-in-the-world, or changing our existence by appropriating fresh instruments" (143). A more intense adaptation, however, seems to occur in our intersubjective relations and experiences. As one body encounters the power and presence of another, it

is infused with new possibilities; it directly incorporates alternative modes
of being-in-the-world into its own activity. For Merleau-Ponty, the body is
at once the origin and recipient of a mutable cultural schema; it creates the
structures which in turn define its potential:

Whether a system of motor or perceptual powers, our body is not an object for an
'I think', it is a grouping of lived-through meaning which moves toward its equi-
librium. Sometimes a new cluster of meanings is formed; our former movements
are integrated into a fresh motor entity . . . our natural powers suddenly come
together in a richer meaning. (153)

These transformations of the body are the transformations of culture and
history. As Merleau-Ponty explains, historical stereotypes "are not a destiny,
and just as clothing, jewellery and love transfigure the biological needs from
which they arise, in the same way within the cultural world the historical
a priori is constant only for a given phase and provided that the balance
of *forces* allows the same *forms* to remain." Fueled by stable, yet mutable
bodies, "history is neither a perpetual novelty, nor a perpetual repetition,
but the *unique* movement which creates stable forms and breaks them up"
(87–8).

   This account of the body as the medium of social and historical significance recalls the expressive strategies we discussed above. For Merleau-
Ponty, the body is that which communicates and perceives desire. It trans-
mits and receives value in its most basic form, as it is informed by material
needs and intentions. In other words, bodily expression cannot be defined
in terms of translation; the body does not express, but creates truth. More
precisely, it "accomplishes" truth. "The body," Merleau-Ponty writes, "does
not constantly express the modalities of existence in the way that stripes
indicate rank, or a house-number a house: the sign here does not only convey its significance, it is filled with it; it is, in a way, what it signifies" (161).
Even speech "is a genuine gesture, and it contains its meaning in the same
way as the gesture contains its" (183). Meaning is "brought to life in an
organism of words, establishing it in the writer or the reader as a new sense
organ, opening a new field or a new dimension to our experience" (182).
In a fascinating turn, this discussion of the expressive body leads Merleau-
Ponty to classical ritual. The Dionysian Mysteries, he claims, "invoke the
gods by miming scenes from his life . . . The god is actually there when the
faithful can no longer distinguish themselves from the part they are playing,
when their body and their consciousness cease to bring in, as an obstacle,
their particular opacity, and when they are totally fused in the myth" (163).
Clarifying what Harrison and H.D. appreciated in ritual, Merleau-Ponty

writes that "The body's rôle is to ensure this metamorphosis. It transforms ideas into things . . . The body can symbolize existence because it realizes it and is its actuality" (164).

Being and thought, thought and language: for Merleau-Ponty, these terms are merely abstractions of a single process whereby the world discloses its always momentary contents. The more radical implications of this theory, which are at once philosophical and political, become clear in "The Intertwining – The Chiasm," part of a work Merleau-Ponty left unfinished at his death.[82] In this essay, the phenomenologist explains that what we perceive as truth is not "a chunk of absolutely hard, indivisible being," but rather a "certain differentiation, an ephemeral modulation of this world – less a color or a thing, therefore, than a difference between things and colors, a momentary crystallization of colored being or of visibility" (132). Moreover, Merleau-Ponty asserts that both the perceiver and the object of perception exist as temporary "modulations" of the same substance. As in H.D.'s "Eurydice," the perceiving body is not simply implicated in the world, but is also shaped or perceived by the world. The body, in other words, always exists in two aspects, at once sensible and sentient, "a being of two leaves, from one side a thing among things and otherwise what sees and touches them" (137). For Merleau-Ponty, this doubled body partakes in the doubleness of the world. Reality is "enfolded" or "coiled" back upon itself and thus makes itself known (146). He writes, "There is vision, touch, when a certain visible, a certain tangible, turns back upon the whole of the visible, the whole of the tangible, of which it is a part" (139). This enfolded or doubled "whole" – tellingly called "flesh" – creates as it distinguishes the aspects of this world. It is at once general and specific, a common experience defined by radically particular moments. For Merleau-Ponty, this quality of the flesh allows us to recognize our positioning within the world, "clear zones, clearings, about which pivot their opaque zones." More importantly, it allows us to recognize our divine power and freedom within that world: "the primary visibility . . . does not come without a second visibility, that of the lines of force and dimensions, the massive flesh without a rarefied flesh, the momentary body without a glorified body" (148).

Merleau-Ponty's work – with its emphasis on the phenomenal body, its conflation of action and expression, its ultimate monism of an "enfolded" or "invaginated" flesh – provides an important link between early twentieth-century feminists and their postmodern counterparts.[83] As this phenomenology consistently positions thought and expression in the experience of the body, it offers a viable counterpoint to the ideological abstractions and regulatory strategies that govern the twentieth century as a whole. Elizabeth Grosz, for example, bases her radical feminism on the body's participation in the negotiation of power. "The body," she writes, "codes the meanings projected onto it . . . Far from being an inert, passive, noncultural and ahistorical term, the body may be seen as the crucial term, the site of contestation, in a series of economic, political, sexual, and intellectual struggles" (18–19). For feminists, however, this phenomenology is most valuable for its implied balance between the need to recognize momentary specificity and the inevitable openness of sexual determination. "The task," Grosz argues, "is not to establish a neutral or objective perspective on the question of sexual difference but to find a position encompassing enough for a sexually specific perspective to be able to open itself up to, meet with, and be surprised at the (reciprocal) otherness of the other sex(es)." This difficult double consciousness, attuned to both difference and continuity, informs an ethics very similar to that advocated by the feminists discussed above. In Grosz's words, "Sexual difference entails the existence of a sexual ethics, an ethics of the ongoing negotiations between beings whose differences, whose alterities, are left intact but with whom some kind of exchange is nevertheless possible" (192).

As I have tried to show, this consciousness underlies classical modernism as a whole. Merleau-Ponty's enfolded landscape, with its mutual pressures and vibrant forms, recalls Hulme's organized cinders, Gaudier-Brzeska's sculpted spaces, and H.D.'s dynamic sea gardens. The phenomenologist's emphasis on touch and contingency recalls the classical object and its ability both to posit and undermine its ecstatic presence. Ultimately, the various systems grouped together in this book – aesthetic, political, or otherwise – share an ethical responsibility toward distinct identities, but they also recognize the ways in which all particularities emerge from a single, dynamic whole. In these systems, phenomena such as art and theory testify to the human ability both to invest the world with significance and to evaluate that significance. This recognition provides at least one critical alternative to the alienation and repetitive violence of modernity. It implies a more inclusive world in which we can both recognize the conditions of our making and then work to reform them.

Notes

INTRODUCTION: ON THE NATURE OF BEING OTHERWISE

1. Wyndham Lewis, *Men Without Art*, ed. Seamus Cooney (Santa Rosa: Black Sparrow Press, 1987), 157. Hereafter abbreviated as *MWA*.
2. Scott Heller, "New Life for Modernism," *The Chronicle of Higher Education*, 5 November 1999, A21.
3. Gianni Vattimo, *The End of Modernity: Nihilism and Hermeneutics in Postmodern Culture*, trans. Jon R. Snyder (Baltimore: Johns Hopkins University Press, 1988), 2, 4.
4. Jeffrey M. Perl, *The Tradition of Return: The Implicit History of Modern Literature* (Princeton: Princeton University Press, 1984), 280.
5. See, for example, H. D., "The Cinema and the Classics," in *Close Up 1927–1933: Cinema and Modernism*, ed. James Donald, Anne Friedberg, and Laura Marcus (Princeton: Princeton University Press, 1998), 105–20; T. S. Eliot, "The Function of Criticism," in *Selected Prose of T. S. Eliot*, ed. Frank Kermode (San Diego: Harcourt Brace & Company, 1975), 59–67; Ford Madox Ford, *The English Novel: From the Earliest Days to the Death of Joseph Conrad* (Manchester: Carcanet Press, 1983), 15ff.; James Joyce, "James Clarence Mangan," in *The Critical Writings*, ed. Ellsworth Mason and Richard Ellmann (Ithaca: Cornell University Press, 1996), 73–83; Wyndham Lewis, "The Terms 'Classical' and 'Romantic,'" in *MWA*, 151–71; Ezra Pound, *Guide to Kulchur* (New York: New Directions, 1970); Gertrude Stein, "Composition as Explanation," in *A Stein Reader*, ed. Ulla E. Dydo (Evanston: Northwestern University Press, 1993), 501; Virginia Woolf, "On Not Knowing Greek," in *The Common Reader: First Series*, ed. Andrew McNeillie (London: Hogarth Press, 1984), 23–38.
6. Walter Benjamin, "The Work of Art in the Age of Mechanical Reproduction," trans. Harry Zohn, in *Illuminations* (Schocken Books: New York, 1968) and "Theories of German Fascism: On the Collection," in *War and Warrior*, edited by Ernst Jünger, trans. Jerolf Wikoff, *New German Critique*, 17 (Spring 1979), 120–8; Rita Felski, *The Gender of Modernity* (Cambridge: Harvard University Press, 1995), 11–14.
7. See, most recently, Paul Peppis, *Literature, Politics, and the English Avant-Garde: Nation and Empire, 1901–1918* (Cambridge: Cambridge University Press, 2000), 11–12.

8. Marshall Berman, *All That is Solid Melts into Air: The Experience of Modernity* (New York: Penguin Books, 1982), 118, 95.

9. See Malcolm Bradbury and James McFarlane, *Modernism: 1890–1930* (London: Penguin Books, 1991), 179.

10. Ezra Pound, *Personæ: The Shorter Poems*, ed. Lea Baechler and A. Walton Litz (New York: New Directions Books, 1990), 186.

11. T. S. Eliot, *The Waste Land: A Facsimile and Transcript of the Original Drafts*, ed. Valerie Eliot (New York: Harcourt Brace Jovanovich, Inc., 1971), 31.

12. See Frank Lentricchia, *Modernist Quartet* (Cambridge: Cambridge University Press, 1994).

13. Wyndham Lewis, *The Art of Being Ruled*, ed. Reed Way Dasenbrock (Santa Rosa: Black Sparrow Press, 1989), 32. Hereafter abbreviated as *AOBR*.

14. Wyndham Lewis, *Time and Western Man*, ed. Paul Edwards (Santa Rosa: Black Sparrow Press, 1993), 12.

15. See excellent commentary in Peter Nicholls, "Apes and Familiars: Modernism, Mimesis, and The Work of Wyndham Lewis," *Textual Practice*, 6, 3 (Winter 1992), 422–3, 425.

16. T. E. Hulme, *The Collected Writings of T. E. Hulme*, ed. Karen Csengeri (Oxford: Oxford University Press, 1994), 62. Subsequent references to Hulme's work pertain to this collection.

17. Hal Foster, "Prosthetic Gods," *Modernism/Modernity*, 4, 2 (1997), 7. For a similar argument, see Jessica Burstein, "Waspish Segments: Lewis, Prosthesis, Fascism," *Modernism/Modernity*, 4, 2 (1997), 139–64.

18. Wyndham Lewis et al., *BLAST* 1 (Santa Rosa: Black Sparrow Press, 1992); hereafter abbreviated as *B*.

19. See Reed Way Dasenbrock, *The Literary Vorticism of Ezra Pound and Wyndham Lewis: Towards a Condition of Painting* (Baltimore: Johns Hopkins University Press, 1985), 33, 36. On the relation of futurism and vorticism, see Richard Cork, "Marinetti and Nevinson's Role in Provoking the Arrival of Vorticism," in *Vorticism and Abstract Art in the First Machine Age*, vol. 1 (Berkeley: University of California Press, 1976); William C. Wees, "'Time for Definition': Futurism in England 1914," in *Vorticism and the English Avant-Garde* (Toronto: University of Toronto Press, 1972); Paul Edwards, *Wyndham Lewis: Painter and Writer* (New Haven: Yale University Press, 2000), 100, 104.

20. See commentary in Cork, *Machine Age*, 1, 31, 215.

21. David Graver, "Vorticist Performance and Aesthetic Turbulence in *Enemy of the Stars*," *PMLA*, 107, 3 (May 1992), 484.

22. Wyndham Lewis et al., *BLAST* 2, *War Number* (Santa Rosa: Black Sparrow Press, 1993), 91. See also Edwards, *Wyndham Lewis*, 114 and Cork, *Machine Age*, 1, 246.

23. Lewis later wrote, "I thought of the inclusion of poems by Pound etc. in 'Blast' as compromising. I wanted a battering ram that was all of one metal. A good deal of what got in seemed to me soft and highly impure . . . My literary contemporaries I looked upon as too bookish and not keeping pace with the visual revolution. A kind of play, 'The Enemy of the Stars' . . . was my attempt

to show them the way." Wyndham Lewis, *Rude Assignment: An Intellectual Biography*, ed. Toby Foshay (Santa Barbara: Black Sparrow Press, 1984), 138–9.

24. See editor's commentary in Wyndham Lewis, *Collected Poems and Plays*, ed. Alan Munton (Manchester: Carcanet, 1979), 220.

25. For a pessimistic reading, see Scott Klein, "The Experiment of Vorticist Drama: Wyndham Lewis and 'Enemy of the Stars,'" *Twentieth Century Literature: A Scholarly and Critical Journal*, 46, 2 (Summer 2000), 232.

26. See Dasenbrock's "Lewis's *Enemy of the Stars* and Modernism's Attack on Narrative," in his *Literary Vorticism*, ch. 4.

27. See Raymond Williams, *Culture and Society: 1780–1950* (New York: Columbia University Press, 1983), 39, 43.

28. Mark Antliff, *Inventing Bergson: Cultural Politics and the Parisian Avant-Garde* (Princeton: Princeton University Press, 1993), 27.

29. Michael North, *The Political Aesthetic of Yeats, Eliot, and Pound* (Cambridge: Cambridge University Press, 1991), 116, 114.

30. This schema has been borrowed and adapted from Eileen Gregory's excellent study, *H. D. and Hellenism: Classic Lines* (Cambridge: Cambridge University Press, 1997), 19–20.

31. See Dasenbrock's competing claim regarding painting's centrality in *Literary Vorticism*, 5.

32. Wyndham Lewis "The Machine," *Modernism/Modernity*, 4, 2 (1997), 172.

33. Karl Marx, "Economic and Philosophic Manuscripts of 1844," in *The Marx-Engels Reader*, 2nd edn., ed. Robert C. Tucker (New York: W. W. Norton & Company, 1978), 76, 89.

34. See Georg Lukács, *The Theory of the Novel: A Historico-Philosophical Essay on the Forms of Great Epic Literature*, trans. Anna Bostock (Cambridge: MIT Press, 1999); Theodor Adorno, "Commitment" and "The Position of the Narrator in Contemporary Fiction," in *Notes to Literature*, vols. 1 and 2, ed. Rolf Tiedemann, trans. Shierry Weber Nicholsen (New York: Columbia University Press, 1991).

35. Charles Altieri, "The Concept of Force as a Frame for Modernist Art and Literature," *Boundary 2: An International Journal of Literature and Culture*, 25, 1 (Spring 1998), 211, 206.

36. Hannah Arendt, *The Human Condition* (Chicago: University of Chicago Press, 1958), 169, 167–8, 5.

I FASCISM AND/OR LIBERALISM: THE AVANT-GARDE
AND MODERN CAPITALISM

1. F. T. Marinetti, *Let's Murder the Moonshine: Selected Writings*, ed. R. W. Flint, trans. R. W. Flint and Arthur W. Coppotelli (Los Angeles: Sun & Moon Classics, 1991), 81, 240, 69, 68. Unless otherwise specified, subsequent references to Marinetti's work refer to *Let's Murder the Moonshine*.

2. Walter Sickert, "The Futurist 'Devil-among-the-Tailors,'" in *Post-Impressionists in England*, ed. J. B. Bullen (London: Routledge, 1988), 310.

3. "Futurism," *Poetry and Drama*, 3 (September 1913), 262–3.
4. C. Lewis Hind, "The Post Impressionists," in Bullen, ed., *Post-Impressionists*, 190.
5. E. J. Hobsbawm, *The Age of Empire, 1875–1914* (London: Weidenfeld and Nicolson, 1987), 9, 188.
6. Russell A. Berman, *Modern Culture and Critical Theory: Art, Politics, and the Legacy of the Frankfurt School* (Madison: University of Wisconsin Press, 1989), 46–7.
7. Andrew Hewitt, "Fascist Modernism, Futurism, and Post-modernity," in *Fascism, Aesthetics, and Culture*, ed. Richard J. Golsan (Hanover: University Press of New England, 1992), 44.
8. Marinetti, *Let's Murder*, 23. Roger Fry, *Vision and Design*, ed. J. B. Bullen (Oxford: Oxford University Press, 1981), 88–9. Hereafter abbreviated as *VD*.
9. F. T. Marinetti and C. R. W. Nevinson, "Vital English Art," *Lacerba*, 15 (July 1914), 210.
10. F. T. Marinetti, "Wireless Imagination and Words at Liberty," trans. Arundel del Re, *Poetry and Drama*, 3 (Sept. 1913), 320.
11. Foster, "Prosthetic Gods," 8–9. See also Tim Armstrong, *Modernism, Technology, and the Body: A Cultural Study* (Cambridge: Cambridge University Press, 1998).
12. P. G. K[onody], "The Italian Futurists: Nightmare Exhibition at the Sackville Gallery," in Bullen, ed., *Post-Impressionists*, 292.
13. See, for example, Caroline Tisdall and Angelo Bozzolla, *Futurism* (London: Thames and Hudson, 1977), 31–2 and Dasenbrock, *Literary Vorticism*, 48–9.
14. Zeev Sternhell, with Mario Sznajder and Maia Asheri, *The Birth of Fascist Ideology: From Cultural Rebellion to Political Revolution*, trans. David Meisel (Princeton: Princeton University Press, 1994), 7.
15. Simonetta Falasca-Zamponi, *Fascist Spectacle: The Aesthetics of Power in Mussolini's Italy* (Berkeley: University of California Press, 1997), 133.
16. Quoted in Sternhell, *The Birth*, 23, 147.
17. See Herbert Marcuse, "The Struggle Against Liberalism in the Totalitarian View of the State," in *Negations: Essays in Critical Theory*, trans. Jeremy J. Shapiro (Boston: Beacon Press, 1968), 11.
18. Quoted in Falasca-Zamponi, *Fascist Spectacle*, 33, 35.
19. Quoted in Dennis Smith, "Englishness and the Liberal Inheritance after 1886," in *Englishness: Politics and Culture 1880–1920*, ed. Robert Colls and Philip Doss (London: Croom Helm, 1986), 254.
20. Samuel Smiles, *Self-Help*, reprinted in *Society and Politics in England, 1780–1960: A Selection of Readings and Comments*, ed. J. F. C. Harrison (New York: Harper and Row, 1965), 212–14.
21. John Stuart Mill, *On Liberty and Utilitarianism* (New York: Bantam Books, 1993), 109.
22. Matthew Arnold, *Culture and Anarchy and Other Writings*, ed. Stefan Collini (Cambridge: Cambridge University Press, 1993), 99.

23. Samuel Hynes, *The Edwardian Turn of Mind* (Princeton: Princeton University Press, 1968), 13.

24. Jonathan Rose, *The Edwardian Temperament 1895–1919* (Athens: Ohio University Press, 1986), chs. 3 and 4.

25. Quoted in Smith, "Englishness," 260.

26. See Rose, *Edwardian Temperament*, ch. 4. Also, D. S. L. Cardwell, *The Organization of Science in England* (London: Heinemann, 1974), and W. H. G. Armytage, *A Social History of Engineering* (Cambridge: MIT Press, 1966).

27. See Rose, *Edwardian Temperament*, 132, 130 and Harold Perkin, *The Rise of Professional Society: England since 1880* (London: Routledge, 1989), 130–2.

28. Quoted in Smith, "Englishness," 260.

29. Richard Cork, *Vorticism and Abstract Art in the First Machine Age*, vol. 1 (Berkeley: University of California Press, 1976), 225. On Marinetti's popularity, see Douglas Goldring, *South Lodge: Reminiscences of Violet Hunt, Ford Madox Ford and the English Review Circle* (London: Constable & Company, Ltd., 1943), 64; Henry Wood Nevinson, *Visions and Memories* (London: Oxford University Press, 1944), 78–9.

30. See "The Aims of Futurism" and Fry, "Art: The Futurists," both in Bullen, ed., *Post-Impressionists*, 305, 298.

31. "The Aims of Futurism," 305.

32. Charles Ricketts, "Post-Impressionism," in Bullen, ed., *Post-Impressionists*, 107.

33. See *The Times* (London), 19 March 1912.

34. George Dangerfield, *The Strange Death of Liberal England* (New York: Capricorn Books, 1961), 8, 217.

35. Robert Ross, "The Post-Impressionists at the Grafton: The Twilight of the Idols," in Bullen, ed., *Post-Impressionists*, 100.

36. See Peter Stansky, *On or About December 1910: Early Bloomsbury and Its Intimate World* (Cambridge: Harvard University Press, 1996).

37. G. E. Moore, *Principia Ethica*, ed. Thomas Baldwin (Cambridge: Cambridge University Press, 1993), 238.

38. Virginia Woolf, "Mr. Bennett and Mrs. Brown," in *A Woman's Essays: Selected Essays*, vol. 1, ed. Rachel Bowlby (London: Penguin Books, 1992–3), 76.

39. Virginia Woolf, *Three Guineas* (San Diego: Harcourt, Brace & Company, 1938), 106.

40. Quoted in Virginia Woolf, *Roger Fry: A Biography* (New York: Harcourt, Brace & Company, 1940), 235.

41. Virginia Woolf, "Middlebrow," in *Selected Essays*, vol. 1, ed. Rachel Bowlby (London: Penguin Books, 1992), 196–7.

42. Lytton Strachey, *The Shorter Strachey*, ed. Michael Holroyd and Paul Levy (Oxford: Oxford University Press, 1980), 178, 39.

43. See commentary in John Maynard Keynes, "My Early Beliefs," in *The Bloomsbury Group: A Collection of Memoirs, Commentary and Criticism*, ed. S. P. Rosenbaum (London: University of Toronto Press, 1975), 52, 57, 64.

44. Raymond Williams, "The Significance of 'Bloomsbury' as a Social and Cultural Group," in *Keynes and the Bloomsbury Group*, ed. Derek Crabtree and A. P. Thirlwall (New York: Holmes and Meier Publishers, Inc., 1980), 49, 54, 59–60.

45. Roger Fry, *A Roger Fry Reader*, ed. Christopher Reed (Chicago: University of Chicago Press, 1996), 98. Hereafter abbreviated as *RFR*.

46. See also Andreas Huyssen, *After the Great Divide: Modernism, Mass Culture, Postmodernism* (Bloomington: Indiana University Press, 1986), chs. 1–3 and Michael Tratner, *Modernism and Mass Politics: Joyce, Woolf, Eliot, Yeats* (Stanford: Stanford University Press, 1995).

47. See similar comments in A. Clutton-Brock, "The Post-Impressionists," in Bullen, ed., *Post-Impressionists*, 198–9.

48. Dmitri Mirsky, "The Bloomsbury Intelligentsia," in Rosenbaum, ed., *Bloomsbury Group*, 384, 387.

49. Marinetti, *Let's Murder*, 100.

50. Virginia Woolf, *A Room of One's Own* (San Diego: Harcourt, Inc., 1929), 41–2.

51. Jesse Matz, *Literary Impressionism and Modernist Aesthetics* (Cambridge: Cambridge University Press, 2001), 185.

52. Virginia Woolf, *To the Lighthouse* (San Diego: Harcourt Brace & Company, 1981).

53. Virginia Woolf, *A Writer's Diary: Being Extracts from the Diary of Virginia Woolf*, ed. Leonard Woolf (New York: Harcourt, Brace & Company, 1954), 87.

54. See North, *Political Aesthetics*, 5–6 and Seamus Deane, "Heroic Styles: The Tradition of an Idea," in *Ireland's Field Day* (London: Hutchinson, 1984), 49. The classic text on this phenomenon is, of course, Raymond Williams, *Culture and Society: 1780–1950* (New York: Columbia University Press, 1983).

55. Ross, "The Post-Impressionists at the Grafton," 104.

56. Ricketts, "Post-Impressionism," 107.

57. Anthony M. Ludovici, "The Italian Futurists and their Traditionalism," in Bullen, ed., *Post-Impressionists*, 320.

58. See Smith, "Englishness," 255 and Perkin, *Professional Society*, chs. 2 and 3.

59. "Futurism and Ourselves," *Poetry and Drama*, 4 (December 1913): 390–1.

60. Walter Benjamin, "Theories of German Fascism: On the Collection of Essays *War and Warrior*, edited by Ernst Jünger," trans. Jerold Wikoff, *New German Critique*, 17 (Spring 1979), 122. Hereafter abbreviated as "TGF."

61. See chapter 4.

62. Susan Buck-Morss, "Aesthetics and Anaesthetics: Walter Benjamin's Artwork Essay Reconsidered," *New Formations*, 20 (Summer 1993), 123–43.

63. Walter Benjamin, "The Work of Art in the Age of Mechanical Reproduction," in *Illuminations*, ed. Hannah Arendt, trans. Harry Zohn (New York: Schocken Books, 1968), 242. Hereafter abbreviated as "WOA."

64. See also Hewitt, "Fascist Modernism," 44–5.

65. Herbert Marcuse, "The Affirmative Character of Culture," in *Negations*, 95. Hereafter abbreviated as "ACC."

66. Peter Bürger, *Theory of the Avant-Garde*, trans. Michael Shaw (Minneapolis: University of Minnesota Press, 1984), 50.

2 "NO END, BUT ADDITION": T. S. ELIOT AND THE TRAGIC
ECONOMY OF HIGH MODERNISM

1. T. S. Eliot, *Selected Poems* (San Diego: Harcourt Brace Jovanovich, 1964), 31. Unless otherwise noted, all subsequent citations to Eliot's poetry refer to this edition.
2. T. S. Eliot, *Inventions of the March Hare: Poems 1909–1917*, ed. Christopher Ricks (San Diego: Harcourt Brace & Company, 1996), 29; hereafter abbreviated as *Hare*.
3. T. S. Eliot, "A Commentary," *Criterion*, 12, 40 (April 1931), 485.
4. Quoted in Lyndall Gordon, *T. S. Eliot: An Imperfect Life* (London: Vintage, 1998), 213.
5. See similar commentary in Gordon, *Imperfect Life*, 226 and Peter Ackroyd, *T. S. Eliot: A Life* (New York: Simon and Schuster, 1984), 160.
6. Quoted in A. David Moody, *Thomas Stearns Eliot Poet*, 2nd edn. (Cambridge: Cambridge University Press, 1994), 9.
7. T. S. Eliot, *The Waste Land: A Facsimile and Transcript of the Original Drafts Including the Annotations of Ezra Pound*, ed. Valerie Eliot (New York: Harcourt Brace Jovanovich, Inc., 1971), xii; hereafter abbreviated as *Facsimile*.
8. T. S. Eliot, *Selected Prose of T. S. Eliot*, ed. Frank Kermode (San Diego: Harcourt Brace & Company, 1975), 49; hereafter abbreviated as *Prose*. See also T. S. Eliot, *The Letters of T. S. Eliot, 1898–1922*, vol. 1, ed. Valerie Eliot (London: Faber and Faber Limited, 1988), 164.
9. See similar comments in Armstrong, *Modernism, Technology, and the Body*, 71.
10. Max Weber, *The Protestant Ethic and the Spirit of Capitalism*, trans. Talcott Parsons (London: Routledge Classics, 2001), 19.
11. Irving Babbitt, *Rousseau and Romanticism* (New York: Meridian Books, 1960) 11, 279; hereafter abbreviated as *RR*.
12. See J. David Hoeveler, Jr., *The New Humanism: A Critique of Modern America 1900–1940* (Charlottesville: University Press of Virginia, 1977), 31.
13. Irving Babbitt, *Spanish Character and Other Essays*, ed. Frederick Manchester, Rachel Giese, and William F. Giese (Boston: Houghton Mifflin Company, 1940), 51; hereafter abbreviated as *SC*.
14. T. S. Eliot, "Origins: What is Romanticism," reprinted in Moody, *Thomas Stearns*, 43.
15. See *RR*, 289. Norman Foerster, "Humanism and Religion," *Criterion*, 9 (1929), 26. *SC*, 56.
16. For Babbitt's accusers see Hoeveler, *New Humanism*, 10.
17. T. S. Eliot, "Second Thoughts about Humanism," *Hound and Horn*, 2, 4 (1929), 343.
18. T. S. Eliot, *Notes Towards the Definition of Culture* (New York: Harcourt, Brace and Company, 1949), 62; hereafter abbreviated as *Notes*.

19. "Liebniz' Monads and Bradley's Finite Centres," reprinted in T. S. Eliot, *Knowledge and Experience in the Philosophy of F. H. Bradley* (London: Faber and Faber, 1964), 204.

20. T. S. Eliot, "A Sceptical Patrician," *The Athenæum* (23 May 1919), 361–2.

21. Letter to Paul Elmer More. Special Collections, Princeton. See Gordon, *Imperfect Life*, 91.

22. See also James Joyce, *A Portrait of the Artist as a Young Man*, ed. Seamus Deane (New York: Penguin Books, 1993), 160.

23. See also Cary Wolfe's "Economies of Individualism," in *The Limits of American Ideology in Pound and Emerson* (Cambridge: Cambridge University Press, 1993).

24. Manju Jain, *A Critical Reading of the Selected Poems of T. S. Eliot* (Oxford: Oxford University Press, 1991), 38.

25. T. S. Eliot, "The Preacher as Artist," *The Athenæum* (28 November 1919), 1252–3.

26. T. S. Eliot, "The Three Voices of Poetry," in *On Poetry and Poets* (London: Faber, 1969), 100.

27. See chapter 4.

28. Ian Watt, *The Rise of the Novel: Studies in Defoe, Richardson, and Fielding* (Berkeley: University of California Press, 1962), 85.

29. Slavoj Žižek, "Why Are There Always Two Fathers?" in *Enjoy Your Symptom!: Jacques Lacan in Hollywood and Out* (New York: Routledge, 1992), 167, 173.

30. Herbert Marcuse, "Industrialization and Capitalism in the Work of Max Weber," in *Negations*, 214. See also Max Horkheimer and Theodor W. Adorno, *Dialectic of Enlightenment* (New York: Continuum Publishing Company, 1996), 152.

31. See representative figures in "Gerontion," "Burbank with a Baedeker: Bleistein with a Cigar," "[Columbo and Bolo verses]," etc.

32. Pound offers a similar critique in Cantos XII, XIV-XV, XLV. Ezra Pound, *The Cantos of Ezra Pound* (New York: New Directions Books, 1995).

33. See Eliot, "Preacher," 1252 and Gordon, *Imperfect Life*, 181–2.

34. See North, *Political Aesthetics*, 97–8.

35. Herbert Marcuse, "Some Social Implications of Modern Technology," in *The Essential Frankfurt School Reader*, ed. Andrew Arato and Eike Gebhardt (New York: Urizen Books, 1978), 142–3.

36. See Lentricchia, *Quartet*, 264.

37. See Lentricchia, *Quartet*, 254, 276.

38. Frank Kermode, *Romantic Image* (New York: Chilmark Press, 1961).

39. Michael Levenson, *A Genealogy of Modernism: A Study of English Literary Doctrine 1908–1922* (Cambridge: Cambridge University Press, 1984), 22.

40. Siegfried Kracauer, *The Mass Ornament (Weimar Essays)*, ed. Thomas Y. Levin (Cambridge: Harvard University Press, 1995), 77–82.

3 THE MODERN TEMPLE: T. E. HULME AND
THE CONSTRUCTION OF CLASSICISM

1. T. E. Hulme, *The Collected Writings of T. E. Hulme*, ed. Karen Csengeri (Oxford: Oxford University Press, 1994), 3. Subsequent references to Hulme's work pertain to this collection.
2. For this and all other biographical data see Alun R. Jones, *The Life and Opinions of T. E. Hulme* (Boston: Beacon Press, 1960).
3. See Kermode, *Romantic Image*, 121, 128–9; Csengeri, "Introduction," in Hulme, *Collected Writings*, ix–xxxvi; Ronald Primeau, "On the Discrimination of Hulmes: Toward a Theory of the 'Anti-Romantic' Romanticism of Modern Poetry," *Journal of Modern Literature*, 3 (1974), 1105.
4. On the relation of Eliot and Hulme, see Ronald Schuchard, "Eliot and Hulme in 1916: Toward a Revaluation of Eliot's Critical and Spiritual Development," *PMLA*, 88 (1973) and Dominic Baker-Smith, "Original Sin: T. S. Eliot and T. E. Hulme," *Centennial Hauntings: Pope, Byron and Eliot in the Year 88*, ed. C. C. Barfoot and Theo D'Haen (Amsterdam: Rodopi, 1990). For Eliot's praise of Hulme, see "The Use of Poetry and the Use of Criticism," in *Prose*, 92; "The Function of Criticism," in *Selected Essays*, 75; "A Commentary" in *The Criterion*, 2, 7 (April 1924), 231–2.
5. See Csengeri on the havoc caused by the editing of T. E. Hulme, *Speculations: Essays on Humanism and the Philosophy of Art*, ed. Herbert Read (London: Routledge & Kegan Paul, Ltd., 1924). Csengari, "Introduction," ix–xxxvi.
6. Jones, *Life and Opinions*, 21.
7. Miriam Hansen, "T. E. Hulme, Mercenary of Modernism, or, Fragments of Avantgarde Sensibility in Pre-World War I Britain," *ELH*, 47 (1980), 370–1, 379.
8. See notes in Hulme, *Collected Writings*, 49, 59, as well as various accounts in the work of Cork, Levenson, Kenner, etc.
9. See Henri Bergson, *Time and Free Will: An Essay on the Immediate Data of Consciousness*, trans. F. L. Pogson (London: George Allen & Unwin Ltd., 1950), 132.
10. On Hulme's sculptural turn, see Kermode, *Romantic Image*, 132–3 and Ethan Lewis, "'This Hulme Business' Revisited or of Sequence and Simultaneity," *Paideuma* 22, 1–2 (1993), 264.
11. Henri Bergson, *Creative Evolution*, trans. Arthur Mitchell (Mineola: Dover Publications, Inc., 1998), 6, 237.
12. Ezra Pound, *A Memoir of Gaudier-Brzeska* (New York: New Directions, 1970), 89. See also Ethan Lewis, "Hulme Business," 256 and Hugh Kenner, *The Pound Era* (Berkeley: University of California Press, 1971), 173ff.
13. See Eliot, "Tradition and the Individual Talent" and Ezra Pound, *Guide to Kulchur* (New York: New Directions, 1970).
14. For an opposing argument see Lewis, "Hulme Business," 259, 262.
15. Henri Bergson, *An Introduction to Metaphysics*, trans. T. E. Hulme (Indianapolis: Bobbs-Merrill, 1949), 27–8.

16. Theodor Adorno, "On the Fetish-Character in Music and the Regression of Listening," in *The Essential Frankfurt School Reader*, ed. Andrew Arato and Eike Gebhardt (New York: Urizen Books, 1978), 274.
17. Theodor Adorno, "Lyric Poetry and Society," in *Notes to Literature*, vol. 1, 42.
18. For more on this backlash against Bergson, see Mary Ann Gillies, *Henri Bergson and British Modernism* (Montreal: McGill-Queen's University Press, 1996), chs. 1–2.
19. On Bergson's facility with language, see R. C. Grogin, *The Bergsonian Controversy in France: 1900–1914* (Calgary: University of Calgary Press, 1988), 107.
20. Sanford Schwartz, *The Matrix of Modernism: Pound, Eliot, and Early Twentieth-Century Thought* (Princeton: Princeton University Press, 1985), 53–4.
21. See Sanford Schwartz, "Bergson and the Politics of Vitalism," in *The Crisis in Modernism: Bergson and the Vitalist Controversy*, ed. Frederick Burwick and Paul Douglass (Cambridge: Cambridge University Press, 1992), 278–9.
22. Georges Sorel, *Reflections on Violence*, trans. T. E. Hulme (New York: Peter Smith, 1941), 11.
23. For debates on Hulme's final "attitude," see Csengeri, "Introduction," xxxiii–xxxiv and Levenson, *Genealogy*, 98–102. Appropriate comments can be found in Hulme, *Collected Writings*, 438, 451.
24. Eliot quoted in Moody, *Thomas Stearns*, 44. See also Baker-Smith, "Original Sin," 274 and Wyndham Lewis, *Blasting and Bombardiering* (Berkeley: University of California Press, 1967), 101.

4 "A FAIRLY HORRIBLE BUSINESS": LABOR, WORLD WAR I,
AND THE PRODUCTION OF MODERN ART

1. Eric J. Leed, *No Man's Land: Combat and Identity in World War I* (Cambridge: Cambridge University Press, 1979), 97.
2. See Modris Eksteins, *Rites of Spring: The Great War and the Birth of the Modern Age* (New York: Doubleday, 1989), 102.
3. Gerard J. DeGroot, *Blighty: British Society in the Era of the Great War* (London: Addison Wesley Longman Ltd., 1996), 81.
4. Exhibit, Imperial War Museum, London.
5. Private R. McPake, diary entry, 6 October 1915, pp. 2–3, Department of Documents, Imperial War Museum, London.
6. Captain E. F. Chapman, to "My Dear Hilda," 9 August 1916, Department of Documents, Imperial War Museum, London.
7. Captain E. F. Chapman, to "My Dear Mother," 2 August 1916, Department of Documents, Imperial War Museum, London.
8. Carl von Clausewitz, *On War*, ed. and trans. Michael Howard and Peter Paret (Princeton: Princeton University Press, 1984), 77.
9. See James L. Stokesbury, *A Short History of World War I* (New York: William Morrow and Company, Inc., 1981), 91.
10. DeGroot, *Blighty*, 110.
11. See J. M. Bourne, *Britain and the Great War 1914–1918* (London: Edward Arnold, 1989), 68.

12. See Trudi Tate, *Modernism, History and the First World War* (Manchester: Manchester University Press, 1998), 128.

13. See "Women are Working Day and Night to Win the War . . ." and "Help Them to Carry On . . ." in Libby Chenault, *Battlelines: World War I Posters from the Bowman Gray Collection* (Chapel Hill: University of North Carolina Press, 1988), 195, 196; DeGroot, *Blighty*, 138.

14. J. H. Leigh, to Mrs. L. Hayman, 15 February 1916, Department of Documents, Imperial War Museum, London.

15. Stokesbury, *Short History*, 238.

16. DeGroot, *Blighty*, 165.

17. Bourne, *Great War*, 171.

18. Captain E. F. Chapman, 28 August 1916, Department of Documents, Imperial War Museum, London.

19. Lieutenant S. A. Knight, 19 June 1915, Department of Documents, Imperial War Museum, London.

20. George Fainstone, to his wife, 19 May 1918, Department of Documents, Imperial War Museum, London.

21. See commentary in Paul Fussell, *The Great War and Modern Memory* (London: Oxford University Press, 1975), ch. 2; Johanna Bourke, *An Intimate History of Killing: Face-to-Face Killing in Twentieth-Century Warfare* (London: Granta Books, 1999); Eksteins, *Rites*, ch. 4.

22. Fussell, *Memory*, 116.

23. Bourne, *Great War*, 38.

24. Arthur Hugh Sidgwick, to Frank Sidgwick, 11 August 1916, 2 February 1916, p. 3, Department of Documents, Imperial War Museum, London.

25. Bourne, *Great War*, 62, 168.

26. Stokesbury, *Short History*, 148.

27. See commentary in Bourke, *Intimate History*, 67, 87.

28. Robert Peyton Hamilton, 5 July 1915, Department of Documents, Imperial War Museum, London.

29. Arthur Hugh Sidgwick, to Frank Sidgwick, 2 February 1916, pp. 2–3, Department of Documents, Imperial War Museum, London.

30. Colonel Sir Lionel Hall, to his father, 24 March 1917, Department of Documents, Imperial War Museum, London.

31. Robert Peyton Hamilton, 20 July 1915, Department of Documents, Imperial War Museum, London.

32. Lieutenant S. A. Knight, 27 February 1915, Department of Documents, Imperial War Museum, London.

33. Captain E. F. Chapman, 17 May 1917, Department of Documents, Imperial War Museum, London.

34. John McCauley, "A Manx Soldier's War Diary," 1920s, p. 6, Department of Documents, Imperial War Museum, London.

35. Leed, *No Man's Land*, 91.

36. Arthur Hugh Sidgwick, 11 August 1916, Department of Documents, Imperial War Museum, London.

37. Quoted in DeGroot, *Blighty*, 171.

38. See DeGroot, *Blighty*, ch. 6.
39. R. P. Hamilton, 30 May 1915, Department of Documents, Imperial War Museum, London.
40. Dr. John D. Hartsilver, "Take that Man's Name," memoir of a "Non-Hero's" service in the London Regiment and RAMC in France and the Balkans, 1916–18, written in 1934, revised in 1960, p. 75, Department of Documents, Imperial War Museum, London.
41. Rupert Brooke, *The Collected Poems of Rupert Brooke* (New York: Dodd, Mead & Company, 1943), 101.
42. Hartsilver, "Take that Man's Name," 1–2, 75.
43. Captain E. F. Chapman, 20 August 1916, 6 March 1917, Department of Documents, Imperial War Museum, London.
44. Quoted in Eksteins, *Rites*, 178.
45. David Lloyd George, "'Through Terror to Triumph!': Speech on the War, Delivered at the Queen's Hall, London, September 19th, 1914," reprinted in *The Great Crusade: extracts from speeches delivered during the war, by the Rt. Hon. David Lloyd George, MP* (New York: George H. Doran Company, c. 1918), 289.
46. See Eksteins, *Rites*, 187.
47. Eksteins, *Rites*, 185.
48. Leed, *No Man's Land*, 60, 62.
49. See Bourne, *Great War*, 231 and Fussell, *Memory*, 120.
50. Quoted in DeGroot, *Blighty*, 44.
51. H. A. Vachell, *The Hill: A Romance of Friendship* (London: John Murray, 1905), 236.
52. Leed, *No Man's Land*, 152.
53. See also Bourke, *Intimate History*, 129ff.
54. Sigmund Freud, "On Narcissism: An Introduction," in *The Freud Reader*, ed. Peter Gay (New York: W.W. Norton & Company, 1989), 554.
55. Sigmund Freud, *The Ego and the Id*, trans. Joan Riviere, ed. James Strachey (New York: W.W. Norton & Company, 1960), 30, 32.
56. Sigmund Freud, *Group Psychology and the Analysis of the Ego*, trans. and ed. James Strachey (New York: W.W. Norton & Company, 1959), 52–60.
57. Sigmund Freud, *Beyond the Pleasure Principle*, trans. and ed. James Strachey (New York: W.W. Norton & Company, 1961), 38.
58. See, respectively, Fussell, "Soldier Boys," in *Memory* and Adrian Caesar, *Taking it Like A Man: Suffering, Sexuality and the War Poets* (Manchester: Manchester University Press, 1993).
59. See Freud, "Narcissism," 559, 562 and *Group*, 73.
60. See Freud, *Group*, 40, 51–2, and *Ego*, 34, 41–2.
61. James S. Campbell offers a slightly different historicized account of modern homosexuality in "'For you may touch them not': Misogyny, Homosexuality, and the Ethics of Passivity in First World War Poetry," *ELH*, 64 (1997), 827.
62. Caesar, *Taking it*, 120.
63. Harold Owen, *Journey from Obscurity: Memoirs of the Owen Family*, vol. 1 (London: Oxford University Press, 1963), 161–2.

64. Wilfred Owen, *Collected Letters*, ed. Harold Owen and John Bell (London: Oxford University Press, 1967), 160–1.
65. Owen, *Collected Letters*, 151.
66. *Ibid.*, 126.
67. Wilfred Owen, *The Complete Poems and Fragments*, vol. 1, ed. Jon Stallworthy (London: Chatto & Windus, 1983), 111. Subsequent references to Owen's poetry are to this collection and appear in the text.
68. Wilfred Owen, *The Collected Poems of Wilfred Owen*, ed. C. Day Lewis (New York: New Directions Books, 1963), 15.
69. See James Campbell, "Combat Gnosticism: The Ideology of First World War Poetry Criticism," *New Literary History*, 30 (1999), 203–4.
70. Owen, *Collected Letters*, 118.
71. Henri Gaudier-Brzeska, "VORTEX GAUDIER-BRZESKA (Written from the Trenches)," BLAST, 2 (1915), 33–4.
72. See Charles Harrison, *English Art and Modernism, 1900–1939* (New Haven: Yale University Press, 1981), 99, 209, 216–17.
73. Ezra Pound, *A Memoir of Gaudier-Brzeska* (New York: New Direction Books, 1970), 92. Hulme, *Collected Writings*, 305.
74. H. S. Ede, *Savage Messiah: Gaudier-Brzeska* (New York: The Literary Guild, 1931), 43. Except where noted, subsequent reference to Gaudier-Brzeska's writings pertain to this book.
75. Gaudier-Brzeska, "VORTEX," BLAST, 1 (1914), 156.
76. *Ibid.*, 158.
77. Quoted in Pound, *Memoir*, 31.
78. See Cork, *Machine Age*, 1, 182.
79. Richard Cork, *Vorticism and Abstract Art in the First Machine Age*, vol. 2 (Berkeley: University of California Press, 1976), 434.
80. Stanley Casson, *Some Modern Sculptors* (London: Oxford University Press, 1928), 98.
81. See commentary by Evelyn Silber, *Gaudier-Brzeska: Life and Art* (London: Thames and Hudson, 1996), 106.
82. Gaudier-Brzeska, "VORTEX," 155.
83. See, particularly, Hulme's "Romanticism and Classicism" and "Modern Art and Its Philosophy," a lecture presented before the Quest Society of London in January 1914, in *Collected Writings*, 268–85.
84. Wilhelm Worringer, *Abstraction and Empathy: A Contribution to the Psychology of Style*, trans. Michael Bullock (London: Routledge and Kegan Paul, Ltd., 1963), 24.
85. Karl Marx, *Economic and Philosophic Manuscripts of 1844*, trans. Martin Milligan, in *The Marx-Engels Reader*, 2nd edn., ed. Robert C. Tucker (New York: W.W. Norton & Company, 1978), 67–125.
86. Herbert Marcuse, "The Foundations of Historical Materialism," in *Studies in Critical Philosophy*, trans. Joris De Bres (Boston: Beacon Press, 1972), 13.
87. See Douglas Kellner, "Introduction to 'On the Philosophical Foundation of the Concept of Labor,'" *Telos*, 16 (Summer 1973), 2–8.

88. For an extended discussion of this distinction see Herbert Marcuse, *Eros and Civilization: A Philosophical Inquiry into Freud* (Boston: Beacon Press, 1966).

5 THESMOPHORIA: SUFFRAGETTES, SYMPATHETIC MAGIC, AND FEMINIST CLASSICISM

1. Christabel Pankhurst, "Speech Delivered by Christabel Pankhurst. Queen's Hall, December 22, 1908," in *Speeches and Trials of the Militant Suffragettes*, ed. Cheryl R. Jorgensen-Earp (London: Associated University Press, 1999), 90–1; Emmeline Pankhurst, "Why We Are Militant: A Speech Delivered in New York October 21st, 1913," in *Suffrage and the Pankhursts*, ed. Jane Marcus (London: Routledge and Kegan Paul, Ltd., 1987), 162.

2. Christabel Pankhurst, *Unshackled: The Story of How We Won the Vote* (London: Hutchinson & Company, 1987), 52.

3. See commentary in Jorgensen-Earp, ed., *Speeches and Trials*, 101, 104; Brian Harrison, *Peaceable Kingdom: Stability and Change in Modern Britain* (Oxford: Clarendon Press, 1982), 51; Antonia Raeburn, *The Militant Suffragettes* (London: Michael Joseph Ltd., 1973), 121, 135–6; Sandra Stanley Holton, "In Sorrowful Wrath: Suffrage Militancy and the Romantic Feminism of Emmeline Pankhurst," in *British Feminism in the Twentieth Century*, ed. Harold L. Smith (Amherst: University of Massachusetts Press, 1990), 21.

4. Christabel Pankhurst, "The Commons Debate on Woman Suffrage," in Marcus, ed., *Suffrage*, 31. Mary Lowndes, "Banners and Banner-Making," in *The Spectacle of Women: Imagery of the Suffrage Campaign 1907–1914*, ed. Lisa Tickner (Chicago: University of Chicago Press, 1988), 263.

5. Jane Ellen Harrison, "Alpha and Omega," in *Alpha and Omega* (London: Sedgwick & Jackson, 1915), 218.

6. Jane Ellen Harrison, *Prolegomena to the Study of Greek Religion* (Princeton: Princeton University Press, 1990), 570–1; hereafter abbreviated as *P*.

7. Elaine Kidd, *Materialism and the Militants* (Hampstead: Macdonald, n.d.), 1. *BLAST* offered the following note of sympathy and encouragement to the suffragettes: WE ADMIRE YOUR ENERGY. YOU AND ARTISTS ARE THE ONLY THINGS (YOU DON'T MIND BEING CALLED THINGS?) LEFT IN ENGLAND WITH A LITTLE LIFE IN THEM." *BLAST*, 1, 18, 151.

8. Janet Lyon, *Manifestoes: Provocations of the Modern* (Ithaca: Cornell University Press, 1999), 94.

9. For a helpful history of the gendered rhetoric of the hard and soft, see Elizabeth Grosz's chapter on "Sexed Bodies" in *Volatile Bodies: Toward a Corporeal Feminism* (Bloomington: Indiana University Press, 1994).

10. Jane Ellen Harrison, *Ancient Art and Ritual* (1913; reprint, Montana: Kessinger Publishing Company, n.d.), 191–2; hereafter abbreviated as *AAR*.

11. George Dangerfield persuasively argues that the Women's Social and Political Union helped to initiate a larger social revolt against liberalism that eventually transformed the face of British politics. Dangerfield, *Strange Death*, 139–213.

12. Emmeline Pethick-Lawrence, "Speech at Albert Hall, November 16, 1911," in Jorgensen-Earp, ed., *Speeches and Trials*, 142.
13. Quoted in Raeburn, *Militant Suffragettes*, 19.
14. Emmeline Pankhurst, "Address at Hartford," in Jorgensen-Earp, ed., *Speeches and Trials*, 332–3.
15. Emmeline Pankhurst, "Great Meeting at Albert Hall," in Jorgensen-Earp, ed., *Speeches and Trials*, 279. See also Emmeline Pankhurst *et al.*, "Closing Days of the Trial," in Jorgensen-Earp, ed., *Speeches and Trials*, 184, and Emmeline Pankhurst, "Window-Breaking: To One Who Has Suffered," in Marcus, ed., *Suffrage*, 183–4.
16. Christabel Pankhurst, "The Political Outlook," in Jorgensen-Earp, ed., *Speeches and Trials*, 93.
17. See commentary in Jorgensen-Earp, ed., *Speeches and Trials*, 272.
18. Emmeline Pankhurst, "The Women's Insurrection," in Jorgensen-Earp, ed., *Speeches and Trials*, 290.
19. Quoted in Tickner, ed., *Spectacle of Women*, 58.
20. Emmeline Pankhurst, "Hartford," 336.
21. Constance Lytton, "A Speech by Lady Constance Lytton," in Jorgensen-Earp, ed., *Speeches and Trials*, 109.
22. As a testament to the effectiveness of this form of protest, it should be noted that the Liberal government responded with every means possible to ensure that women were fed and remained "healthy." Significantly, the most violent of these efforts, force-feeding, often appears in suffragette accounts as an act of mechanized rape, a process of cold, alienated instrumentalization. See commentary by Jorgensen-Earp, ed., *Speeches and Trials*, 103–4 and June Purvis, "The Prison Experiences of the Suffragettes in Edwardian Britain," *Women's History Review* 4, 1 (1995), 103–33. Also, Djuna Barnes, "How It Feels To Be Forcefully Fed," in *New York*, ed. Alyce Barry (Los Angeles: Sun and Moon Press, 1989), 174–9.
23. Quoted in F. W. Pethick-Lawrence, "The Trial of the Suffragette Leaders," in Marcus, ed., *Suffrage*, 77.
24. Quoted in Susan Kingsley Kent, *Sex and Suffrage in Britain 1860–1914* (Princeton: Princeton University Press, 1987), 94.
25. Cicely Hamilton, *Marriage as a Trade* (London: Women's Press, 1981), 86.
26. Christabel Pankhurst, *The Great Scourge and How to End It* (London: E. Pankhurst, 1913), 20.
27. C. Pankhurst, *Unshackled*, 153, 108.
28. Olive Schreiner, *Woman and Labour* (New York: Frederick A. Stokes Co., 1911), 4.
29. Cicely Hamilton, *Life Errant* (London: J. M. Dent & Sons Ltd., 1935), 282.
30. Emmeline Pethick-Lawrence, *The Meaning of the Women's Movement* (London: Woman's Press, n.d.), 4–5.
31. Emmeline Pethick-Lawrence, *My Part in a Changing World* (London: Victor Gollancz, 1938), 215.

32. Caroline J. Howlett, "Writing on the Body? Representation and Resistance in British Suffrage Accounts of Forcible Feeding," in *Bodies of Writing, Bodies in Performance*, ed. Thomas Foster, Carol Siegel, and Ellen E. Berry (New York: New York University Press, 1996), 30, 33, 41.

33. E. Pankhurst *et al.*, "Closing Days," 252.

34. *Ibid.*, 238.

35. Quoted in Tickner, ed., *Spectacle*, 102.

36. Emmeline Pankhurst, "Emmeline Pankhurst's Speech in the Portman Rooms, London. March 24, 1908," in Jorgensen-Earp, ed., *Speeches and Trials*, 31.

37. Emmeline Pethick-Lawrence, "The Rune of Birth and Renewal," in Jorgensen-Earp, ed., *Speeches and Trials*, 283, 285.

38. E. Pankhurst, "Women's Insurrection," 290.

39. Quoted in F. W. Pethick-Lawrence, "Trial," 77.

40. Christabel Pankhurst, "Broken Windows," in Marcus, ed., *Suffrage*, 124.

41. F. W. Pethick-Lawrence, "Trial," 78.

42. Sylvia Pankhurst, "How Shall We Get the Vote?" in Marcus, ed., *Suffrage*, 254.

43. Mary Jean Corbett, *Representing Femininity: Middle-Class Subjectivity in Victorian and Edwardian Women's Autobiographies* (Oxford: Oxford University Press, 1992), 14.

44. See North's discussion of these opposed kinds of community in *Political Aesthetics*, 3–4.

45. Mary R. Richardson, *Laugh A Defiance* (London: George Weidenfeld & Nicolson, 1953), 46–8, 84.

46. Constance Lytton, *Prison and Prisoners: Some Personal Experiences* (London: William Heinemann, 1914), 42.

47. E. Pethick-Lawrence, "Rune," 283.

48. *Ibid.*, 284.

49. Elizabeth Robins, *The Convert* (1907; reprint, Old Westbury: Women's Press, 1980), 87; May Sinclair, *The Tree of Heaven* (New York: MacMillan Co., 1917), 229.

50. See commentary in Raeburn, *Militant Suffragettes*, 77.

51. Quoted in Constance Lytton, *Letters of Constance Lytton*, ed. Betty Balfour (London: William Heinemann Ltd., 1925), 129.

52. *AAR*, 152.

53. Harrison, "Alpha," 202.

54. In this critique, Harrison offers a theory of language evolution very similar to that found in Horkheimer and Adorno, *Dialectic of Enlightenment*, 15, 10–11.

55. Jane Ellen Harrison, "Homo Sum," in *Alpha*, 81. Hereafter abbreviated as *HS*.

56. Jane Ellen Harrison, "Scientiæ Sacra Fames," in *Alpha*, 133. Hereafter abbreviated as *SSF*.

57. Susan Stanford Friedman, *Psyche Reborn: The Emergence of H. D.* (Bloomington: Indiana University Press, 1981), 17, xi.

58. *Ibid.*, xi.

59. Susan Stanford Friedman, *Penelope's Web: Gender, Modernity, H. D.'s Fiction* (Cambridge: Cambridge University Press, 1990), 19. Friedman, *Psyche*, 10.

60. Friedman, *Penelope's Web*, 32.

61. Laity's work, it should be noted, is also aware of the dangers posed by these oppositional or revisionary strategies, the manner in which they tend to resurrect the very logic they sought to oppose. Cassandra Laity, *H. D. and the Victorian Fin de Siècle: Gender, Modernism, Decadence* (Cambridge: Cambridge University Press, 1996), xiii, xv.

62. Rachel Blau DuPlessis, *H. D.: The Career of that Struggle* (Bloomington: Indiana University Press, 1986), 41.

63. Susan Stanford Friedman, "Modernism of the 'Scattered Remnant': Race and Politics in the Development of H. D.'s Modernist Vision," in *H. D. Woman and Poet*, ed. Michael King (Orono: National Poetry Foundation, 1946), 104.

64. Susan Stanford Friedman, "Exile in the American Grain: H. D.'s Diaspora," in *Agenda: H. D. Special Issue*, 25, 3–4 (Autumn–Winter 1987/8), 47.

65. Friedman, "Exile," 13.

66. Friedman, "Scattered Remnant," 115. Fortunately, several scholars have begun to recognize the manner in which this criticism obscures not only H. D.'s thought and writing, but her contribution to modernism in general. See, for example, Michael Kaufmann, "Gendering Modernism: H. D., Imagism and Masculinist Aesthetics," in *Unmanning Modernism: Gendered Re-readings*, ed. Elizabeth Jane Harrison and Shirley Peterson (Knoxville: University of Tennessee Press, 1997), 59. Eileen Gregory, *H. D. and Hellenism: Classic Lines* (Cambridge: Cambridge University Press, 1997), 1, 6. Mary E. Finn, "The Need for a New Modernism: H. D. and Our Present Critical Fictions: A Review Essay," *South Atlantic Review*, 56, 1 (January 1991), 98.

67. Quoted in Barbara Guest, *Herself Defined: The Poet H. D. and Her World* (Garden City: Doubleday & Company, Inc., 1984), 218.

68. H. D., *Collected Poems 1912–1944*, ed. Louis L. Martz (New York: New Directions Publishing Corporation, 1983), 5, 14, 25–6, 21. Subsequent citations to H. D.'s poetry refer to this collection.

69. Eileen Gregory, "Rose Cut in Rock: Sappho and H. D.'s *Sea Garden*," in *Signets: Reading H. D.*, ed. Susan Stanford Friedman and Rachel Blau DuPlessis (Madison: University of Wisconsin Press, 1990), 133.

70. H. D., "H. D. by Delia Alton," *Iowa Review*, 16, 3 (Fall 1986), 184.

71. H. D., *Notes on Thought and Vision and The Wise Sappho* (San Francisco: City Lights Books, 1982), 52, 22; hereafter abbreviated as *NTV*. On H. D.'s poetics and the issue of restraint, see also Helen Sword, *Engendering Inspiration: Visionary Strategies in Rilke, Lawrence, and H. D.* (Ann Arbor: University of Michigan Press, 1995), 131, 133, 138.

72. H. D., *Tribute to Freud* (New York: Pantheon Books Inc., 1956), 74; hereafter abbreviated *TF*.

73. Although we are focusing on H. D.'s poetry, we could just as easily trace these themes through her autobiographical fiction of the 1920s. In both *HERmione*

and *Asphodel*, we find a doubled subject caught in the manifold tensions and pressures of the material world. See H. D., *HERmione* (New York: New Directions Publishing Corporation, 1981), 8–9, 25. H. D., *Asphodel* ed. Robert Spoo (Durham: Duke University Press, 1992), 182.

74. For this debate, see Friedman, *Penelope's Web*; DuPlessis, *Career*; Susan Stanford Friedman and Rachel Blau DuPlessis, "'I had two loves separate': The Sexualities of H. D.'s *HER*," in *Signets*, 205–32; Dagny Boebel, "The Sun Born in a Woman: H. D.'s Transformation of a Masculinist Icon in 'The Dancer,'" in *Unmanning Modernism*, 14–30; Laity, *H. D. and the Victorian Fin de Siecle*, xiv; and Sword, *Engendering Inspiration*, 138.

75. H. D., "Responsibilities," *Agenda: H. D. Special Issue*, 51–3.

76. Gary Burnett, *H. D. Between Image and Epic: The Mysteries of Her Poetics* (Ann Arbor: UMI Research Press, 1990), 10, 11, 8.

77. Adalaide Morris, "Signaling: Feminism, Politics, and Mysticism in H. D.'s War Trilogy," *Sagetrieb* 9, 3 (Winter 1990), 121–2.

78. Jane Ellen Harrison, "Art and Mr. Clive Bell," in *Alpha*, 215, 217. On aesthetic deathliness, see also Hulme, *Collected Writings*, 274; Lewis, *Art of Being Ruled*, 349–50 and *Tarr: The 1918 Version*, ed. Paul O'Keefe (Santa Rosa: Black Sparrow Press, 1990), 298–300.

79. H. D., *Collected Poems*, 330.

80. H. D.'s own suffragette story, while certainly topical, seems derivative and rather perfunctory; it barely sustains careful analysis. That said, the story, one of conversion and transformation, suggests the same arousals and restrictions found throughout H. D.'s writing. H. D., "The Suffragette," *Sagetrieb*, 15, 1–2 (1996), 7–11.

81. M. Merleau-Ponty, *Phenomenology of Perception*, trans. Colin Smith (New York: Routledge, 2000).

82. M. Merleau-Ponty, "The Intertwining – The Chiasm," in *The Visible and the Invisible*, ed. Claude LeFort, trans. Alphonso Lingis (Evanston: Northwestern University Press, 1968), 130–55.

83. Merleau-Ponty, "Chiasm," 152. See Luce Irigaray's discussion of "invagination" in *An Ethics of Sexual Difference*, trans. Carolyn Burke and Gillian C. Gill (Ithaca: Cornell University Press, 1984), 151–84. Commentary in Grosz, *Volatile Bodies*, 103–7.

Index